Expl

and

Lea

DEREK ROWNTREE

**KOGAN
PAGE**

had ideas and encouragement
...wis Elton, David Hawkridge,
Clive Lawless, Fred Lockwood, Dave Perry, Peter Raggatt,
Marilyn Saddington, Sandy Sieminski, Nick Small,
Mary Thorpe, Joyce Walmsley, David Zeldin and Bob
Zimmer. Many thanks to them all.

First published in 1992

Kogan Page Limited
120 Pentonville Road
London N1 9JN

© Derek Rowntree, 1992

British Library Cataloguing in Publication Data

A CIP record for this book is available from the British Library.

ISBN 0 7494 0813 8

Typeset by the author
Printed and bound in Great Britain by
Biddles Ltd, Guildford and King's Lynn

Contents

About this book . . .

> OPEN LEARNING: ". . . an imprecise phrase to which a range of meanings can be, and is, attached. It eludes definition. But as an inscription to be carried in a procession on a banner, gathering adherents and enthusiasts, it has great potential." (MacKenzie *et al*, 1975)

This book is about a family of approaches to education and training that mostly call themselves "open learning" or "distance learning". But there are many offspring and sundry relatives going by a profusion of other names—flexible learning, supported self-study, technology-based training, and so on.

All these names may change, and have changed over the years, but the issues we explore in this book will remain important in any kind of education or training. Basically, the book is about teaching and learning.

Who might benefit?

I have written this book for people with a professional interest in open learning. I am assuming you are, for example:

- a teacher or trainer or guidance worker, or a book author or media specialist, or a manager or consultant
- involved in, or preparing to become involved in
  - ~ supporting learners and/or
  - ~ selecting or preparing learning materials for them and/or
  - ~ managing the work of others who do so
- in education, in industry or in a public sector organisation.

Or, of course, you might describe yourself entirely differently. However, you should, ideally, have in mind an organisation in which you might be applying open learning—and the kind of system you might be wanting to introduce or modify. I am assuming that you will already have some experience in teaching or training or working with other people to help them do things. I also assume that you will know other people (not necessarily experts) with whom you can discuss the ideas in this book.

What the book aims to do

This book is meant to help you in your work. However, it is not a "How to do it" book. Rather, it is more of a "What might be worth doing?" book. My chief aim is to help you critically reflect on current practices (both your own and those of other people) in open learning—and be able to act more confidently and competently as a result.

Indeed I hope to encourage you as a "reflective practitioner". In Donald Schon's book of that title (1983), he suggested we should be constantly reflecting on what we do, why we do it and how it might be done differently. As reflective practitioners we never allow our work to become a matter of routine. We remain alive to new issues, new theories, new knowledge, new technologies, new controversies that touch upon our field. We expect to go on learning and developing new approaches of our own as long as we practice.

Through practice we may develop competence. Through reflection we may develop wisdom as well.

Possible objectives

How might your professional competence improve as a result of working on this book? You could be better able to:

- Take part in critical discussion of the nature and use of open learning in education or training.

- Explain your own vision of open learning.

- Justify your design for an open learning scheme appropriate to specific circumstances.

- Implement your scheme effectively.

- Evaluate and improve your scheme.

Each of the nine "units" in the book could help you, one way or another, towards all five general objectives above. In addition, you'll find that each unit suggests its own, more specific objectives. These I list at the beginning of each unit.

How to use the book

There is no one best way of using this book. Different people will use it in different ways. That's fine. All our needs are different.

Decide your own sequence

The body of the book is divided into nine units. The nine units are numbered, but this is simply for ease of reference. You don't need to read them in that order—just as I didn't write them in that order. I've printed them in what seems to me a reasonably sensible sequence. But it may not be appropriate to your immediate needs and interests.

So, start with whatever unit you wish and decide your own sequence through the rest of the book. I wrote the units in such a way that each is independent of the others. None of them assumes that you will have read any of the others first.

This does mean, however, that I've had to raise certain issues in more than one unit. But you shouldn't find this unduly repetitive because you'll be viewing them from a rather different angle each time you meet them. And if you want to find out what I've said in other units about an issue that interests you, then of course you can always look it up in the index.

How the book is structured

The book starts with this introduction and ends with a list of sources, a bibliography and an index. In between are the nine units that form the body of the book. Each unit has the same structure:

- introductory page with suggested objectives
- several pages giving an overview of the topic
- suggested follow-up work
- portfolio prompts
- reflection checklists.

Objectives

Notice that these are "suggested" objectives. You may have others of your own that you want to pursue. Notice also that the objectives imply that you could get "better" at doing the various things mentioned—not that you'll achieve perfection.

Overview

Each overview offers you a base from which to explore. It aims to point out some of the chief features of the topic and help you decide which aspects might be worth pursuing further. You may want to look at some topics in more detail, relating them to your own experience and context.

Also, the overviews present just one person's view of the topic—mine. Other authors might have taken quite different lines. So may you. I know my own vision of open learning altered considerably in the course of writing this book. Yours may too in the course of reading it.

Indeed, open learning itself is constantly changing—new aims, new learners, new providers, new technology, new problems—even new names for itself. By the time you come to read the overviews, I may be wondering why I laid so much emphasis on this and that or completely ignored something else. So I hope you will feel free to develop your own overview of each topic—and of open learning as a whole. I expect it will be quite different from mine.

Suggested follow-up work

If you want to get maximum benefit from your explorations in open and distance learning, you will want to do more than just read this book. So, at the end of each unit, I have suggested some follow-up work— both "desk work" and "field work".

Desk work

By "desk work" I mean using published materials—books, journals, videos, audio-cassettes. As an example, I pay special attention to four books that I have found to be useful companions while exploring open learning. You also may find one or more of them worth reading as a supplement to this book. At the end of each unit, I give you some idea about what each one might have to say on the subject of that unit.

Field work

By "field work" I mean exploration that requires you to go off to talk with other people. Even the best of desk work materials can't talk back at you or respond to your very specific concerns. Other people can. You may want to find a number of people—whether in your organisation or outside it—who can, for example, between them:

- let you bounce ideas off them
- tell you of their experiences
- show you their system in operation
- let you talk with their learners or staff
- comment on draft plans you produce
- join with you in a planning workshop.

Two unusual features

Here I must mention two features that aren't common in books of this kind. I have included them because I think they will help you get more "value for money" from your explorations and also aid your development as a reflective practitioner. They've certainly helped me in those ways.

Portfolio prompts

While you are working on this book I would urge you to keep a portfolio. By a "portfolio", I mean simply a ring binder (or maybe a box file) in which you keep a personal record of your explorations. If "portfolio" sounds too much like art college, you can call it your "log" or "personal file" or whatever you prefer.

Whatever you call it, it might include, for example:

- your thoughts and feelings about the topic of each unit as you work through it
- any notes you make about the contents of each unit
- whatever notes you make or draft materials you produce during your field work
- your reflections about your own self-development
- publishers' catalogues, book reviews, clippings from newspapers, copies of magazine articles—indeed any item that seems relevant to your needs in open learning
- anything else you think is useful.

The box below is one you'll see at intervals in the book. I call it a "portfolio prompt". It is meant to suggest to you that this might be a good moment to write something in your portfolio.

 Why not make a start on your portfolio by writing yourself a note about what you want from this book?

Reflection checklists

At the end of every unit you will find a "reflection checklist". These checklists encourage you to look back over your work on the unit—what and how you learned during it, and how you feel about it—and make notes in your portfolio.

The checklist poses the same questions each time. But you don't have to answer all of them. It's not a questionnaire and only you will see how you respond. Use just the questions that seem relevant to you on a particular topic. Also, you may have questions or concerns of your own you'd prefer to reflect on.

Bon voyage

So, I wish you well on your voyage of exploration. You'll find, if you haven't already, that open learning is a realm whose boundaries are constantly shifting and whose natives don't all speak the same language. Nor, you may come to believe, do we always say what we mean, do what we say, or know what we do. You have been warned!

If you feel like writing to tell me how you got on with this book, I'll be very pleased to hear from you. In particular, I would be interested to hear how the book might help in your professional work and how you think it might be improved for the benefit of future readers. Here is how to reach me:

Professor Derek Rowntree
Institute of Educational Technology
Open University
Milton Keynes
MK7 6AA

Unit 1

What are open & distance learning?

What's the difference between open and distance learning? Are they just the latest boisterous bandwagon to trundle through education and training? Or do they represent a new philosophy of teaching and learning?

In this unit we look at where open and distance learning have come from, the ideas behind them and the forms they take. We also ask whether open learning anywhere is as open as it ought to be.

Suggested objectives

As a result of working on this unit you could be better able to:

- Distinguish between open learning and distance learning.
- Give examples of different purposes and approaches among different open learning systems.
- Suggest ways in which learning might be made more open in a context you know well.
- o *Any objectives of your own to add?*

N.B. Remember—there is no need to start with this unit if you would prefer to start elsewhere in the book.

I suggest you now start a new section in your portfolio in which to keep a record of your ideas about the nature of Open and Distance Learning. From time to time, I'll print a box like this (with the symbol alongside) to prompt you to write something in your portfolio. I expect you will use some of these prompts and not others; and also that you will make occasional notes without my prompting.

The variety of forms

Whatever open and distance learning are, they certainly take many forms. The brief examples on the opposite page hardly begin to suggest the variety that is possible.

Are any of them similar to the kind of open or distance learning you are most familiar with? Which of them would you think of as open learning and which as distance learning? (That is, if you think there is any difference between the two.) Maybe you think some of them are neither one nor the other.

Before we go any further in this unit, I suggest you make a note about what you see as the key features of open learning and distance learning. What differences do you see between them?

 Please make a note in your portfolio. (You may find it useful to look back at this when you have finished your work on the unit.)

Where did it all come from?

I am always having to tell people that the name of the town in which the Open University is based—Milton Keynes— existed long before Milton the poet and Keynes the economist. Similarly, open learning was known, and named, long before the Open University. One issue of *Pitmans Journal* spoke of distance learning and open learning as "one of the most interesting developments of recent years in the educational world"—and that was on 6 December 1924.

Even then, the basic idea—in the form of correspondence education—had been around for some time. Isaac Pitman started to teach shorthand by post in 1840 and, in 1856, language teaching by correspondence started in Germany. During the second half of the 19th century, correspondence education became well-established in the USA and Europe.

In fact, there have been many forerunners to open learning during the first three quarters of this century—e.g. the Dalton Plan, progressivism, adult education, programmed learning,

Some open and distance learners

JANET, a police sergeant, is doing an Open University degree, taking a range of courses from arts to technology. She likes learning from the printed materials and audio-tapes but, working shifts, she rarely views the television programmes and has only once been to a tutorial. She says she gets all the regular help she needs from her tutor in writing and on the telephone. But she does make a point of choosing courses with summer schools because she enjoys what she calls the "hothouse academic experience".

BOB is taking advantage of a lull in production at his steel mill to carry on where he left off with an interactive video near his work-station. He is learning about a new manufacturing process. He calls over his manager to discuss a tricky point. They decide to bring it up at the weekly session when all members of the work-group get together to discuss what they have been learning during the week.

ALVIN, a partially disabled 24 year old, is studying GCSE subjects as a FlexiStudy student attached to a local FE college. His work is based chiefly on printed materials produced by the National Extension College and he is supported by a tutor in the college who comments on assignments by post and is available at set times on the telephone. He is entitled to a personal tutorial once a month, but he has agreed with some fellow students and the tutor to pool their time and meet once a fortnight for a longer group session and a spell in the library.

KIM is one of a group of young mothers talking animatedly in the back room of a pub in Glasgow. Their discussion centres around some Open University booklets on child care, and today the main topic is children's illnesses. They are eager to swop their experiences and get one another's advice and support. They even suggest ways of improving the materials. As one says to the group leader: "It's nice to know we're not as daft as they made out at school".

WAYNE is logging on to the computer in his high street building society office. He is going to learn about probate from a CBT module. No-one else in the office is studying this at present, but others have done it earlier and he can talk to them if he gets stuck. His branch manager will give him a certificate when he passes the end-of-module test.

ELLIE, in the sixth year at a rural comprehensive, knows more about economics and sociology than any teacher in the school. She is one of three in her school who would be unable to study these subjects were it not for self-study materials—and, of course, the specialist teacher from a local 6th-form college whom she meets once a week for a class with students from four other schools.

SUSHMA has been persuaded to try out her local Basic Skills Open Learning Centre. During an "initial assessment" with a tutor she was able to sort out her needs in learning to use English as a second language, and she has already chosen some learning materials to start on and agreed some goals. She feels very welcome at the centre and is relieved to find she can talk with others who share her difficulties.

educational technology, Keller Plan, Nuffield resource-based learning projects—to name but a few.

These approaches had many differences from one another, of course. But between them they foreshadowed most of the intentions or features that have come together in open learning, e.g.:

- learners taking responsibility for their own learning
- learning alone or in small groups
- learning at their own pace and in their own time
- learning from materials
- use of audio-visual media
- active learning rather than passive
- self-assessment
- less frequent help from a teacher
- a more individual-centred role for teachers
- learning from other people besides teachers
- plenty of hype.

Some key institutions

The history of open learning in the UK has been largely the history of some influential institutions and initiatives. Here are the chief ones, in the order they appeared on the scene:

1963   **National Extension College.** NEC was set up by Michael Young (who also founded the Consumers' Association) as a self-financing non-profit trust. Its purpose was to give home-based adults a "second chance" at academic or vocational studies, using specially written correspondence materials, broadcast television and support from local tutors.

Among NEC's many innovative schemes was FlexiStudy—a partnership with local further education colleges who would provide NEC students with face-to-face tuition, practical facilities and support with examinations. There are now about 200 colleges in the scheme.

NEC claims more than a quarter of a million successful students so far and it is still enrolling about 8,000 new students each year.

1971   **The Open University.** The Open University (OU) was the
          world's first university to teach only at a distance—and
          admitted more than 24,000 students in its first year. Its success
          has spawned many other similar institutions around the
          world. Among the many unusual features it pioneered were
          admission without qualifications, degrees built up from
          credits obtained by taking a number of modular courses, and
          a team approach to developing courses.

          The undergraduate programme (£89 million annual
          funding) is still the main business—with some 77,000
          students in 1992. But the continuing education programme is
          expanding fast. The Open Business School, for example, has
          18,000 managers taking its courses in 1992 and has an annual
          turnover of £17 million. More than a million and a half
          people have studied with the OU and it now admits students
          in mainland Europe.

1983/7   **Open Tech Programme.** Unlike NEC and OU, the Open Tech
          was not an institution but an initiative. The then Manpower
          Services Commission pumped almost £45 million into 140
          projects intended to develop, deliver and support open
          learning in vocational training. By 1987, some 28,000 hours of
          learning material had been produced and more than 27,000
          students had benefited from the programme. Some people
          question whether Open Tech got adequate value for its
          money; but it undoubtedly created a fund of expertise and
          commitment that is still growing and fuelling many of the
          developments in open learning today.

1986   **Open College of the Arts.** Another creation of Michael
          Young (by now Lord Young of Dartington). The college offers
          practical courses in such areas as painting, sculpture, textiles,
          photography, and creative writing. Its students (10,000
          claimed in the first four years) work at home from specially
          prepared course books backed up by correspondence tuition
          and/or occasional class sessions in local centres.

1987   **Open College.** This initiative was set up by government to
          carry on where Open Tech left off. It was meant to transform
          vocational education and training much as the OU has
          transformed higher education. Its £100 million funding
          enabled it to buy in or develop a wide range of high quality
          courses. But it has not achieved the hoped-for success in
          marketing these to individual learners and is now dependent
          on corporate clients who will pay for their employees to

learn. Its funding ended in 1992 and we must wait to see whether it can become self-financing.

N.B. Beware of confusing this Open College with the quite separate "Open College Networks"—an association of local colleges dedicated to providing accreditation and credit transfer for all kinds of adult learning (UDACE, 1990).

1988   **Open Learning Foundation** (formerly Open Polytechnic). This is a consortium of more than twenty institutions in higher education who have agreed to invest in producing open learning packages which all can use—largely in association with on-campus classroom-based courses. The Foundation will not itself enrol students but will market its materials to member institutions (and others) and support their implementation through staff development and consultancies.

1989   **Open School**. Yet another Michael Young initiative. It aims to bring open learning to the aid of learners whose needs might not otherwise be met—e.g. children in hospital or in schools with no specialist teachers of certain subjects.

Many other institutions have played and are playing a major part in the development of open learning—not least the government funded National Council for Educational Technology and Scottish Council for Educational Technology. Since 1988, more than £3m of government funding has also gone into setting up 75 Basic Skills Open Learning Centres in cities and rural areas of England and Wales. An initial evaluation by the Basic Skills and Adult Literacy Unit (ALBSU, 1991) suggests that the centres have already proved successful at reasonable cost and that more are needed.

Despite all this activity, open learning is a long way from realising its potential. Many colleges (in the still-appropriate words of Dixon, 1987) "have yet to appreciate the advantages of using open learning methods within their mainstream courses" and many companies, particularly small firms, are still unaware that open learning might have anything at all to offer them.

 You might like to make a note of any of the above organisations you think worth getting in touch with. (Addresses at the back of this book.)

So what is open learning?

Before we go any further, perhaps we should try to agree
what it is we are talking about. Our problem here was clearly
stated some time ago by the observers (MacKenzie *et al*, 1975)
who called open learning:

> ". . . an imprecise phrase to which a range of meanings
> can be, and is, attached. . . It eludes definition. But as an
> inscription to be carried in a procession on a banner,
> gathering adherents and enthusiasts, it has great
> potential."

All these years later it is still imprecise. It still eludes
definition. And it has certainly gathered plenty of adherents
and enthusiasts. They may all have their own views about
what is special about open learning. And so may you.

I have printed a number of definitions in the boxes overleaf.
Thinking about them, and many other words that people
have uttered on the subject, it seems to me that open
learning is two different things. It is:

- a philosophy—a set of beliefs about teaching and learning
- a method—a set of techniques for teaching and learning.

Much of the confusion arises because people don't always
realise that the philosophy can be practised without using the
method. And, more commonly, the method can be applied
without the philosophy.

Open learning—the philosophy

In one sense, "open learning" is a rallying cry—a slogan that
implies commitment to shared educational beliefs. But
people in open learning express a variety of different beliefs.
They can be beliefs about the purposes or ends of education
and training—the Why? They can be beliefs about the best
means of achieving such purposes—the How? People may
agree about the means but disagree about the ends, and vice
versa.

The most widely agreed beliefs are about opening up learning
opportunities to a wider range of people and enabling them
to learn more congenially and productively. This involves
reducing barriers to access and giving learners more control
over their own learning.

Some definitions of open learning

"An open learning system is one in which the restrictions placed on students are under constant review and removed wherever possible. It incorporates the widest range of teaching strategies, in particular those using independent and individualised learning." (Coffey, 1977)

"Open Learning: arrangements to enable people to learn at the time, place and pace which satisfies their circumstances and requirements. The emphasis is on opening up opportunities by overcoming barriers that result from geographical isolation, personal or work commitments or conventional course structures which have often prevented people from gaining access to the training they need." (MSC, 1984)

"'Open learning' is a term used to describe courses flexibly designed to meet individual requirements. It is often applied to provision which tries to remove barriers that prevent attendance at more traditional courses, but it also suggests a learner-centred philosophy." (Lewis & Spencer, 1986)

"... a wide range of learning opportunities that both aim to assist learners in gaining access to knowledge and skills they would otherwise be denied and to give learners the optimum degree of control over their own learning." (Dixon, 1987)

"Open learning is a state of mind rather than a method with particular characteristics." (Jack, 1988)

"Open learning is not just about access alone, it is also about providing people with a fair chance of success." (Holt & Bonnici, 1988)

But why do we want a wider range of learners? Some may say: "Because we need more students/skilled workers." Others may say: "Because we must try to meet the needs of individuals who are not getting the education or training opportunities they could benefit from." The former may be hoping to find additional learners who can cope with whatever programmes are currently being offered. The latter perhaps admit the possibility that they may need to develop radically different programmes.

And why do we want open learners to have more control over their learning? Is it simply a means of making the learning more palatable to them—and thus helping keep them in the system? Or is it something to do with the respect we have for them as people with their own preferences and purposes—and with encouraging them to take responsibility for their own lives? Does it touch on what we'd like to see our learners become (the Why?) as well as on how we believe they might best learn (the How?)

Desirable aims?

You may like to consider the following aims for open learning, suggested as desirable by Lewis & Spencer (1986). Would any of them be important to YOU in setting up your open learning programmes? If so, is there one you would give top priority to? And are there any you could not accept?

☐ "A focus on the learner's own purposes and on helping the learner to articulate these at every stage."

☐ "A focus on the learner's own environment and experience—domestic, social, communal and work-based— and on its potential for learning."

☐ "The belief that the learner is self-directed, that individual learning styles need to be respected and used, that learning involves the whole person."

☐ "A commitment to helping the learner to acquire independence and autonomy."

Lewis and Spencer's learner-centred aims reflect the "progressive" strand in education. They don't imply merely that learner-centredness is an appropriate spur to learning. They also imply—especially in their final aim—that the purpose of learning is to produce independent and autonomous people.

Some people in open learning go along with the first of these implications without accepting the second. For example, Hilary Perraton (1987) points out that:

> ". . . development of the autonomous ability to learn would be an inappropriate measure for a distance-teaching activity like the Tanzanian radio campaign on health whose aim was to stimulate co-operative action by groups of villagers."

 You may like to make a note about the kind of aims you would think important for open learning.

Open learning—the method

Learner-centred aims could be pursued through a variety of different methods. For instance, they can be, and are, pursued in adult education classes, in one-to-one literacy coaching, and in community development projects. There seems no reason why such experiences should not be called open learning. But usually they are not.

The role of packages

For most people, open learning implies that the learner's work is based around self-study materials—the **package**. As Lewis & Spencer (1986) pointed out: ". . . in nearly every case specially prepared or adapted materials are necessary."

These packages may involve any of a variety of media—e.g., print, audio-cassettes, television, computer "courseware" and practical kits. And the learners using them will be provided with various amounts and kinds of help from other human beings—e.g. tutors or line managers.

Packages are designed to help the learner learn with less help than usual from a face-to-face teacher. They can contribute to openness by:

- enabling more people to learn—by economising on the amount of teacher time required
- using a variety of media appealing to different learners
- enabling learners to study when and where they choose.
- enabling them to work at their own pace.

- setting learning activities in the learner's home, community or workplace.

- giving learners responsibility for their own progress.

- *Any others that occur to you? (What?)*

How packages are used

How will learners use packages? Some will be using self-teaching packages on-site—in colleges or training centres, or at their workplace. Others may be using them at home, in pubs or on buses. And all of these may be using them alone or in company with fellow-learners.

And what proportion of their learning will come from the package rather than through contact with other people? Some learners will be using "stand-alone" packages with no organised support. Some will keep in touch with a tutor by telephone or correspondence. Others may be supported with occasional face-to-face coaching sessions or classwork. Yet others will be using packages as one element in a programme that involves as much or even more learning in a class.

YOUR learners may be using packages on-site or at home (or both)—and they may or may not have contact with other learners and tutors. Which of the following sounds most like your practice or intention?

☐ "They'll be using STAND-ALONE packages—e.g. no organised contact with tutors or other learners."

☐ "They'll be using packages with SUPPORT—e.g. they will be backed up by correspondence tutoring, occasional tutorials or classwork."

☐ "They'll be using packages ALONGSIDE regular class teaching—e.g. as preparation or follow up for class meetings."

☐ *Some other use? (What?)*

Packages are not enough

Some companies have tried stand-alone packages (bought in or home-made) as a means of training staff. Usually, as the Open Tech programme clearly demonstrated (Tavistock, 1987), unless the students are highly motivated, the drop-out rate is unacceptable. For example, Austin Rover set up an open learning centre at its Cowley works, using CBT packages but with no-one for learners to turn to if they had problems. The trainers soon found it necessary to add tutorial support.

All the national providers—e.g. Open College, Open University and National Extension College—can make packages available to users on a stand-alone basis. But their reputation depends on supported packages—e.g. using FlexiStudy or correspondence tuition.

Packages used in the third way mentioned above—alongside class sessions—can be an important means of saving on expensive contact time. They can also ensure such time is reserved for activities that learners cannot do on their own. At present, the Open Learning Foundation expects its packages to be used largely in this way.

So, learners need not only packages but also support. In addition, to some degree or other, they may need the "real world". Although its potential role in open learning programmes is rarely highlighted, the learner's world—of work, family or community life—may be both a rich resource to draw on in learning and a test-bed for trying out new ideas. (After all, most of us do get much of our most important learning out of this local world, unaided by either packages or support.) Packages and support systems that do not tie in to what the learner can draw on locally may be neglecting a vital means of helping him or her become autonomous.

 You may like to make a note about how packages are or might be used in the system you have in mind.

How open is open learning?

No learning system or programme is ever fully open. Nor is any fully closed. Openness is an ideal for which we must keep striving rather than a state we can expect to attain.

Open v closed systems

What might a fully **open** system look like?

- Whatever you wanted to learn about, you would be able to get a programme tailored to your wishes and at an acceptable price.

- You would get it when you wanted it, where you wanted it, and at your own pace.

- You would be able to set your own objectives, choose the content and sequence of your programme, and decide when and how your learning was to be assessed.

- You would also be able to decide how you wanted to learn —e.g. with others or on your own, from books or from videos, with the emphasis on theory or on practice—and who might help you in what kind of ways.

And how would you get on in a fully closed system? Strictly speaking, you wouldn't get in at all—you'd be too old, too young, short of the required educational background or of the required fee, or you'd be in the wrong organisation (or in the right organisation but the wrong job). But if you did get in—and you might find you'd been put in whether you wanted to be in or not—then you'd have few of the choices mentioned in the previous paragraph.

- The programme organisers would tell you what you had to learn about, the objectives you were expected to attain and how you would be assessed.

- You'd have to learn in a specified place, at specified times and the pace would be set by the organisers.

- The learning methods and sequence would also be set by the organisers and they would decide who might help you and what sort of help they might give. Your wishes or preferences would not be taken into account when these decisions were made.

The open learning continuum

Clearly, these are two extreme scenarios. Most learning programmes and systems lie somewhere on a **continuum** (Lewis & Spencer, 1986) between these extremes. Some systems and programmes are more welcoming and accommodating than others. Those that are more welcoming and accommodating—that is, more open—may be so in a variety of ways.

So how do we compare the openness of one system with that of another? Lewis & Spencer (1986) suggest some 30 questions to help decide how far a system lies along along the Closed-Open continuum. I find it more revealing to ask about a smaller set of factors under three main headings: WHO? WHAT? & HOW?

WHO?   How easy is it for someone to become a learner without restrictions of age, qualifications, wealth, job, etc? And to what extent will success depend on the learner possessing already the same learning skills and motivation and cultural background as the learners the system is used to dealing with?

WHAT?   To what extent is the learner free to decide the content and objectives of the programme and when and how he or she will be assessed?

HOW?   To what extent is the learner free to decide where, when and at what pace he or she will learn, the teaching/learning methods to use and the routes to take, and how he or she will call on other people for support?

For each separate factor we might question under these three headings, a learning system or programme will lie somewhere along the continuum from very closed to very open. For example, under the WHAT? heading, consider the factor of programme content. A programme is:

- **very closed**   if all learners must study exactly what they are told to study

- **not quite so closed (or somewhat open)**   if they can make up their programme by choosing from a range of modules

- **even less closed (more open)**   if the range of modules is very varied and each module is quite short

- **yet more open**   if they can choose topics within a module

- **very open**   if the entire content is tailored to suit the wishes of each individual learner.

I leave you to think up your own 5-point scale for each of the other factors mentioned—together with any additional factors that occur to you.

If you haven't considered such factors before you may like to apply them to a learning system you know—e.g. the system you are working in or a programme you are thinking of setting up. Towards which end of the continuum does it lie on each of the factors under each heading—and overall?

 You may think this is worth a note in your portfolio.

I think I'd be safe in betting that your system is some way from the open end. There aren't many systems that are open enough for learners to decide exactly what and how they want to learn. For comparison, try imagining the learning programme you might devise for yourself if you wanted to learn how to grow your own vegetables or find out more about antiques. Where would that lie on the continuum?

How open is the Open University?

Many people assume that, given its name, the Open University must be pretty open. But is it? As a matter of fact, I don't remember any of my colleagues using the term open learning before the early 1980s. Prior to that we always said we were in distance education—and most of us still do.

So let's ask just how open the OU actually is. We'd get a rather different answer according to which of the university's activities we looked at. But let's consider how the questions above relate to the OU's undergraduate programme (which covers about 70% of its students):

Who can learn?

The Open University has no entry requirements, so anyone over the age of 18 can enrol for undergraduate courses—if they can afford the fees and other expenses. They may have to wait a year or more though, because applications always far exceed the number of places available.

What can they learn?

OU students have free choice among courses from a wide range of disciplines. Within a course, however, there is rarely any chance for students to choose or negotiate what to study in the light of their personal interests. Once embarked on a course (some entailing 100, some as much as 400 hours of learning), students usually cannot risk omitting any of it.

What they learn is heavily constrained by the objectives implicit or explicit in the assessment requirements. And they have little or no control over that. Courses have both continuous assessment (usually through essays but often with computer-marked objective questions as well) and an examination. Students have to perform satisfactorily on both. Except on some project-based courses, there will be little opportunity for them to negotiate an individual assessment theme to fit in with their own interests.

How can they learn?

OU students are mostly free to learn wherever they like. Occasional attendance at tutorials and day-schools is optional. However, the compulsory attendance at summer school on some courses remains a barrier that may exclude many potential students.

But undergraduates have no choice as to when they start and finish. All undergraduate courses start in February and end in November. Once in, students have some day-by-day choice of when to study, but their overall pace may be influenced by the timing of television and radio broadcasts and will be heavily controlled by the cut-off dates (ominous term!) for assignments.

Nor do they have much choice of teaching and learning method. At least 90% of their learning on most courses is driven by specially developed workbooks and published texts. Television, audio, practical work and computers may also be used—but typically to present additional content rather than provide an alternative approach for those who don't take easily to reading. In addition, course structures are usually quite controlling—students are constrained to follow a fixed sequence, reinforced by the order in which batches of material are sent to them and by the sequence in which assignments are to be completed.

OU undergraduates are allotted a succession of tutors depending on which courses they take. They do not have a choice and tutors vary in how responsive they are to the needs of an individual student.

The overall reckoning?

So even the Open University is open only to a limited extent, and scarcely at all in some aspects. Compared with most other institutions of higher education, the OU is much more open on Who? and to a lesser extent on What? and How? But the gap is less wide than it was when the OU took in its first students in 1971. The need to attract more students, and the successful example set by the OU, have prompted many other institutions to allow easier access and enable more learner choice by offering shorter, modular courses.

How open is in-company training?

For comparison, let's consider the openness of a typical in-company open learning scheme:

Who can learn?

Most in-company programmes are open only to people in the company. In fact, they are probably not even open to everyone in the company. For example, few training departments would consider it wise (even if they could afford it) to let everyone join a management training scheme. Furthermore, even those who are eligible may need to be nominated. They may even be put on the programme whether they desire it or not. (I remember running workshops for one group of professionals who told me they had, in their local parlance, been "warned to attend".)

What can they learn?

Nor do in-company schemes usually offer much choice over objectives, content or assessment. The employers decide what knowledge and competence will suit their objectives, and the programme is tailored accordingly. From the employer's point of view, this is one of the advantages over sending people away for courses elsewhere.

How can they learn?

Trainees are not likely to have much choice about teaching and learning methods, or about who might help them. In fact, the openness of most in-company schemes lies solely in the aspects of "time, place and pace" promoted by Open Tech.

Though even this is limited if the programme is based on computers and other kit or involves attendance at a learning centre.

There may be little sign of the four learner-centred aims listed by Lewis and Spencer. The focus is usually on satisfying the needs of the employer and the job rather than the needs of the learner.

Are they open?

Is "open learning" something of a misnomer for such schemes? Some organisations seem to think so, preferring to use the term "flexible learning" or—as at British Gas, the Post Office and the police service—"distance learning" or, where appropriate, "computer-based training".

Perhaps we could say that they are using open learning **methods** but without drawing much on the philosophy. With a few interesting exceptions—e.g. the "personal development" approach at Ford, Rover and Lucas—open learning in industry may be more clearly described as "packaged training" or, to varying extents, "supported packaged training".

This is not meant to disparage such programmes. Supported packages are usually a more cost-effective way of achieving the employer's objectives than trying to get people onto classroom-based courses. This may suit the learners' purposes better, also—providing them with a more user-friendly means of attaining new competences and greater confidence in their work.

But are they open enough to be called open learning? And is the OU undergraduate programme for that matter?

 Where would you want to draw the line in calling a learning programme "open"? You may think this worth a note in your portfolio.

The Rumble-Lewis debate

During 1989/90, such questions as those above gave rise to a fascinating tussle for ownership of the term "open learning". It took the form of a debate that ran over four issues of *Open*

Learning. Writing from the Open University, Greville Rumble (1989) started it with an article that concluded thus:

> "The term 'open learning' is now being used to describe systems which are anything but open. This is a monstrous misuse of language which needs to be stopped now."

Roger Lewis (1990), writing from the Open College and with an interest in industrial training as well as education, scolded Rumble for suggesting that the OU's access policy set the standard for openness. He quoted another OU writer, Ian McNay (1988), to the effect that the OU's admissions policy "skews the entry towards the socially adept systems players". In any case, he suggested, openness in terms of "choice over the content of learning and over the means by which it is delivered is currently more important" than being open to the general public. As he said:

> "There may be little use in gaining access to a scheme when, once in it, choice is restricted at almost every point."

Lewis also reminded Rumble that changes in the use of language cannot be "stopped". People will apply the term open learning to systems as they see fit. Rumble (1990) replied that certain uses would be "misleading" as when "dictatorships are called democratic republics". The Rumble-Lewis debate continued through numbers 2 and 3 in volume 5 of *Open Learning* with new pundits entering the fray. If you haven't yet looked at these articles, you may think them worth your attention. Their clash of viewpoints caused quite a few of us to re-examine our prejudices.

What sort of openness do YOU want?

Of course, we could all go on for ever with the sophisticated equivalent of "We're more open than you"—"No you're not"—"Yes we are". But none of us can afford to be complacent. However differently we define openness, we all need to ask ourselves: Are we open **enough**?

What might we do to become more open? Is it enough just to let more people have a go at the same old standard programmes? Or must we develop new programmes to ensure the success and satisfaction of the newcomers?

Think about the system you are working in, or the particular programme you are developing for your learners:

- How might it be made more welcoming to learners who are not at present being attracted?

- Might it be possible to give learners more choice about what they are learning and how it might be assessed?

- What more might be done to enable perhaps new kinds of learners to learn in the ways that are best for them?

 Perhaps you might find it helpful to write some notes about these questions in your portfolio.

Opening up

There is plenty that we in the Open University might do to make our undergraduate courses more open—as a former colleague has been telling us for some time (Harris 1976, 1987). For example, here are just a few of the ways of further opening our system that have been suggested over the years:

- Get more funding so that we can lower the fees (At present, studying for a degree costs at least £2000.)

- Have several start dates during the year (as we do on some of our continuing education courses) rather than just one.

- Break our introductory courses (now demanding at least 12 hours study a week for 32 weeks) into shorter modules that learners could spread over a longer period.

- Make summer schools optional rather than compulsory.

- Have more courses in which learners are given room to develop their own content—e.g. by means of a project.

- Allow students to negotiate more of the assignment topics on their courses and be more flexible about the deadlines by which assignments must be completed.

- Make our packages less controlling and enable learners to find their own best routes through the course.

Many colleagues from various institutions who've examined their openness on workshops with me have started to feel rather despondent. "We don't seem to be giving learners much in the way of autonomy," they say. "Are we really doing open learning at all?"

For myself, I try not to be too sniffy about who is entitled to march behind the banner. It's all relative: we're none of us as open as we might be. If the kudos or funds provided by the slogan can help teachers and learners to work more productively and enthusiastically—and perhaps allow us to remind them that they are not yet as open as their banner might imply—then I wouldn't want to "Rumble" them.

Or will you settle for flexibility?

Some providers have begun to hedge their bets (fudge the issue?) by saying they're offering "open or flexible learning". This leaves us to decide which of the two is on offer in a particular programme—or whether all their programmes offer both at once. And it still begs the question : "Flexible in what ways, and to what degree—compared with what?"

An approach labelled "flexible learning" (without explicit mention of openness) is now very much up and coming in schools and colleges. It has been propelled by the Employment Department's TVEI Flexible Learning Development programme. Already it has inspired a minor flood of publications, many of them government-sponsored (e.g. Eraut *et al*, 1991; FEU, 1992: Tomlinson & Kilner, 1991). The chief aims of the TVEI Flexible Learning Development programme are:

> ". . . to meet the learning needs of students as individuals and in groups . . . and to give the student increasing responsibility for his/her own learning within a framework of support."

You may wish to investigate the literature with a view to finding out how far and in what ways flexible learning differs from open learning—and other forms of learning.

What are the limits to openness?

We cannot expect any one institution to be wide open to all potential learners in every aspect. We are all limited by what our budgets and talents enable us to offer. Besides which, we may be daunted by certain tensions and contradictions within the ideals of openness. What may make the system more user-friendly for some learners may make it less so for others.

For instance, suppose we let anyone enrol, regardless of whether they have already gained the prior competences that the programme has previously reckoned to build upon. If we are to help them catch up and keep up, we'll need to divert resources from the teaching of other students. But this may impoverish the teaching we can offer them and so make it less responsive, less open for them.

Again, we may decide not to pace our learners with timetabled meetings and regular assignment deadlines. This flexibility may appeal to learners who are already experienced and well-organised. But what about those who have not yet acquired the self-discipline needed for truly independent learning? Might they suffer by losing this encouragement to find time for study?

And how much control over what and how they learn are our learners ready to take? If we insist they make too many choices, too soon, some may be frightened off. Reporting his experience with mature learners, Lewis Elton (1988) says: ". . . many students find the greater freedom and responsibility given to them hard to handle." He recommends offering learners gradually more and more openness as they progress through a programme (or through their learning careers).

As open learning providers, we are all entitled to set our own limits: "These are the learners to whom I can open new opportunities. These are the ways in which I will make learning more productive and satisfying for them. More than that I cannot do—as yet."

How far might we reach?

But we must remain aware of the gap between our rhetoric and reality. And I don't just mean that learner-centred, autonomous, self-directed learning is more talked about than practised. I mean also that there are still many potential learners whose needs we have not begun to consider. So far, as Winifred Hirst (1986) pointed out:

> "the practice of open learning has had little impact on movement toward learning appropriate to an open society."

Even though each of our institutions limits itself, we are entitled to raise our eyebrows if the open learning movement as a whole fails to provide learning opportunities that might help transform the lives of people who are not attracted to what we currently have to offer. I'm thinking here of people who don't have much clout in the market-place—e.g. people who are homeless, housebound, imprisoned, retired—the unwaged, unwooed and often unwanted.

Many large organisations are looking to open learning to cut training costs and/or increase productivity. Perhaps some of them will be public-spirited enough to invest a little of the proceeds in promoting open learning in the community around them—starting perhaps with their redundant ex-employees or by helping local people improve their basic skills. (Marks & Spencer has already made some money available to promote local open learning.)

Do you think open learning should reach out to people who are not even aware that learning might help them improve their lives? Can you identify groups that your organisation might work with? Can you imagine what kind of provision you might be able to offer them?

 You may want to record some thoughts in your portfolio.

What is distance learning?

So far, I have scarcely needed to mention distance learning. Perhaps, it is now time we defined it and compared it with open learning.

Distance learning is learning while at a distance from one's teacher—usually with the help of pre-recorded, packaged learning materials. The learners are separated from their teachers in time and space but are still being guided by them.

The biggest and best-known distance learning systems are part of the **distance education** movement. This embraces the hundreds of world-wide schools, colleges and universities who cater for learners studying at a distance. The movement has spawned several specialist journals and numerous books. Oddly enough, with the exception of the journal *Open Learning*, which was once called *Teaching at a Distance*, the literature on distance education rarely refers to the literature on open learning, or vice versa.

Desmond Keegan (1990) prefers using the term "distance education" because it includes both distance learning and distance teaching. Unfortunately it doesn't include all distance learning. Distance learning is used not only in education but also in much industrial and professional training.

How open is distance learning?

And what is the connection between open learning and distance learning? Simply this—if the **philosophy** of open learning is to do with improving access and learner-control, then the **method** (thanks to self-study materials) usually involves some element of distance learning.

However, while open learning usually involves distance learning, not all distance learning systems are particularly open. As I said earlier, it is possible to use the method without the philosophy.

Theoretically, distance learning needn't be open at all. A few years ago, the film *Superman* demonstrated an extreme example of distance learning. Our infant hero, on his solitary spaceship journey from Krypton to Smallsville, USA, was kept occupied with a packaged course that taught him all he would need to know about Earth and its inhabitants. The learning programme was totally closed.

In the real world, most distance education programmes are fairly open, as we've seen with the British Open University. But they may be open in different ways and to different extents. For example, the equivalents of the Open University in Germany and Spain demand exactly the same entry qualifications as other universities. Where distance learning is used in vocational and professional training it may be even less open.

What kind of distance?

As with openness, a learner's learning may be more or less **distant**, and in a variety of ways. We need to ask exactly what the learner is distant from and for how long.

There is often some element of distance even in a classroom-based, on-site course. For example, which of the following will YOUR learners be distant from?

☐ the teachers/trainers who developed their programme

☐ someone who can respond to their individual concerns or difficulties (e.g. a tutor or mentor)

☐ the people who will assess their learning for accreditation

☐ other learners with whom they might pursue joint learning and mutual support

☐ equipment or facilities that might aid their learning

☐ the context in which, or "clients" with whom, their learning is meant to be applied (e.g. student teachers learning in college rather than in school).

☐ *Anything else? (What?)*

The feeling of distance

Not all distance learning systems involve all these kinds of distance. The demands and opportunities within a learning system will differ according to which factors the learner is at a distance from and for how long.

Notice that it is accessibility rather than geographical distance that matters here. The on-site learner having difficulty with a CBT package may know that the people who wrote it are in the next office. But if they are not available for consultation, he or she may feel as distant as if they were on the other side of the moon. Conversely, the learner in a Basic Skills Open Learning Centre may be happy to work alone with workbook and tapes knowing that a tutor is within call if needed.

Similarly, learners who can telephone a tutor any evening or get face-to-face feedback once a week may feel less distant than those who can only get written comments once a month. And learners who can easily meet other learners learn differently from those who are working alone. A hutful of villagers in China or Africa watching a satellite television broadcast in company with a trained animateur are experiencing "distance" differently from the Open College student watching a video alone at home.

Such factors help explain why some on-site learners can feel "distanced". Many higher education students are very much aware, especially in these days of worsening staff-student ratios, that they are largely having to teach themselves, with sparse and infrequent feedback from tutors.

I also remember one course for third world health workers—a lengthy residential course held in Europe—whose organisers were turning it into a distance learning course so that (paradoxically) the new approaches would not have to be learned at a distance from the patients and co-workers with whom they were to be used. For them, the "real world" would play a more potent role in the package-support-world "triangle" than it does in many open learning programmes.

Is there a **key** factor among those I've listed? I suspect one's sense of distance depends chiefly on how quickly and satisfactorily one can get individual help or feedback from another human being whose viewpoints seem relevant—e.g. a teacher, an assessor, another learner or a co-worker.

 At this point you may want to look again at the ideas you wrote down earlier about the key features of open and distance learning. Have your ideas changed at all?

Final remarks

- All open learning (even on-site) involves some degree of distance learning.

- Not all distance learning involves much openness—except perhaps of time, place and pace.

- But many so-called open learning systems don't involve much of any other kind of openness either.

- And some learning systems that don't call themselves open are actually more open than some that do.

I leave you to ponder how much more open our learning systems might have to become if they are to cater for the world of "new work" envisaged by Michael Young (1988):

> "Quite soon over half the adult population will be over 50, and with earlier and earlier retirement, coupled with increased life expectancy, many millions of people are going to have over 25 years of active life ahead of them without much prospect of getting ordinary paid work again. There is going to be a second society and second careers, still based on 'work' but on a different kind of work in which people help themselves to new skills, new

disciplines and new fulfilments. The old education fed by the acquisition of book knowledge will not be appropriate for many of them.

. . . In the new era, people will not be limited by the habits and timetables they have for centuries been drilled into at school and in their ordinary workplaces. They will be less the creatures of the greater and lesser bureaucracies and more their own men and women, still working but to unfold more of their own span of capacities, their own ability to create, their own sense of beauty, their own sympathy for each other than any society has ever before tolerated."

 What remaining concerns, fears or questions do you have about the nature of open and distance learning? Make a note of any that seem important enough to bear in mind when you do your desk work and field work on this topic.

Suggested follow-up work

Desk work

Thorpe & Grugeon (1987) has several useful chapters, some
setting the scene, some defining the field, and some
illustrating uses of open and distance learning in
educational and industrial contexts.

Robinson (1989) has two chapters setting the scene and
defining terms, together with several chapters that give
examples of open and distance learning in nurse training.

Paine (1988) provides an excellent range of chapters on the
social, political and educational background of open
learning (including several critical voices) and also gives
some useful glimpses of open learning in practice in both
educational and industrial settings.

Temple (1991) spends little time philosophising about open
learning, but it is rich with examples of open learning in
industrial settings and it does have a final chapter entitled
"What is open learning?"

In addition, you may find other sources you want to look at
in the bibliography at the end of this book. One of the best
ways of keeping up to date in this field is to devote a little
time every few weeks to regular publications like *Open
Learning* and *OLS News*.

Field work

- If your organisation has already embarked on open
  learning while you are new to it, try to establish what the
  prevailing philosophy is. Maybe there is a published
  statement of purpose or intent (e.g. a "mission
  statement")? Maybe you'll have to ask around. Look out
  for discrepancies between public and private beliefs.

- Find some people (teachers or learners, inside or outside
  your organisation) who will tell you about their open
  learning experience. How does it rate for openness on the
  WHO?/WHAT?/HOW? continuums?

- Begin building up your own contacts, case studies and
  reference materials by writing off to organisations that

seem to developing or supporting open learning of the kind you are interested in.

- Join together with other colleagues who are at much the same stage as yourself in exploring open learning. Consider basing discussions on materials from this book or others you find useful; and maybe you can get more experienced colleagues to present some workshops.

 Remember to make a record of your desk work and field work in your portfolio.

Reflection checklist

 When you have completed your desk work and field work on this unit, please make notes in your portfolio using some of the following questions as a guide:

o What are the most important things you have learned during this unit? (You may want to look back at the objectives suggested at the beginning.)

o What has given you most satisfaction in this unit?

o What do you feel least satisfied about in this unit?

o Does this unit leave you with any unresolved questions or difficulties you feel you want help with?

o How might you try to get the help you need?

o What have you learned in your work with other people during this unit?

o In what ways were you able to draw on your previous experience during this unit?

o What have you learned about yourself—your own feelings, ideas and competences?

o What do you feel you need to do next?

Unit 2

Open learners & their learning

What sort of learners are you hoping for? People pretty much like those you're used to dealing with? Or are you ready to respond to new kinds of learners with interests and needs quite different from those you are used to? Either way, what do you need to know about them in order to help them learn with satisfaction?

And what will your new learners be learning? Whatever you choose to teach? Or will your learners have a say in deciding the content and purpose of their own learning?

Suggested objectives

As a result of working on this unit you could be better able to:

- Find out things about your learners that will affect the way you design the learning system.

- Make the learning system appropriate to what you know of your learners.

- Help them develop their own abilities to learn.

o *Any objectives of your own to add?*

 I suggest you now start a new section in your portfolio in which to keep a record of your ideas about Open Learners and their Learning. From time to time, I'll print a box like this (with the symbol alongside) to prompt you to write something in your portfolio. I expect you will use some of these prompts and not others; and also that you will make occasional notes without my prompting.

Know your learners

Open learning—more than other kinds of learning—is supposed to be learner-centred. Traditional education, like traditional industry, has long been producer-centred. That is, teachers and institutions developed the product they wanted to develop and there was never any shortage of customers.

We didn't need to know much about them—so long as they had the right amount of cash (or A levels) in their pockets. That alone was sufficient guarantee that most of them would cope reasonably well and if some of them didn't, well, that was their look-out. A few failures were nothing to worry about and even testified to the high value of the product.

Choice and variety

In the last two or three decades, however, people have come to expect choice. In industry, the emphasis has shifted from selling (getting people to buy what producers feel like producing) to marketing (finding out what they want and providing it). As Richard Edwards (1991) puts it:

> "Shops no longer keep large stocks of a narrow range of items. They have small stocks of a large range of items. Any walk down a High Street will confirm this change. Shops respond to the consumer demands of particular market segments. Products have a shorter lifespan and there is a greater need for innovation and design. . . The mass market is dead, supposedly replaced by consumer choice and power."

In education too, the mass market seems to be a thing of the past. People's needs can no longer be met by an educational assembly-line that picks them up as infants, bolts on various modules of knowledge and skills at successive ages as they pass along it and then drops them off at this age or that according to whether the system decides to put them on the road as basic models or as top-of-the-range.

New learning, new learners

This front-loading, "preparation for life" conception of education has been made redundant by the huge changes wrought in society by economics and technology. Thirty years ago, it was possible to greet the fresh concept of "lifelong education" as a lifestyle option for an age of increased leisure. Now it is becoming a necessity for survival. Whether we are simply trying to understand the world or are trying to hang on to paid employment, we realise that there's no way but to keep on learning, throughout our lives.

But people's lives run different ways. Hence the education and training market has become segmented and diversified. Providers are facing new demands from a greater variety of learners—more mature ones, especially—and from new sponsors like the Training and Enterprise (or Local Enterprise) Councils.

Satisfying our consumers

These new consumers want a wider range of products, they want relevance, they want it when they want it, and they want value for money. In short, consumers more and more expect a product that is tailored to their individual needs. However, we'd do well to notice that some of these customers (the people who put up the money and therefore call the shots) are not the individual learners themselves but their employers or sponsors. (More about that in Unit 8.)

Open learning is just one expression of this new consumer-orientation in education and training. Other new devices—like accreditation of prior learning, credit accumulation and transfer, and modularisation of courses—are all part of the same shift. If we are to make them work—so that they really do meet the requirements of the individual learner—we'll need to know a lot more about that individual learner than we've ever needed to know in the past.

How do you and your colleagues feel about regarding learners as consumers or as your customers or clients? What benefits might it have—for them and for you? What drawbacks?

 You may think this worth a note in your portfolio.

What might you need to know?

What do you need to know about your learners? The short answer is—anything you might use to help them enjoy the most productive and satisfying learning experiences. Even if you are developing programmes for learners you will never meet, there is much you need to know about them. If you are supporting individual learners who are working on a programme, you may need to know yet more.

Knowledge about your learners may help you in:

- counselling prospective learners about their programmes
- preparing packaged learning materials that relate to their needs and preferences
- planning a support service and delivering it in a humane and responsive way once learners have begun on their programmes
- adjusting the programme to suit the needs of different individuals as they work through it
- counselling learners about ways of building on what they have learned.
- *Others? (What?)*

Consider the factors mentioned in the following checklist. Which of them might you find it useful to know about in the case of your learners? Which of the questions do you feel you can already answer satisfactorily? Are there any additional questions you would want to ask?

Demographic factors

☐ How many learners are you likely to have?

☐ How old?

☐ What sex and race?

☐ Any personal handicaps?

☐ Occupations (if any)?

☐ Whereabouts in (or out of) the country will they be learning?

Motivation

☐ Why are they learning?

☐ How might your programme relate to their lives or work?

☐ What do they want from the programme?

☐ What are their hopes and fears?

Learning factors

☐ What are their beliefs about learning?

☐ What learning styles do they prefer?

☐ What learning skills do they have?

☐ What experience of **open** learning?

Subject background

☐ How do they feel about the subject of the programme?

☐ What knowledge and skills do they already have in that subject?

☐ What personal interests and experience might they have that are relevant?

Resource factors

☐ Where, when and how will they be learning?

☐ Who will be paying their fees?

☐ How much time will they have available?

☐ What access will they have to media/facilities?

☐ What access to human support—tutors, mentors, colleagues, other learners?

☐ *Other factors? (What?)*

You may want to make some notes in your portfolio after reading through the checklist above.

Clearly, there are many things we might want to know about our learners. And it would not be idle curiosity. The fact is, such knowledge could have implications for our teaching. Knowing more about our learners would help us remove barriers to their learning. We could thus make it more open.

How to find out?

When much our teaching will be done through packages—especially when learners are studying at a distance—we need to obtain information about them **before** they begin. Otherwise it cannot affect the teaching as much as it should. There are three main ways of building up a picture of your prospective learners:

- Reflect on your previous experience of those learners, or broadly similar ones, and consult colleagues.

- Meet some of the prospective learners and discuss with them (individually or as a group) what they would like from the programme, and what they already know/feel about the subject.

- Send a questionnaire to prospective learners, trying to elicit the information you need. If this can be followed up by discussion with learners, whether face-to-face or on the telephone, so much the better.

Using what you know

What we discover about our learners may reveal numerous barriers, or potential barriers to learning. Some of these will be within us, some within our learners, and some in the relationship between them and us (or our organisations). Let's see if we can identify some of these barriers and consider ways we might avoid them or lessen them.

The demographic factors

Here it is important to know whether you are dealing with a couple of dozen learners or a couple of thousand. With small numbers it may be easier to respond to the needs of individuals; with large numbers it may be possible to develop special learning packages. These two outcomes may be mutually exclusive. Which of them better suits your philosophy of openness?

Does age make a difference?

How might your learners' ages influence the learning programme? Most open learners are adult learners. Compared with children, adult learners are more likely to be:

- rich in experience (or attitudes) relevant to the subject of their learning programme

- goal-oriented—with their own agendas to attain
- self-aware—wanting their own view of things taken into account
- haunted (benignly or otherwise) by memories of schooling
- more various in their beliefs and feelings about learning
- more concerned with getting value for time and money—especially if the time and money is their own.

Adults may differ greatly among themselves. Aspects of a programme that suit one adult learner will not suit another. So how far can you give each one what they need or want? If you are doing flexible learning or supported self-study in school, you may take issue with me here. You may argue that younger learners can be just as various, but in different ways. And the learning programme needs to be individualised for them also.

Equal opportunities?

Will you try to ensure that your programme doesn't make access unduly difficult for people of one sex rather than the other, or for people of certain races or with certain physical handicaps? If you are providing open learning within industry, you may wonder whether you can justifiably deny access to people from certain jobs or ranks—e.g. to supervisory or management training.

Even if access is unimpeded, open learning material can alienate some learners if they think the writers regard them as inferior or invisible. For instance, the material may show certain people in stereotyped or derogatory roles or ignore their perspective altogether when they think it should be represented.

I remember a police training package in which—as some women officers were quick to point out—the word "policeman" had been used (instead of "police officer") throughout and all the examples showed male officers at work. On the other hand, I remember one packaged course on child-rearing whose authors were careful to include many photographs of black and Asian parents as well as white ones tending their children. Unfortunately, all the parents shown were women. (The oversight was corrected in the next edition.)

Where are they?

The whereabouts of your learners may make a big difference to the shape of the programme. Are they all working on oil rigs in the North Sea—able to meet with one another but not with a tutor? Do they travel throughout Europe—distant from both tutors and other learners? Or are they all within easy reach of you and one another so all can get together easily for tutorials or group activities?

 Do you have any thoughts to note in your portfolio?

Motivations

No problem here, some may think. Open learners are all thrilled to bits to be given new opportunities and they're highly motivated, aren't they? Don't be misled by the rhetoric. Not all beneficiaries of so-called open learning are learners by choice. Some, especially in vocational training, have open learning thrust upon them.

Many feel insulted that they are being asked to undertake training at all. "Training is for the unemployed," they say. They may be particularly resentful (and resistant) if they are expected to do any of the training in their own time.

Orientations to learning

Even if your learners are volunteers, it will pay you to know what they might want from their learning. Some of my colleagues (see Taylor *et al*, 1981) have identified four common attitudes—or "orientations" as they call them—to studying. They labelled these as follows:

* "vocational"—to do with the learner's present or hoped-for job

* "academic"—to do with interest in study or education for its own sake

* "personal"—to do with developing oneself as a person

* "social"—to do with partying, playing sports and having a good time.

And all but the last of these can be pursued either for "intrinsic" or "extrinsic" purposes. That is, a person may be (intrinsically) interested in what they are learning. Or they may be (extrinsically) interested in what they hope will **result** from the learning—e.g. promotion, a pay-rise, a degree, the respect of their spouse. The fourth orientation seems purely extrinsic—showing no real interest in studying at all, other than as an excuse for being in congenial company.

You may want to ask your own learners why they are studying. Some may have several reasons but they will probably be able to tell you the main reason. Here are some reasons I've been told. (See if you agree with the way I've classified them.)

- *"I felt I was vegetating, so this should give me a chance to get my mind into gear."* (Personal-intrinsic)

- *"It should help me cope better with difficult people at work."* (Vocational-intrinsic)

- *"If I pass this course I'll be able to prove I'm not rubbish."* (Personal-extrinsic)

- *"They said I'd need the certificate to protect me against redundancy."* (Vocational-extrinsic)

- *"I've always been interested in this subject, but I've never had time to study it in depth."* (Academic-intrinsic)

- *"I want to complete my qualification."* (Academic-extrinsic).

Learners may also develop new orientations once they have started on a programme. Gary may start on a course only because he's been told to, yet find to his surprise that he is actually enjoying it and finding it useful. Conversely, Karen may come in search of personal growth only to be disappointed and thereafter settle, cynically, for just doing enough to collect her "piece of paper" at the end.

Improving learners' orientations

Two researchers (see Sagar & Strang, 1985; Strang, 1987) interviewed some adult learners on an Open Tech engineering programme about their reasons for studying. They found that learners with intrinsic interests tended to get higher grades than those with extrinsic interests. This is not surprising. Extrinsically motivated learners are rather inclined to study as little as they can get away with.

So can we—in marketing our programmes, in developing materials, and in talking with individual learners—promote the **intrinsic** benefits that learners might expect to get from their learning? How might what they learn help them in their work, their family or social life, or in their development as persons?

Such an approach may also help learners to realise that they may have several reasons for studying—e.g. personal as well as academic or vocational. Eileen Sagar and Alison Strang confirmed that learners with several reasons for studying are more likely to do better than those with one only. This could be a useful part of pre-programme counselling. You may be interested to look at one of my books (Rowntree, 1988), in which I try to get learners to reflect about their purposes in studying.

How might you explore such issues with your learners?

Learning beliefs, styles and skills

Learners not only have orientations to studying and learning. They also have beliefs about learning—not to mention styles and skills of learning—that we may need to know about.

Conceptions of learning

To begin with, what would your learners think of as learning? In Rowntree (1988) I discuss four conceptions of learning:

1. Learning as memorising
2. Learning as understanding
3. Learning as application
4. Learning as personal development

1st—I suggest that learners (and teachers?) who hold the most basic conception of learning (1) will be concerned largely with facts and procedures that can be reproduced under test conditions. This is the *Mastermind* conception of learning.

2nd—Learners holding the second, more sophisticated conception will not be satisfied simply to remember and reproduce the facts and procedures they've been working with. They will search for ways of making them meaningful—perhaps looking for the ideas that lie behind them, or the patterns and relationships that help make sense of it all, or the links with their own beliefs and values.

3rd—Learners who've reached the third conception will go further still. They will expect to apply what they are learning in some context of their own—and in the process develop new ideas and procedures of their own. They expect their learning to help them see the world differently and perhaps find new ways of making things happen in it.

4th—From there it is but a short step to the most sophisticated conception of all (4). Here the learner recognises that they themselves are part of the world they might come to see or act upon differently. The learner expects to be changed as a person by the experience of learning. Even when the detail is forgotten, something will remain to leave them, in some sense, a wiser and more capable person.

Learners with this fourth conception might agree with Robert Pirsig (1972) who remarks, in his book *Zen and the Art of Motor Cycle Maintenance*, that "the motor cycle you are working on is yourself". (By the way, if you've not come across it, this is a book by a philosophy teacher with an intriguing way of discussing quality in teaching and learning.)

You may or may not accept that these four conceptions would be found among your learners. You may suggest a different set of conceptions. (For one alternative set, see Strang, 1987.)

But one thing I think we shall be able to agree on. Learners may conceive learning differently from their teachers. And this could present a barrier to learning. If, for example, the assessment system is operating at level 1 or 2 when your learners yearn to be at 3 or 4, frustration looms.

So it may be worth asking your learners what they think of as learning and helping them see how their conception relates to what might be happening in the programme. It may even be one of the aims of the programme to help them acquire more sophisticated notions of learning.

Styles of learning

What do you know about your learners' learning styles? Learning styles have been categorised in many different ways. Learners have been identified as, for example:

- Convergers, Divergers, Assimilators or Accommodators (Kolb, 1984).
- Serialists or Holists (Pask, 1976).
- Surface-level or Deep-level processors (Marton & Säljö, 1976).
- Activists, Theorists, Pragmatists or Reflectors (Honey & Mumford, 1986).

Let's consider, for example, the last of these distinctions. What are these four styles of learning? How might knowing about them influence the learning programme you develop?

Honey & Mumford (1986) have developed a questionnaire that asks you whether you agree or disagree with 80 statements such as these:

- I often "throw caution to the winds".
- Quiet, thoughtful people tend to make me uneasy.
- I like to relate my actions to a general principle.
- I steer clear of subjective or ambiguous topics.
- I am careful not to jump to conclusions too quickly.
- On balance I do the listening rather than the talking.
- What matters most is whether something works in practice.
- Most times I believe the end justifies the means.

Your answers enable them to suggest the strength of your preference for each of the four styles they identify. Few people are likely to favour one style to the exclusion of all others. But it is common for one to predominate, with the others being used less often or not at all. None of the styles is inherently superior to the others. All are of value in different contexts.

Teachers too, of course, have their own preferred learning styles. In our traditional producer-centred way, we may tend to design courses that reflect our own preferred learning styles. These may or may not tally with those of our learners.

Honey & Mumford give many detailed suggestions about the kinds of learning activities that people with each learning style are likely to respond well or poorly to. For instance:

STYLES	respond WELL to, e.g.	respond POORLY to, e.g.
Activists *"Here, let me do that."*	New problems, being thrown in at the deep end, team work. . .	Passive learning, solitary work, theory, precise instructions. . .
Theorists *"Yes, but how do you justify it?"*	Interesting concepts, structured situations, opportunities to question and probe. . .	Lack of apparent context or purpose, ambiguity and uncertainty, doubts about validity. . .
Pragmatists *"So long as it works."*	Relevance to real problems, immediate chance to try things out, experts they can emulate. .	Abstract theory, lack of practice or clear guidelines, no obvious benefit from learning. . .
Reflectors *"I need time to consider that."*	Thinking things through, painstaking research, detached observation. . .	Being forced into the limelight, acting without planning, time pressures. . .

If you are developing a learning programme, you may want to check out Honey & Mumford's suggestions in more detail. In the meantime, if you are producing a programme that must suit all comers, try, at least, to make sure that it is:

- novel and participatory enough for the Activists
- intellectually rigorous enough for the Theorists
- practical enough for the Pragmatists
- leisurely enough for the Reflectors.

As with conceptions of learning, you may also plan to help your learners acquire new learning styles. To do so would make them more flexible and open as learners. This would lower yet more barriers between them and what they might learn.

Learning skills

You may also wonder what learning skills your learners have—especially if it is some time since they have done any formal studying. To build up their confidence, you may need to get them thinking about the skills and approaches they use in their everyday, informal learning. For example, how do they learn about D-I-Y tasks, cooking or gardening, or new technology at work? What is the connection between such approaches and those they'll need on the programme?

In particular, you may want to know what experience your learners have of **open** learning. Are they prepared for the demands it is likely to make on their self-discipline (and maybe on their families)? And do they have the skills to learn from the media you plan to use?

For example, if your programme demands they work with printed materials, how competent are they at learning from text? It could be useful to know what newspapers they read and what kind of reading they do as part of their jobs or social life. If they read nothing more taxing than the *Daily Tabloid*, it may be unwise to offer learning materials written at *Guardian* or *Times* level.

Familiarity with open and flexible learning is likely to accelerate over the next few years—not least because young people will meet them before they leave school. But, with so many different approaches to open and flexible learning, can you be sure that your learners will be familiar with yours? If not, you may need to help them learn about learning as well as whatever else you are teaching. Two of my earlier books (Rowntree, 1988 and 1991) may help you with this.

 Any thoughts to note in your portfolio?

Subject background

What do your learners know already about the subject they'll be studying? How do they feel about it? Do they have any relevant interests or experience?

It's most unlikely that the subject will be totally new to them. Even if they don't have knowledge and skills, they are likely to have ideas, attitudes, even prejudices. They may even have more experience than you of some aspects. Knowing their present familiarity with the subject can be a great help in developing a programme that they can truly engage with.

At the very least, you can help them avoid repeating work that they are already familiar with. Or you may need to recommend some prior study to get them "up to speed".

More positively, you may be able to focus the programme on common misconceptions or conflicts of viewpoint.

Building on what they know

You may be able to build on what people already know. You can look for ways of helping them make their own experience part of what they are studying.

Some of my colleagues (Gibbs *et al*, 1980) did this when planning an introductory psychology course. They found that the learners they spoke to had several valid notions about the role of a psychologist; though it would be news to most that psychology was a scientific, experimental discipline. Similarly, another colleague has used intending learners' answers to the question "Is Britain capitalist?" to help decide how to introduce and handle the concept of capitalism in an introductory social science course.

If you are tutoring open learners, you may need to help them relate what they are learning to their prior understandings of the subject. They may want to use their own experience—e.g. at work or in the community—in their assignments. If their learning is project-based, it might involve their bringing new concepts and methods to bear in analysing or exploring their prior (or current) experience.

Learners as contributors

If you are developing a packaged course, it is also worth asking your intending learners (or people like them) about their experience of the subject. They may be able to offer you examples and anecdotes that you can quote in the material. This can help make the package more user-friendly and accessible—because users will recognise that people like them have been seen to have a valid viewpoint.

Roy Webberley (1987, 1988) and his team built this idea into their course production system when producing materials for supervisor training under Open Tech. They developed their packages out of workshops with the target learners:

> "We began by collecting anecdotes—snippets of the supervisors' job experiences in their own words—and we sought to draw up an anecdote bank from which we could draw these experiences (often verbatim)."

This bottom-up approach apparently led to a high level of street credibility. One of the learners summed it up like this:

"It isn't stuffed shirt or jargonese; it's plain and deals with real issues."

Resource factors

No need, I guess, for me to say much about the final items in our checklist. If you don't take them into account, you could end up with a course that will be overloaded, too expensive, badly timed, and based on media inconvenient for learners to use or unsuited to their preferred learning styles. Providers sometimes have.

Do you have a typical learner?

Clearly, there are many ways in which our learners can differ. It could be fatal to regard them as a homogeneous mass. If you are tutoring learners or acting as mentor, there is little danger of this. Your every contact with them will bring home to you their differing needs and responses.

The big challenge is for someone writing a distance learning package? How can one write it in such a way that different learners can each feel welcome in it and get what they want out of it?

Personally, I follow the advice of the poet Robert Graves and imagine a crowd of the prospective learners I have already met are looking over my shoulder as I write. Periodically, I look at something I have written and say to myself: "How would this relate to Khatija's family" or "How would Ron in his wheelchair carry out this activity?"

The danger here, of course, is that I might make the materials too relevant to the few learners I have met at the expense of the many I have not. So I often find it useful to draft a "thumbnail sketch" of my **typical** learner. This gives me a concise summary of all the key facts I've gleaned about my learners. The example on the next page (from a course for farmers and market gardeners) also points out some of the implications of these key facts.

The trick in using a thumbnail sketch is to remember that none of your actual learners will exactly match it. One needs to remember the range as well as the average. In this case, for example, I had to ensure the course was not unwelcoming to the small percentage of women among the learners.

Thumbnail sketch of typical learner
—for *Managing your Farm's Finances*

The typical learner runs a small farm or market garden.
He is male, between 30 and 40 years of age, and is
married with one or two children living at home. He
left school at 16 with a few examination certificates
and has done no systematic studying since. His most
regular reading will be at *Daily Mail* level.

He will not be worried about the cost of books or
travelling to course meetings and will be ready to obtain
playback machines for audio- and video-cassettes if he
does not have them already. However, he is unwilling
to commit himself to attending even occasional class
meetings at a fixed time (because of the unpredictable
demands of his work). This, in fact, is why he is
choosing an open learning course.

He is enrolling for the course in hope of improving his
efficiency and profitability and avoiding hassle from his
bank manager, accountant and tax inspector. He will be
perfectly capable of learning on his own, provided the
materials are flexible enough for him to find his own
level and he is allowed fairly ready access (at least by
telephone) to a tutor or other learners if he gets into
difficulties. The tutor will need to be scrupulous in
providing support rather than criticism.

Needless to say, the learner is very familiar with the
subject-matter of the course. He will be scathing about
anything he regards as "unrealistic" in our examples or
suggestions, and will not stick with the course unless it
remains clearly relevant to what he perceives as his needs.

N.B. A FEW of those "he"s are "she"s.

Any thoughts you want to note in your portfolio?

What will they learn?

This question is little debated in open learning circles. By and large, the nature of our learners' learning seems taken for granted. Our concern seems chiefly with form rather than with content. People worry about the Who? and the How? of learning, but rarely question the What? and the Why?

We have already considered how different learners think about learning. But how do the providers see it? Again, different providers see it differently. And their conceptions of learning don't always match up with those of their learners.

In a moment we'll look at what may be the most important difference of viewpoint—between those who are teaching a subject and those who are teaching learners. But first, let's consider what it is possible to learn with open learning and how the idea of objectives can help the learner make decisions about his or her learning.

What can be learned?

Some people's first reaction on hearing about open learning is to say: "That's all very well, but it wouldn't work in my subject." I have heard this said about any number of subjects from counselling to philosophy, from painting to learning a musical instrument, from vehicle maintenance to appraisal interviewing. In recent years, I have almost always been able to point to a programme that was already operating successfully in that subject.

Such early rejectors are usually equating open learning with solitary packaged learning. How can print and audio-visual packages enable one to learn practical or interpersonal skills? In fact, such packages can do a great deal to aid the learners— preparing them for a learning encounter with the real world of things or people, guiding them through it and helping them reflect on it afterwards.

Powerful open learning materials can change the way people see the world. For instance, Wendy Stainton Rogers (1987) describes a package containing a moving audiotape of a woman talking about her life caring for her mother who was suffering from senile dementia. It helped transform staff attitudes in an old people's home. As the head of the home commented:

> "To make the change I had to know how it felt to be a
> daughter. . . It was hearing a real person, all the emotion
> in her voice, hearing her crying and describing breaking
> point. It was that which convinced me."

Learning alone from a pre-recorded package is not necessarily
impoverished compared with classroom learning. A package
can provide experiences that few classroom teachers could
offer. Furthermore, the permanence of the medium enables a
learner to revisit it as often as she or he wishes. And being
free to do so without "interference" from the reactions of
one's classmates can sometimes be an advantage.

But, of course, there is a limit to what can be learned from
packages alone. Distance learners usually need to converse
regularly with a tutor—either by correspondence or on the
telephone. If learners are on-site, or can meet occasionally,
or can get out and about in the world, various amounts of
practical work, class work and collaboration with other
people can also be built into the system—however much is
needed for the objectives that learners are seeking to attain.

In theory, anything that can be learned via "conventional"
learning may also be learned via open learning. After all, an
open learning programme can include all the approaches
used in conventional teaching plus a few that aren't.

There is certainly no excuse for assuming that open learners
can be offered only a pale shadow of "real" learning. Nor is
there any escape from helping our learners confront the
problem of what learning is most worthwhile.

The role of objectives

Objectives have a particular significance in open learning.
Indeed, they can contribute to its openness. Traditional
syllabuses talked only of the content to be covered. Likewise,
teachers tended to talk largely in terms of aims—what they
planned to do for the learners.

Thanks to the objectives movement—which has been
beavering away for at least seventy years (e.g. Bobbit, 1924)—it
is becoming normal practice to say, in addition, what learners
might be expected to be able to DO as a result.

Thus, the syllabus for a history course might have described
one of its topics simply as "Historical research and
communication". What are potential learners to make of

that? They might get more of a clue if the teacher added that the aim of the course was "to introduce students to the efficient and critical use of all the sources available".

But students would be in a much better position to decide whether this was really the course they wanted—and to organise their work on it—if they were, in addition, told the intended objectives, e.g.

> "By the end of this course, the student should be able to:
>
> (a) Distinguish between primary and secondary sources.
>
> (b) Identify primary sources appropriate to the various kinds of historical data he/she requires.
>
> (c) Assess the likely bias and credibility of a secondary source.
>
> (d) Determine the usefulness of a source.
>
> (e) Distinguish between valid and invalid inferences that might be made from a source."

Such objectives, or "outcomes" as they are sometimes called, make one's proposed programme more transparent—more open. If the view of learning held by the developers of the programme is trivial or irrelevant, nothing will reveal this more quickly than a glance at their suggested objectives.

Once the objectives are out in the open, learners are the more empowered. They can say? "No thanks, I can do that already" or "Those objectives are too narrow for me" or "I would rather you helped me achieve these other objectives instead". If they can show—through Accreditation of Prior Learning— that they have attained the objectives already, they may even be able to get credit for that programme without taking it, and go straight on to whatever they want to do next.

Again, if they accept the objectives, they may be able to negotiate the content. For instance, the above objectives do not specify a particular period of history. Might these basic skills be learned just as well if some learners chose to work on World War II sources, some on the Tudors and some on the early development of the organisation they work in?

Furthermore, once started on a programme, its openly stated objectives enable them to monitor their own progress. They may ask how effective is the programme in helping them attain those objectives. Are they getting the help they need?

Objectives can also make the assessment less of an unknown quantity. Learners will naturally expect to be assessed on how well they can demonstrate the abilities listed as objectives. In the above example, they will expect to be assessed on how well they can handle sources. They will not expect to be assessed on how well they can write an essay about handling sources or about how other historians have handled them. Those assessment tasks would relate to different objectives.

It is only proper to remind you that some commentators are highly critical of objectives (especially in their dreaded "behavioural" form)—and of other "outcomes" approaches. (See, for example, Eisner, 1967: Macdonald-Ross, 1973; Marshall, 1991). Unfortunately, I have no space in this book to debate the pros and cons or tell you about my own reservations and provisos. Perhaps this is an area you'll want to explore further yourself.

Which objectives?

Since they explicitly state what is to be learned and—by implication—what is to be assessed, objectives can help demystify learning and enable the learner to take more responsibility for his or her own decisions.

However, some objectives are more empowering than others. Much depends on whether learners have a say in deciding them. In three earlier books (Rowntree, 1982, 1985, 1987), I have contrasted the many kinds of objectives we might develop—e.g. content objectives, methodological objectives and life-skill objectives; content objectives v. process objectives; mastery objectives v. infinitely improvable objectives.

I have no space to run through all that again here. But there are two related themes I do want to pick out from it. These are:

- the distinction between teaching a subject and nurturing a learner; and

- the value of negotiating objectives with our learners.

Dissemination or development?

Both of those themes are foreign to many teachers. Some see themselves as guardians of the sacred flame—the craft or discipline—whose time-honoured body of knowledge must be passed on intact to their learners. Similarly, others see themselves as the medium through which learners will achieve the "competences" laid down by some authoritative "lead body".

This is what Richard Boot and Vivien Hodgson (1987) have called the "dissemination" model of learning:

> "knowledge can be seen as a (valuable) commodity which exists independently of people and as such can be stored and transmitted (sold)."

The objectives will be framed in terms of the subject—or of the job if we are teaching work-based competences. There will be no room for different learners to have individual objectives each according to his or her own personal angle on the subject.

Very often, our learners will fall in with this point of view. But only, perhaps, because they have not been encouraged to consider any other, more open, viewpoint. Consequently, many so-called open learners are being allowed to go at their own pace, and perhaps in their own way—but towards someone else's objectives. Packaged learning lends itself only too well to the dissemination model.

Boot & Hodgson offer, by contrast, what they call the "development" model. The aim of this, they say, is:

> "the development of the whole person, especially the continuing capacity to make sense of oneself and the world in which one lives."

Here the teacher shifts from saying, "This is what I'm going to teach you and it's your job to learn it" towards saying, "How can I use my interests and expertise to help you build on whatever your interests and strengths may be?"

Where disseminatory teachers are primarily concerned with their **product** (e.g. a package), developmental teachers are primarily interested in **process**—the on-going relationship with a learner. As I have suggested elsewhere (Rowntree, 1975), the former are concerned only with one-way "munication", the latter with two-way "co-mmunication".

The latter expect that they too will learn in the tutor-learner relationship. As one of my literature colleagues told me: "I expect my students to say things which make me radically rethink my own conception of an author or literary work."

The developmental approach can also have explicit objectives. These may be framed in terms of the subject but are more likely to put the learner in the frame also—e.g. not "identify the causes of conflict in organisations" but "identify the causes of conflict in **your** organisation". The learner's perceptions and their family, social or working life become part of the **content** of the programme. (The "motor-cycle" they are working on is themselves.)

And it is more likely to have objectives that can be pursued **whatever** the subject-matter. Consider, for example, these "self-actualisation" objectives suggested by the humanistic psychologist and teacher, Carl Rogers (1961):

"•   The person comes to see himself [sic] differently.

•   He accepts himself and his feelings more fully.

•   He becomes more self-confident and self-directing.

•   He becomes more the person he would like to be.

•   He becomes more flexible, less rigid in his perceptions.

•   He adopts more realistic goals for himself.

•   He becomes more acceptant of others.

•   He becomes more open to the evidence, both of what is going on outside of himself and what is going on inside himself."

Except in certain work with adults, such objectives are rare in education. (See the Open University course, *Personal and Career Development*, for a distance learning example.) Another humanistic psychologist, Abraham Maslow (1968), commented as follows:

". . . education makes little effort to teach the learner to examine reality directly and freshly. Rather it gives a complete set of prefabricated spectacles with which to look at the world in every aspect, e.g. what to believe, what to like, what to approve of, what to feel guilty about. Rarely is each person's individuality made much of."

By startling contrast, developmental objectives are becoming not uncommon in training. Many organisations have begun to recognise that what distinguishes superior from average performers is not technical knowledge but generic "soft skill competencies". Lyle Spencer (1979), reporting on a five year study of people in a variety of careers, gives some examples:

- The ability to discern themes and patterns in large amounts of disparate information.

- The ability to explain the different sides of a controversial issue

- The ability to learn from experience by reflecting on it and forming ideas about how one might do things differently.

- The ability to see beneath the surface features of someone else's behaviour and diagnose the concerns that drive it.

- The ability to promote feelings of efficacy in other people.

- The proactive ability to influence and make an impact on other people.

As Lyle Spencer points out, such generic abilities do not emerge from task-functional analysis—the kind pursued by the UK "competence movement". There, "the unit of analysis is the job, not the person who performs the job well". He suggests that detailed lists of job tasks are of limited use "without supplementary information about the competencies a superior job incumbent uses". If you are concerned with NVQs or SVQs, you might want to ask "Yes, but what are the competencies that are needed to perform these elements of competence?"

To quote one of Spencer's colleagues, George Klemp (1977):

> "Perhaps the most consistent—yet counter-intuitive—finding that we have discovered is that the amount of knowledge of a content area is generally **unrelated** to superior performance in an occupation and is often unrelated **even to marginally acceptable performance**. Certainly many occupations require a certain level of knowledge on the part of the individual for the satisfactory discharge of work-related duties, but even more occupations require only that the individual be willing and able to learn."

When I began working with police trainers around 1986, I found that the training culture was in transition. The emphasis, at least in the training of probationer constables, was shifting from the learning of law and procedures (dissemination) to a more developmental curriculum in which "soft skills competencies" like those mentioned above are now argued to be no less important. (See UEA, 1987.)

It took me a while to sort out my own position in relation to dissemination and development. I wonder where you stand:

- Do you accept that there is a distinction between dissemination and development?

- If so, which do you and your colleagues favour?

- Which would your learners prefer? (You may want to bear in mind what you know of their "orientations".)

- If you and your learners disagree, how might you resolve the conflict of views?

- Could you, within your programmes, combine dissemination and development?

 Perhaps you will want to make some notes in your portfolio.

Fostering learner autonomy

According to Lewis & Spencer (1986), one of the key features of open learning is "a commitment to helping the learner to acquire independence and autonomy". Learners are autonomous to the extent that they can make their own decisions about:

- their learning objectives or intended outcomes

- the subjects, themes, topics, issues they will study

- the learning and teaching resources and methods they will make use of

- when, how and on what they will be assessed.

How does autonomous learning fit in with the distinction between dissemination and development? I suggest that dissemination leaves little room for learners to exercise autonomy, except perhaps in their choice of resources and methods. Developmental approaches, on the other hand, are much more likely to encourage autonomy—and autonomous learning is, by its nature, developmental.

Increasing learners' choice

The traditional (dissemination) model in education and training has been "top-down". The "powers-that-be" have made all the decisions about the four aspects of programme design that I've listed above. Learners are then selected on the grounds of how well they are likely to cope with what the provider has decided to offer—and they are expected to master whatever they are presented with.

In recent years, however, a "bottom-up" approach has begun to make itself felt. In much basic adult education and employment training, it is common for the goals of a programme to be negotiated between learners and tutors— sometimes resulting in individual "learning contracts".

In higher education, learners are being offered a little more choice through the use of modular courses. And some institutions have experimented with "independent learning"—helping learners to design their own diploma or degree programme (see Boud, 1988). Even in fairly conventional programmes, it is not uncommon nowadays to find "options" or "projects" where learners can, at least for part of the programme, negotiate what they are to study and be assessed on.

Learner attitudes

Not all learners will want to influence the shape of their programme, of course. Some—especially those who are learning because it's required of them—will stoutly reject that responsibility. Their attitude may be: "You told us we **had** to learn so you'd better tell us **what** to learn."

Others may feel that, since what they want to do is master the subject they've volunteered for, only someone who's already mastered it can tell them what they need to learn. Some of these may even be autonomous learners who are choosing, for the time being, to surrender some of their independence —a little dissemination may suit their present purposes. The point is, the choice will be theirs, not the teacher's.

Yet others may be so dominated by top-down memories of earlier education that they feel bewildered—to begin with, anyway—by the idea that they might have some say in what they learn. Thus may arise what Lewis Elton (1988) calls "the well known educational paradox that students have to be led to autonomy".

The quotations opposite remind us how people's conception of learning—and of themselves as learners—can change over time.

How learners can change

Year 1

". . . if I look through a book, it's still sort of learning facts and dates and names rather than the content. And if I have read something I'm so bothered about taking in what is said."

"I got worried at the tutorial because the tutor was picking the unit to bits and questioning it—I said to her 'Look, I'm a foundation student. I don't pull this unit to bits, I accept what they have told me.' Sometimes I may not like something that is said, but I must accept what is there because I assume they know what they are talking about and [why] they are putting it to me this way—spoon-feeding me—[after all, I'm] someone who is unlikely to understand any other way."

Year 5

"Real learning is something personal and it's also something continuous, once it's started it carries on and on, and it might lead to other things. . . The unit of work you are given is only the catalyst really, it is only one hundredth of the learning and the rest goes on once you put the book down. And the next time you talk to someone or read something in the newspaper, that's when the rest happens because it's been started and you carry it on for yourself because you want to and you get something lasting from it."

Year 6

"So I suppose I have learned that there are no real right answers and if you get that in your mind to begin with then you can end up agreeing with some theory if you like but you don't have to. It makes you realise that you can take control of your own life. I used to think that life just took hold of you and did what it wanted with you but you come to realise that you should take hold of it and make it go your way."

"The OU is definitely less important now, but it is only less important because I'm more important and I'm more important because of it. Because of what it has done for me or shown me —it might just be the confidence that I can look back and say well I've got through thick and thin and come out on top and pleased with myself. But it has got a lesser place now, but only because it's given me more scope, more ammunition, more confidence. It has definitely led to other things. It has been a self-realisation I suppose of what I can do and be."

from interviews reported in Beaty & Morgan (1992)

What can be done?

Autonomy is always a matter of degree. Not just because different learners are ready only for different amounts but also because there is a limit to the amount of learner-autonomy that any teacher or system can support. Lewis Elton (1988) describes the practical limitations:

> "The most obvious is that of resources. Students may have to adapt their learning objectives to the learning resources— teachers, materials, peers, etc—available and this will also affect content. A second limitation arises if students wish, as is almost always the case, for some certification to document their learning achievement. The extent to which assessment can then be negotiated rather than imposed is perhaps the most difficult area of autonomy learning in practice."

There will always be a compromise between what "the system" requires, what our learners might want to learn about, what we feel they "really ought" to learn and what we feel capable of supporting them with. So—how far, and in what ways, might you foster autonomy among your learners?

Learners usually do exercise some choice about what they learn, anyway. For instance, they may ignore bits of a package (or skip class sessions) they are not interested in—so long as they don't fear retribution from the assessment system. David Harris (1987) presents a case study depicting the blatant "instrumentalism" of students who leave certain units of their course materials literally unopened if they believe they will not help them with their assignment answers. Perhaps you can help your learners exercise choice more creatively?

Assessment the key?

I have described elsewhere (Rowntree, 1987) how the assessment tail so often wags the curriculum dog. So maybe assessment is the place to start encouraging autonomy?

Perhaps, for example, there are assignments that must be completed and marked during the programme. Are the assignment topics specified in advance by the course developers? Or can they be negotiated with individual learners? Can the learner even specialise, to some extent, on an aspect of the programme she or he is particularly interested in? (This would imply that your learner could spend less time on certain other aspects without being disadvantaged by the assessment procedures.)

Can you, in addition, allow individuals some choice as to how they'd like to be assessed—e.g. by written work, oral interview, workplace observation, or some combination? Can the individual's self-assessments, or the assessments of peers and work-colleagues, be taken into the reckoning?

Some learners may get all the autonomy they want or can cope with by building their own programme from package-based courses. You may be able to help them make better-informed choices.

Product v process?

But even a well-designed package will not provide enough autonomy for some learners. We may need to help them formulate and pursue their own questions rather than those posed by the package developers. If so, we may need a form of open learning that emphasises "process" (regular interaction with tutors and peers and colleagues)—rather than "product" (the package).

You and your colleagues may be able to support learners in pursuing self-directed **projects**—either as part or as the whole of their programme. Many open learning programmes—even those operating at a distance—now include or take the form of a project in which learners (with guidance from a tutor) define their own objectives, content and approach which they then pursue with the tutor's continuing guidance. (See Elton, 1988; Henry, 1989; Morgan, 1983, 1987.)

Such learners are likely to need a lot more help than package-driven learners. For example, someone may need to help them track down and get access to appropriate local learning resources—e.g. libraries or laboratories they can use, organisations they can visit, people they can talk to. They may also need regular counselling—e.g. about trying to cover too much ground (a common occurrence) or overlooking areas or approaches that seem relevant to their objectives. Additionally, since each learner may be working on something different, assessment will need to be individually negotiated.

Apropos that last point—autonomous learning does not necessarily mean solitary learning. People who are pursuing their own purposes can still **choose** to seek feedback or even guidance from one another. They may even choose—as an autonomous **group**—to negotiate a programme design that suits the purposes of the collective.

Package-based or project-based, the ideal open learning programme should allow what Paolo Freire (1974) calls a "convivial dialogue" between you and your learners. This would enable content, objectives, methods and assessment to be continuously renegotiated. As Boot & Hodgson (1988) point out, this involves:

> ". . . a commitment to engaging with the aspirations, demands and experience of those whose learning interests we are claiming to serve. This implies a continuous process, not a one-off piece of 'market research'."

Questions worth considering:

- To what extent would you be able and willing to share control of the design of a programme with your learners?
- How would you enable them to exercise their autonomy?
- What would you expect their attitude to be?
- What problems and opportunities might arise?

 Perhaps you would like to record some thoughts in your portfolio?

Final Remarks

Perhaps we can end with a metaphor from the world of horse-racing. Are we chiefly interested in horses for courses or courses for horses? The former approach aims to select the horses that are most likely to cope well with the conditions prevailing on a given course. The latter approach starts with the strengths and weaknesses of a known horse and considers what sort of course conditions it needs if it is to have its best run.

Traditionally, in education, our attitude has been "horses for courses". We have developed a course and then selected those learners whose prior qualifications suggest they should have the skills required to cope with its demands. Or, we may have let anyone start the course, knowing that only those with the appropriate prior skills (not all of whom will have the prior qualifications to prove it) will survive to the end.

As you will have gathered, I favour the "courses for horses" approach—trying, as far as possible, to negotiate a programme in line with the needs of the individual learner. It is not easy, I know, especially if you are dealing with distance learners and large numbers of them. But trying to make our programmes client-centred rather than producer-driven is the supreme challenge of open learning.

You may or may not find such a switch of emphasis easy to accept. Even if you accept it as an ideal, you may not see how you can implement it within your context. However, even if you are restricted to offering programmes that **look** the same for all learners, perhaps you may wish to individualise them along the lines suggested by Nathaniel Cantor (1972):

> "No two students will learn in the same way. Every individual will take out of the course what he [sic] feels he wants or needs and will put into it whatever efforts his capacity and willingness to learn allow. The [teacher] who is aware of these differences in learning will permit different students to use him, and the material of the course, in their own unique ways. As long as the student is sincerely trying to do something with himself and struggling to learn, he should be permitted to move at his own speed and on his own level."

 What remaining concerns, fears or questions do you have about Open Learners & their Learning? Make a note of any that seem important enough to bear in mind when you do your desk work and field work on this topic.

Suggested follow-up work

Desk work

Thorpe & Grugeon (1987) has several chapters that focus on open learners and their learning, especially those by Woodley, Thorpe, Jack, and Northedge.

Robinson (1989) has three chapters (by Clark, Johnston and Green) in which the voices of the learners are heard.

Paine (1988). Learners' voices are somewhat distant in this book which is largely provider-centred—but chapters by Tuckett and Young do raise questions about who is being provided with what.

Temple (1991). No one section is devoted to learners and what they learn but the learners' angle is kept in focus throughout.

In addition, you may find other sources you want to look at in the bibliography at the end of this book. Journals like *Educational and Training Technology International, British Journal of Educational Technology* and *Open Learning* sometimes carry articles that look closely at open learners and their learning. The only source I know in which the direct voices of learners can regularly be heard is the Open University newspaper, *Sesame*, which is sent to staff and students seven times a year.

Field work

- Interview some learners. Get them to tell you about some of their learning experiences, whether formal or informal. What does learning mean for them? What kinds of learning do they get on best with and which worst? Why do they think this is?

- Interview some colleagues—especially some who have tutored open learners. What is their image of learners and their learning? What do they feel the learners' needs are and how well do they feel they are being satisfied?

- Interview some prospective learners to get their suggestions as to how a proposed programme might best meet their needs and interests. How much choice might they like about what they are to learn?

- Try to draw up a profile of your "typical" prospective learner—or, if they're just too various for that, list the implications of what you know about them for the design and delivery of your open learning programme. Check this out by discussing it with some colleagues and with prospective learners.

 Remember to make a record of your desk work and field work in your portfolio.

Reflection checklist

 When you have completed your desk work and field work on this unit, please make notes in your portfolio using some of the following questions as a guide:

o What are the most important things you have learned during this unit? (You may want to look back at the objectives suggested at the beginning.)

o What has given you most satisfaction in this unit?

o What do you feel least satisfied about in this unit?

o Does this unit leave you with any unresolved questions or difficulties you feel you want help with?

o How might you try to get the help you need?

o What have you learned in your work with other people during this unit?

o In what ways were you able to draw on your previous experience during this unit?

o What have you learned about yourself—your own feelings and competences?

o What do you feel you need to do next?

Unit 3

Supporting open learners

Open learners usually work with packages of materials. But the package is rarely enough. Most open learners will need support from human beings—people who can help them with their learning and respond to them as individuals.

Whatever your connection with open learners—whether as producer, deliverer or sponsor—you are likely to have an interest in how your learners might need supporting. If you have not yet started in open learning, this unit should help you see what may be needed. If you are already involved, you may want to consider how your support system might be improved.

Suggested objectives

As a result of working on this unit you could be better able to:

- Identify some of the reasons why your learners may need support.
- List some of the types of support they might be given—before, during and after their learning programme.
- Identify people who might provide such support.
- Plan a support system for an open learning programme that you are developing.
- o *Any objectives of your own to add?*

I suggest you now start a new section in your portfolio in which to keep a record of your ideas about Supporting Open Learners. From time to time, I'll print a box like this (with the symbol alongside) to prompt you to write something in your portfolio. I expect you will use some of these prompts and not others; and also that you will make occasional notes without my prompting.

Why learners need support

The package is the eye-catcher in open learning. Glossy workbooks, videotapes and audiotapes—even computers and interactive video. It can look so accessible, so easy—and (sometimes) relatively cheap. Many colleges, and not a few industrial firms, have said: "All we need do is buy in a few packages and we'll be able to recruit dozens of new students/halve our training costs."

Packages are not enough

But it's not that easy—as many organisations have found to their cost. Both the final report on the Open Tech programme (Tavistock, 1987) and the Coopers & Lybrand (1989) report on open learning in industry indicate why. Learners without support are most liable to delay their completion of a programme or to drop out altogether. They simply have no-one to turn to when they run into problems.

And the sad thing is that their problems would often have been solved by a few minutes of a supporter's time—perhaps just enough to say "Yes, of course you can take longer over the project" or "You're doing fine; everybody has trouble with that section". Reassurance is often all a learner needs to keep them in the system.

What David Sewart (1987) has to say about learning at a distance may be true for most package-based learning:

> "It does not seem unfair to suggest that there is an overwhelming tendency within the field of teaching at a distance to offer systems from the viewpoint of the institution teaching at a distance rather than from the viewpoint of the student learning at a distance. The response to the individual needs of the student learning alone and at a distance has become lost in the overriding requirement to produce a grandiose package of materials.
>
> I have argued that the standard teaching package cannot provide a wholly satisfactory individualised learning system for students and also that such a package suffers from a tendency towards tight curriculum control. It is only the introduction of the human element, capable of adapting to the great variety of student needs, which can counteract this sort of bias."

Few learners can survive on the package alone—whether they are working on it at home or in some sort of learning centre. They need help and support from other people—the human element. This support needs to be planned at least as rigorously as the package materials. And providing it may turn out to be a lot more expensive.

Offering D-I-Y learning through packages without offering learners a decent support system can look very attractive to those who are hoping to pay fewer teachers or trainers to process greater numbers of learners. But paying for less tutorial time can turn out to be a costly economy.

The problems learners face

The fact is, learners can run into all sorts of anxieties, problems and difficulties when trying to learn under their own steam. Here are some that have been mentioned by learners I've worked with:

~ *"I'm having trouble finding the time."*

~ *"I'm nervous about learning from these computers."*

~ *"I'm not sure my memory will be good enough."*

~ *"My mates think I'm getting above myself."*

~ *"I was never any use at school."*

~ *"It's costing me an arm and a leg."*

~ *"Some parts of the course seem beyond me.".*

~ *"Am I really making the progress I should be?"*

~ *"I'm not getting a chance to apply it at work."*

~ *"What if I fail?"*

~ *"Why should I bother with this anyway?"*

Might any of those concerns be voiced by some of your learners? If you've already talked with your learners, do you know of any additional concerns they may have?

Perhaps most of your learners' concerns will fall into one or more of these three categories:

• whether the learning is worth the time and effort

• how other people react to their learning

• how successful they feel they are at it.

Such problems may simply cause your learners minor or occasional anxiety. Some may seem so crushing that they think about dropping out. Open learning's open door can easily become a revolving door that deposits them back on the pavement. Can we help them before a problem gets too much to cope with?

What kind of help and support?

Your learners may need help of various kinds. They may need help before they even begin learning, as well as during and after a learning programme.

You may like to tick any items in the checklist below that you think will be true of your learners. If I've missed out any that you think important, write them in.

Might your learners need help and support with . . .

Before they begin:

☐ recognising that they need to learn

☐ deciding what they want from learning

☐ deciding the best way of achieving it

☐ assessing their present experience and abilities

☐ selecting an appropriate open learning package

☐ finding other learners who have worked through it

☐ negotiating a personal open learning project

☐ deciding what support they might need

☐ obtaining financial help.

☐ *Others? (What?)*

To do with tackling the work:

☐ planning a timetable

☐ getting themselves organised

☐ improving study skills—e.g. reading, noting, number-work

☐ learning from new media—e.g. computers

- [ ] overcoming a technical problem—e.g. a machine breakdown
- [ ] making the most of class sessions
- [ ] learning from other people informally
- [ ] reflecting on what and how they are learning
- [ ] producing assignments to be marked by a tutor
- [ ] taking tests and examinations.
- [ ] *Others? (What?)*

To do with the content of the programme:

- [ ] making sense of it
- [ ] sorting out misunderstandings
- [ ] challenging its viewpoints
- [ ] getting an alternative viewpoint
- [ ] relating the content to their own experience
- [ ] deciding which bits to concentrate on and which they can leave out.
- [ ] *Others? (What?)*

To do with their jobs:

- [ ] seeing how what they are learning might relate to their jobs
- [ ] getting financial or other support from their employers
- [ ] getting to use facilities at work
- [ ] setting up work projects that let them practise what they are learning
- [ ] having their competence assessed in their workplace
- [ ] getting their employers to recognise their new competence.
- [ ] *Others? (What?)*

To do with assessment:

☐ understanding or negotiating how they are to be assessed and by what standards

☐ getting expert comment on how well they are progressing

☐ learning to assess their own progress realistically

☐ deciding when they are ready to take a competence test or final exam

☐ psyching themselves up for a test or final exam

☐ deciding what to do next in the light of how well they have done.

☐ *Others? (What?)*

To do with them:

☐ getting a realistic idea of their own ability and prospects

☐ keeping things in proportion

☐ coming to terms with new beliefs or values

☐ coping with stress

☐ enjoying the learning

☐ sorting out conflicts (e.g. between work, home and the programme)

☐ keeping going when they begin to wonder if the sacrifices are worthwhile.

☐ *Others? (What?)*

 Perhaps you have thoughts you will want to jot down in your portfolio at this point?

You may want to remember this list and come back to it again when next you are writing up a proposal for an open learning programme. It should remind you of the kinds of help that open learners are most likely to need. Fortunately, most learners don't need every kind I've listed. (On the other hand, your learners may need some additional kinds of help that aren't mentioned above.)

I'll ask you to come back to it in a moment anyway. Because we need to consider who might provide the kinds of help listed above.

Providing personal help

Different people mean different things when they talk about support. Some would point out that learners will get support from the package, if it is properly structured. Some would say that a well-equipped learning centre—with access to computers or other kit, and maybe also some peace and quiet—is also supportive. Some would mention newsletters, learning centre notice-boards, or other means of keeping learners up to date with what is going on in the system.

All the above are undoubtedly supportive—in a **general** sense. Learners won't get far if the materials are poor and they can't get access to vital equipment. And they may work more enthusiastically if we help them to feel part of a learning community—part of a training culture within a company or, in the case of distance learners, of an "invisible college". Users of the open learning centres at Jaguar Cars, for example, mentioned "the family atmosphere" and the feeling that "the company is concerned about you" (Cox & Hobson, 1988).

General v personal support

Such general support is undoubtedly necessary. But is not sufficient. Most learners also need **individual** support. They need feedback that relates to their specific and unique concerns. To a limited extent, this can be provided mechanically. Both the National Extension College and the Open University, for example, send individualised comments to learners based on their answers to computer-marked tests.

Learners often find such computerised feedback very useful, and at least they know it is impartial. However, the impartiality means it is also impersonal. Anyone who answered as they did would have received the same standard comments. And, besides, they can't answer back.

So, beyond this, learners may also need **personal** feedback—a response from someone who knows more about them than simply which boxes they've ticked in the latest test. This could be anyone with whom they can have a dialogue—face to face, on the telephone or by correspondence. Most open learning systems of any worth will enable learners to get personal help and support from a variety of people.

Think about your own system. Which of the following people might be available to talk with your learners about their individual concerns?

Possible helpers

- [ ] an adviser or counsellor
- [ ] a tutor
- [ ] a mentor
- [ ] their line manager
- [ ] technicians or workshop demonstrators
- [ ] librarians
- [ ] learning centre receptionists
- [ ] other learners
- [ ] friends, colleagues, etc.
- [ ] *Others (Who?)*

You may wonder why I've included "other learners" and "friends, colleagues, etc". It's true that you probably won't have any control over how they operate. But you'd still be wise to keep an eye on how they might be influencing your learners' learning—for good or ill. Be prepared to help learners benefit from their influence or, if necessary, to survive in spite of it.

Who might do what?

What kind of support might be provided by each of the people on the list above? This will differ from one open learning system to another. Some colleges may not have separate tutors and advisers (or counsellors). The same person will perform both roles. Nor will all systems use all the terms above. For example, some industrial training set-ups don't use the term "mentor" even though they do expect certain colleagues (formally or informally) to give mentor-type support. (I'll be outlining the typical mentor role, among others, in a few moments.)

The question is, if you think a particular sort of help is essential for your learners, who might best provide it? I suggest you now look back over the earlier list on which you've already ticked the kinds of help your learners may need and consider who might do what.

 You may want to make a note of your ideas.

Ways of providing support

You may be familiar already with the variety of ways in which people can provide learners with support. These ways usually depend on the person's role within the particular learning system. We'll look below at the most common roles—particularly at that of the tutor, which is usually the most crucial.

Remember that, within a particular open learning system, the person providing the kind of support I mention may not actually have the title I've given that role. For instance, some of the tutoring help I mention will sometimes be provided by a line manager or a mentor.

Tutoring

This sounds like the easiest role to understand. It sounds like that of a teacher or trainer or lecturer in a "traditional" learning system. But it may be quite different. After all, open learning usually depends on the learners taking responsibility for teaching themselves—with help from a self-instructional package. So the initial teaching will already have been done. For the tutor to "do the basics" all over again would be to promote just the kind of dependence in learners that open learning is pledged to overcome.

Strengthening and challenging

In the Inland Revenue's open learning system—where trainee tax inspectors work on packages by themselves before coming together for group tutorial days—new tutors are warned against re-teaching all the contents of the package. They are encouraged to check whether learners have had any difficulties with the ideas in the package and to give remedial help if necessary. But the main function of the scarce and expensive time face to face with learners is to help them build on what they have already learned—and achieve objectives that are not so easily attained on one's own.

Tutoring is certainly a role for someone expert in the subject that learners are learning about. But that person also needs to be knowledgeable about learners. They need to know how to help learners make their own sense of the subject—and about the kinds of difficulty they may have and the kind of approach they might find helpful from tutors. Margaret Miers (1984, 1987) tells how signing up as an open learner oneself can be an effective way for a tutor to get such knowledge.

Tutors may also need to help learners challenge the package. Learning from packages can easily take the form that Richard Boot & Vivien Hodgson (1987) call "dissemination". That is, the learner may be encouraged to soak up what is presented on page or screen without questioning whether it truly accords with his or her experience of the world. Tutors may need to help learners critique the package in terms of their own values and experience. Alan Tait (1989) argues that such an approach can give learners more control over their learning and is:

> ". . . an essential rather than an optional element in open learning delivered by distance education methods, if the title open learning is not to be a cruel reminder of its contrary."

You may want to challenge this assertion. How desirable might it seem to your open learners? And to their sponsors?

Forms of tutoring

Face-to-face tutoring is usually done in groups. The tutor may prefer to act as what is now being called a "facilitator". That is, he or she will usually be helping groups to collaborate in a learning task and benefit from one another's insights and experience (Gibbs, 1988; Northedge, 1987). Learners will sometimes urge their tutor to lecture them about his or her own insights and experience. But this may not always be what they need if they are to get all they might from one another and from themselves.

Some systems allow for occasional one-to-one sessions with a tutor—e.g. where the tutor is helping the learner develop workplace competence. The cost makes this uncommon. But one nurse tutor, quoted in Wright (1989) suggests how important such sessions can be:

> "I have an 'open door' policy anyway as far as I am concerned, with my office. I made it clear to Janet that she could come back to me if she got stuck anywhere in the programme. We had two or three particular occasions when we had to work quite hard at some subjects, but I think it helped her get beyond them, then she was OK for a while and would come back to me if needs be."

Much important tutoring is done at a distance. It is usually done via telephone or correspondence. In addition, some tutors send personally recorded audio-tapes to their learners and some exchange messages via a computer network. Many systems operate a "help line" enabling learners to telephone their tutor if they have a problem.

In some distance learning systems, the tutor's most crucial and demanding task is to read and assess the regular assignments that learners send them—and write constructive feedback that will help the learner overcome any weaknesses and build on his or her strengths. Such "correspondence teaching" has been a major factor in the success of the Open University.

If this aspect of support is one that concerns you, you will find useful chapters by tutors in Thorpe & Grugeon (1987). Also, the journal *Open Learning* frequently carries articles by tutors about their experience of assessment and teaching through assignments.

Tutoring project-based learning

Some open learning programmes, even at a distance, enable learners to do a "project" (see Henry, 1989; Morgan, 1983, 1987). This term can mean anything from an hour's foraging in the library to a piece of action-research lasting several weeks. In its full form, a project will enable a learner to choose his or her own topic, find relevant sources of information, decide his or her own way of grappling with it and present the results for assessment.

Such a learner-directed project can enable learners to escape the domination (and "dissemination"?) of pre-digested packaged learning. The learner takes control and, through experiential learning in their "real world", will often develop a special, enduring kind of confidence and self-reliance.

However, not all learners will take easily to the demands of truly independent learning. They, in turn, are likely to make quite taxing demands on the tutor for support at all stages— choosing a topic, collecting data, working it up, and presenting their results for assessment. Besides helping them cope with anxiety and frustration, the tutor will need to give them varying amounts of help in planning and carrying out the work. If the tutor is also responsible for assessing the outcome, she or he will have the difficult task of weighing the amount of help given against the difficulty of the learner's topic and the problems they faced in tackling it.

Why have I thought it worth saying so much about projects here? Because they are a special case—where support (rather than packages) is the main thing the programme offers to learners. (If there are any packaged materials they will probably offer guidance on doing projects rather than information about the subject matter.) Tutors may find it a refreshing change to help learners make their own sense of the world rather than always helping them respond to someone else's pre-recorded teaching.

Where tutors come from

By now, large numbers of people have tutored open learners. The Open University alone has several thousand tutors— some of them freelance or self-employed but the great majority of them with teaching or training jobs in other organisations. The Open College and National Extension College also rely on other institutions and freelance tutors to provide support for the learners who use their materials.

In industry, tutorial support may be available from within— e.g. from the training department. But staff who have not tutored open learners before may need training themselves if they are to tutor in an appropriate manner. This will be equally true of staff in a college that is introducing open learning—especially if it involves home-based learners. (I say more about staff development for tutors in Unit 9.)

Some organisations will buy in tuition, perhaps from a local college. In the open learning scheme for zoo keepers (Everiss, 1984), each student has two tutors. One is provided by National Extension College: he or she marks assignments and deals with assessment. The other is usually on the staff of the student's own zoo: his or her role is to encourage learners and help them relate what they are learning to their work in the zoo. In many organisations, this role would be that of someone called a "mentor".

 How might you like to see tutoring develop within your open learning system?

Advising/counselling

Open learners often need help and advice on matters that are nothing to do with the subject matter they are learning about. They may need help in getting started, organising their time, coping with self-doubt, and deciding on the next step after completing their learning programme—to name but a few. You'll see other needs in the checklist we looked at earlier.

Distance learners may be in particular need of help because they are usually in no position to pick up cues from other learners or from frequent face-to-face contact with their teachers. Too easily they can become "out of sight, out of mind" unless proper support is designed into the system.

Here is one Open University tutor and counsellor (Fage, 1987) talking about the telephone calls she made after the induction meeting for her new students:

> "In the following weeks I contact those who did not come, or with problems to follow up. Pat needs to talk about summer school: how does she feel about going? What are her fears? Can or should they be overcome? With young children she could be excused, but would deprive herself of a valuable academic experience, as well as the social contacts she misses as a single parent. Granville needs help with essay writing: we discuss local courses and work he could do at home. My young unemployed student, John, is facing depression and has a problem with fees. I cannot cure his depression, though I try not to add to it. I can listen to him, and give him practical advice on financial help. I do listen— and listen—and as my projected 15-minute phone call extends to 45, I am conscious of my increasingly clamorous children needing supper. Winding up phone calls graciously is a difficult counselling skill, but one which I need increasingly with John, who will be telephoning me almost weekly over the next few months."

Some college-based open learning systems employ advisers or counsellors to provide this help for learners at various stages of their learning "career". Some, as in the Open University, combine the tutorial and counselling roles.

According to Hilary Temple (1991), company open learning providers may not be convinced of the need: "'I'm here to help them with their studies, not marriage guidance', sums up the attitude of many managers, tutors and mentors." But she points out that advice will, nevertheless, be needed in less contentious areas like those I've mentioned above. And she warns:

> "Trainers, personnel staff, line-managers, tutors and mentors can all contribute to fulfilling these functions, but responsibilities need to be clearly allocated in advance if large cracks are not to appear in the system, through which a small but significant minority of the learners could disappear."

For a review of the various forms of guidance and counselling in work-based open learning, see Bailey (1988).

 Will your learners need guidance or counselling? If so, what kinds, and who will give it?

Line manager support

Do your learners need or wish to apply what they are learning to their work? If so, the role of their line manager can be crucial. It may, in fact, be their boss who has suggested (or demanded) they do the learning in the first place. In which case, we might hope that he or she will provide appropriate help and resources while they get on with it—and give them a chance to apply what they are learning in their jobs.

In some organisations, like the Royal Bank of Scotland, line managers are trained to be coaches to their staff. And there are many others (like the hotels and restaurants using the Caterbase scheme) where managers play a big part in the workplace assessment of trainees. In British Airways, according to Chris Pike (1990):

"Managers must take an active part in any nomination process and an active interest in participants' work and progression. It is not enough to sign a form and ask 'How's it going?' occasionally. Participants need to feel their learning is important and relevant to the business, the department and the manager."

Yet there are many organisations where line managers have no involvement at all in training their staff. For them, training and staff development is the responsibility of a training or personnel department. Some line managers may even regard training as a nuisance—as disruptive to production or the smooth running of their department. Yet others may be unaware that a member of their staff is doing an open learning course that might be relevant to their job.

The difference managers can make

Clearly, the attitude of line managers can make or break open learning in a vocational context. This will be especially true if staff are rather reluctant learners to start with. Where line managers think the programme is disruptive they certainly won't support, and may well discourage, the learners. ("You don't want to bother with that stuff; I didn't need it to get where I am today." Or simply "Do it if you want—so long as it's in your own time.")

But if line managers are well-disposed (and themselves given appropriate training, time and support) they can help in many ways. Perhaps the spread of VQs and the assessment of workplace competence will mean that more and more managers will be expected to support their open learners.

Some Open College packages include guidance notes for line managers. One package—in a series for learners aiming at a Certificate in Management Studies (OC, 1990)—suggests several ways in which the line manager can support (in addition to helping with workplace assessment):

"There are. . . a number of other ways in which you may be able to help learners succeed with the course. These include:
- discussing the new concepts and ideas introduced in the workbooks
- helping learners relate their learning to their work
- creating learning opportunities at work
- reviewing the results of the learner's activities and self-assessment exercises
- discussing the assignments the learner will be submitting

to the tutor
* enabling the learner to carry out research activities by providing access to resources not normally available
* allowing the learner time for study at the workplace
* talking over any problems and difficulties that may arise."

By 1991, the packages in that Open College series were addressing such suggestions to the "Line Manager/Mentor" —recognising a new support role that had emerged (or at least become more widely talked about) since the earlier publication.

 Will your learners have line managers who might influence their learning? If so, what might you need to do to ensure that they give maximum support?

Mentoring

The idea of mentoring is still new to many organisations. Yet in others, like Jaguar Cars and many health authorities, it has become so much part of the system that regular training is provided for potential mentors. They may even get help from an open learning package (Flexitrain, 1990).

The most important function of the mentor is to give the learner someone to talk to. He or she might be:

* someone on whom the learners can try out new ideas

* someone who will encourage the learners to reflect on what they are learning and how it relates to their life and work and

* someone who will look out for their interests in the organisation.

He or she is the learners' ally and perhaps their champion.

Ideally, one should perhaps have someone other than one's line manager as mentor. In civil service training, people sometimes call this the "grandfather/grandmother" role—to distinguish it from the perhaps more parental role that people may ascribe to their line manager. Learners should be able to talk freely with their mentor, knowing that she or he has no direct power to retard or advance their career.

If learners also have a tutor, then there may be no need for their mentor to be an expert in the subject they are studying. They may even look outside the workplace for a mentor and enlist a friend or relative in the role.

But the role of mentor is still evolving. Often she or he is an unplanned amalgam of tutor, adviser and ally—sometimes with an uncomfortable supervisory element thrown in. Organisations setting up an open learning support system may want to consider what the learner needs that cannot be provided by tutors, line managers, trainers and other staff. And, if someone is to be asked to meet such needs as a mentor, how are they to be prepared for and supported in that task—and what might be in it for them?

Perhaps you yourself have a mentor at present, officially or unofficially, while you are exploring open learning. If so, what kind of support are you expecting her or him to provide? Might any role conflicts arise?

Learning centre staff

Might your learners need to visit some sort of learning centre, whether frequently or very occasionally? This might be a "drop-in" or "learning by appointment" centre in a college or company. It might be a "practical training facility". It might be a residential period or a weekend workshop. It might be a library.

In such a learning centre, your learners might meet people besides those mentioned above who may give them support. For many open learners, a centre administrator or receptionist, or a technician or librarian, may be a key supporter. The centre receptionist may be a fund of advice and information. The technician may be able not simply to help computer-based learners unglitch their programmes but also to jolly them out of their fear of information technology.

Remember also that libraries, whether in colleges or in the high street or in large public or private sector organisations, have always been resources for open learning. Hence, as Dixon (1987) reminds us:

"In some institutions, librarians provide first-level
tutorial support—in the form of counselling,
encouragement, motivation and study skills—leaving
second-level support in the form of advice on subject
content and assessment to tutorial staff."

The potential of libraries as open learning centres was
formally recognised by the Employment Department (then
Training Agency) in 1990. That is when it funded ten local
authority libraries to "offer members of the public access to
open learning programmes on terms that are attractive to
unsponsored individuals". Harris (1991) reported that "the
project appears to be a great success" and the scheme is now
being extended.

 You may want to jot down some thoughts about the possible
support role for people like those discussed above.

Support from other people

Open learning usually involves self-study, but it does not
have to mean learning entirely on one's own. Even distance
learning does not have to mean solitary learning. Apart from
"official" supporters, open learners often get support of one
sort or another from:

• other learners

• family and friends

• the people they work with.

Other learners

Many open learning systems make a deliberate attempt to get
learners in touch with one another. To quote Chris Pike
(1990) of British Airways again:

"Participants must be given the opportunity to support
each other through meetings and newsletters. It is often
through sharing experiences that long-term learning
occurs and short residential periods in open learning
programmes are a particularly effective mechanism."

Offering occasional classes and residential sessions are
common ways of enabling learners to support one another.

In fact, such sessions may be the only way of ensuring that learners meet and learn to handle viewpoints other than those put across in the published package.

Another approach is to encourage learners to set up their own self-help groups (see Fanshaw, 1990). Marion Jack (1987) tells about groups of young mothers in depressed areas of Strathclyde meeting in Women's Aid centres, playgroup premises and pubs to talk about Open University booklets and tapes on bringing up children.

Family and friends

Family and friends can have a powerful influence on an open learner. Some learners embark on open learning to impress their companions ("I'll show 'em!"); some to distract themselves from an unsatisfying home life; some to keep up with their children.

Once started, some open learners have the active support of their family and friends. Spouses and children may even find they can join in or contribute to the learner's studies. But other learners face scorn and resentment, if not hostility.

Many open learning programmes take up more of the learner's time and do more to alter her or his attitudes than family and friends may have expected. The learner may no longer be either as available or as easily dominated as she or he once was. What is seen as liberation by the learner may look like mutiny to the learner's nearest and dearest. In this latter case, the "official" supporters may have a role in helping the learner ride the storm.

Workmates

With vocational open learning programmes, it is helpful if learners can get support from workmates and other professional contacts. At the very least, it should help them if their colleagues respect what they are doing and encourage their efforts. Using open learning with YTS trainees in its retail electrical stores, Rumbelows found that it was the attitude of other staff that determined whether the approach was successful. "If staff do not support the introduction of the new approach then they will ruin it" (Rossetti, 1988).

This reminds me of a trainer in another retail chain who told me how attempts to introduce open learning too quickly had run into difficulties. Apparently the experienced sales staff resented having to handle extra business while the learners were sitting about the staffroom with their training packages. They scornfully dismissed the trainees as "wozzocks".

Such unsupportive attitudes seem less likely in organisations like Rover, Ford, Jaguar, Short Brothers and Blue Boar Services (Temple, 1991). In recent years, these organisations have developed a climate in which staff seem to welcome training as an opportunity for self-development rather than resist it as a threat to their self-esteem.

Indeed, colleagues may work together on open learning packages. Catering assistants at Blue Boar service stations form into study groups of between three and seven people and work out their pattern of study between them. Such collaboration between workplace colleagues is also common in professional education—not least in the National Health Service where hundreds of managers, nurses, midwives and health visitors are doing their open learning in groups.

For all I know, you may be using this book as part of a staff development exercise with colleagues. Even if you aren't, you'll have noticed that I often suggest you approach your colleagues (and learners and other contacts) for their ideas and feedback. It is quite common nowadays for open learning packages to encourage such consultations.

In that respect, at least, package learners have an advantage over learners who go off-site to attend a conventional course. That is, they can try out new ideas in the real work-situation straight away and get feedback. This allows them to practise and fine-tune their new ideas rather than commit them to memory as neat abstractions for future reference.

 You may want to jot down some thoughts about the possible support role for people like those discussed above.

Final remarks

I believe that the issue of support can reveal quite different assumptions among people in open learning. At one extreme are people with a **product** focus. For them, the package is paramount—and, if support is necessary, its purpose can only be to help learners cope with the product. At the other extreme are those with a **process** focus. They see the creative relationship between supporter and learner as paramount—and, if packaged materials are necessary at all, they need to be selected, modified or developed to suit the immediate needs of an individual learner.

The former are concerned with helping the learners cope with an existing body of knowledge; the latter with helping them create meanings and capabilities of their own. Most people in open learning operate somewhere between these two extremes of coping and creating—usually nearer the former than the latter.

But what if we wish to reach out to potential learners who've had little worthwhile experience of organised learning and whose self-esteem as learners is low? Offering them open access to packages (however "well designed") may not be productive. Such open learning programmes might need to be support-led rather than package-driven. We might need to budget for a far greater amount of support than would be needed by people who are already successful learners.

Such an approach—potentially threatening to open learning's image as a low-cost option—would also run counter to the "unto those that hath, more shall be given" philosophy that seems to underlie most educational resourcing. That, however, is just the kind of challenge that a slogan like "open learning" will keep taunting us with.

One final caution. However much support learners might need to begin with, they may not need it for ever. Here is an opinion from Hilary Temple (1991). Do you agree with her?

> "The object of the exercise is not, after all, to induce learners to accept as much support as possible, even though that may warm the cockles of the supporters' hearts, but to ensure that they are assisted to become as independent as possible."

 What remaining concerns, fears or questions do you have about Supporting Open Learners? Make a note of any that seem important enough to bear in mind when you do your desk work and field work on this topic.

Suggested follow-up work

Desk work

Thorpe & Grugeon (1987) contains many articles by open learning supporters. They cover student problems, counselling, tutoring at a distance, commenting on assignments, projects, and group work. Mostly they draw on Open University experience, but the material is thought-provoking and has many applications elsewhere.

Robinson (1989). Most of the chapters in Part 3 ("The ecstasy of delivery") have something to say about supporting nurses who are using open learning packages.

Paine (1988) contains only one chapter devoted to support (by Diane Bailey) but several others (especially those by McNay, Sewart, Rossetti and Crawley) raise issues you may need to consider in developing a support system.

Temple (1991). Issues of learner support arise in many chapters; but one chapter "Supporting learners: is your learning centre really necessary?" is devoted to the subject.

The journal *Open Learning* is also an excellent source of articles by people writing about their experiences of supporting learners. If you can get hold of back numbers, you may find that articles written 20 years ago are as relevant today as they were then.

Field work

- Interview one or two people who give support to learners who are as much like your learners as possible. Here are the kinds of question I would be asking them. You may have a quite different agenda. What do they regard as their main tasks? What sorts of skills or qualities do they bring to those tasks? How do they judge the effectiveness of the support they give? What kinds of training and support do they get themselves in carrying out their duties?

- If you can get hold of some learners who've used open learning programmes, ask them (individually if possible) about the kinds of problems they ran into and the kinds of support they were given (or not given).

- Run a workshop for your colleagues asking them to discuss the likely support needs of your learners and how they might be met. (You may want to prompt them with material photocopied from this unit.)

 Remember to make a record of your desk work and field work in your portfolio.

Reflection checklist

When you have completed your desk work and field work on this unit, please make notes in your portfolio using some of the following questions as a guide:

o   What are the most important things you have learned during this unit? (You may want to look back at the objectives suggested at the beginning.)

o   What has given you most satisfaction in this unit?

o   What do you feel least satisfied about in this unit?

o   Does this unit leave you with any unresolved questions or difficulties you feel you want help with?

o   How might you try to get the help you need?

o   What have you learned in your work with other people during this unit?

o   In what ways were you able to draw on your previous experience during this unit?

o   What have you learned about yourself—your own feelings and competences?

o   What do you feel you need to do next?

Unit 4

Media in open learning

Open learning depends on the use of media. Rarely do teachers speak directly to learners. Mostly the teaching is pre-recorded and delivered through a medium—through print, through audio-visual devices and, increasingly, through a variety of computer-based systems.

Whatever your interest in open learning, you will probably need to make decisions about media—or cope with other people's. Which media are available? Which are most suitable? And how can we enable learners to get access to them at an acceptable cost? This unit should help you make your own decisions and evaluate those made by other people.

Suggested objectives

As a result of working on this unit you could be better able to:

- Consider a wider range of media for open learning.
- Decide on a set of criteria for use in choosing media.
- Suggest how you might use particular media.
- Identify some of the costs and practicalities of using particular media.
- Outline the benefits your learners might get from some medium that you have not previously explored.
- o *Any objectives of your own to add?*

 I suggest you now start a new section in your portfolio in which to keep a record of your ideas about Media in Open Learning. From time to time, I'll print a box like this (with the symbol alongside) to prompt you to write something in your portfolio. I expect you will use some of these prompts and not others; and also that you will make occasional notes without my prompting.

Which media might we use?

Newcomers to open learning are often surprised at the variety of teaching and learning media available. There's no reason they should be, of course. Open learning can use all the media available in ordinary, classroom-based courses plus a number of others besides.

If you are about to write some open learning materials, you need to know which media are available to you. If you are setting up an open learning system, you need to decide which media to use—perhaps even which hardware to buy. Even if you are simply deciding which of several published packages to use with learners, you may decide partly on the basis of whether they use acceptable media.

You may like to scan through the list on the opposite page and consider which media you might be able to use in your open learning system—perhaps after finding out more about them.

In most open learning—whether on-site or at a distance—the main medium is **print** (the written word, together with pictures). This may be supported by **audio-visual** material—especially audio-cassette tapes, and slides or filmstrips. Quite often, moving pictures in the form of video or film will be used. In some cases, video or audio teaching will be broadcast.

Computers are a key medium in some open learning. They may provide pre-structured teaching as in computer-based training. They may be used to explore databases on compact disc, e.g. CD-ROM and CD-I. And they may allow learners and tutors to keep in touch with one another through "computer conferencing".

Practical work may be relatively easy to arrange if learners are doing their open learning at work or in a college. Otherwise, more distant learners may need to be provided with their own "kits" of material and equipment, or be allowed the use of laboratory or workshop facilities at a learning centre or some other convenient location.

Some of the media available in open learning

Print

o Books, pamphlets, etc—already published, or specially written

o Specially written "wrap around" study guides to already published material

o Specially written self-teaching texts, e.g. "tutorials-in-print"

o Workbooks for use along with audiotape or videotape, CBT, practical work, etc

o Self-tests, project guides, notes on accreditation requirements, bibliographies, etc

o Maps, charts, photographs, posters, etc

o Material from newspapers, journals and periodicals

o Handwritten materials passing between learners and tutor.

Audio-visual

o Audio-cassettes/discs/CDs
o Radio broadcasts
o Slides or filmstrip
o Film or film loops
o Video-cassettes
o Television broadcasts
o Computer based training —CBT
o Interactive video.

Practical or project work

o Materials, equipment, specimens for learner's own use—e.g. home experiment kits, keyboards, official forms

o Field-work or other use of learner's local environment— e.g. observation, interviews, collection of evidence, etc

o Projects in local offices, farms, workshops, etc

o Assignments based on learner's workplace

Human interaction

At-a-distance

o Telephone conversation between learner and tutor (supplementing written communications)

o Learner-learner telephone conversations

o Several learners in telephone contact at the same time, with or without a tutor, by means of a "conference call"

o Video conferencing

o Computer conferencing.

Face-to-face

o Learners' self-help groups

o Help from line managers/ "mentors"/technicians/others

o Occasional seminars, tutorials, lectures by tutors or other group organizers

o One-day, one week, weekend, or other short group sessions (residential or otherwise).

Others? (What?)

o

o

o

o

Most open learning needs to involve the "human media"—**personal interaction**—amongst learners or between learners and a tutor. This may be done through frequent or occasional face-to-face contact or else through telephone discussions or through computer conferencing. (I deal with human media chiefly in Unit 3: "Supporting open learners".)

How shall we choose media?

The chief mistake people can make with media is to decide on the medium before they've thought about the message. They may say : "We've got all these computers, so let's run the course on them." Or: "We can afford the most complex multi-media, so why should we make do with less?"

But the most appropriate medium is not necessarily the first one that comes to mind. And low-tech media can be more powerful than high-tech media. It all depends on the circumstances. Even in a company at the forefront of technology which has also pioneered high-tech training approaches like two-way video delivered by satellite (Gange, 1986):

> "The book is a technology that can be overlooked (perhaps because of its very familiarity) but which can stand up remarkably well to critical appraisal as a distance learning medium. . . . Books are widely used at IBM as part of distance learning packages."

How can we decide which media to use in an open learning programme? Here are some of the criteria you may want to take into account. Which do you think are most important in your situation?

Possible criteria for choosing media

☐ Do any of your learning objectives dictate certain media?

☐ Which media will be physically available to the learners?

☐ Which media will be most convenient for learners to use?

☐ Are any media likely to be particularly helpful in motivating learners?

☐ Are you under pressure from the organisation to use/avoid certain media?

☐ Which media will you (the teacher) be most comfortable with?

☐ Which media will learners already have the necessary skills to use?

☐ Which media do you and your colleagues have the necessary skills to use?

☐ Which media will you be able to afford to use?

☐ Which media will the learners be able to afford to use?

☐ Which media might you need to back up the main media and/or to ensure variety?

☐ *Other criteria. (Which?)*

You may want to jot down some thoughts in your portfolio.

Suiting media to objectives

Most media can give learners some sort of help towards the achievement of most learning objectives. But, with certain objectives, some media may be more helpful than others. For instance, print alone might be sufficient for someone learning to read and write a foreign language. But what if they hoped to converse in the language? Then the addition of sound—e.g. on audio or video tape—preferably with some opportunity for human interaction—would surely be necessary.

Similarly, certain other objectives may demand that learners study moving pictures, handle real objects or bounce their ideas off other people in a workplace. Different media have unique characteristics that give them advantages and disadvantages for different kinds of learning. We look at these later on in this unit.

What suits the learners?

What you know about your learners may influence your media choice in a number of ways. To begin with, which media can your learners get access to? If they are learning "on-site", perhaps in an open learning centre, then you will know which media are available to them. But if they are learning at home (or even at work) they may not have access to computers, video-players and other hardware. Nor may they be able to meet with other people for human interaction.

Even if you were prepared to give them or loan them the equipment, they might not find it convenient to use. Someone planning to do most of their studying on long train journeys would not thank you for a course involving frequent use of video-tapes or ("laptops" apart) a computer. Someone learning at a workplace computer might not be able to find desk space for A4-size workbooks as well.

Skills and preferences

You might also ask yourself what you know about your learners' media skills and preferences. Most people can read and few have trouble watching television with their feet up and a relaxing beverage by their side. But do they have the skills for using print and television as **learning** tools? Some of the early Open University evaluations, for example, revealed that some students' leisure use of radio was hindering their learning from it. Even with the most everyday media (let alone with high-tech approaches) you may need to teach your learners how to learn from the medium before you can teach them anything else with it.

Your learners may also have preferences—some detesting books ("too much like school"), others being turned on by computers, some being happy only in class, and so on. These may be based on the individual's realistic assessment of their existing talents (or former humiliations). Or they may simply be hoping that television or computers or whatever will be more fun.

Perhaps you can't give every one of your learners the medium they might prefer. But if you know something of their preferences, you may find ways to convince them of the benefits of whatever media you are forced to choose on other criteria.

What suits you and your colleagues?

There are several issues here. For one thing, you may feel under pressure to use certain media rather than others. You may pick up the message that only print plus audio-cassette are acceptable in our system or, conversely, that only the most expensive, high-tech media will suit the public image that our organisation seeks to maintain. For instance, Hilary Temple (1991) reports that British Steel got into CBT and interactive video because the directors were sufficiently impressed to sell it to the rest of the company.

Such pressures cannot be ignored. Often there is a valid non-educational reason for choosing certain media—e.g. when the use of broadcast television increases recruitment or when use of high-tech media attracts sponsorship money that can be used to help learners on other programmes. But, if you feel that any of your learners might be adversely affected by the organisation's favoured media, you may want to argue the case for alternatives.

It is quite reasonable, however, and only realistic, to consider which media you and your colleagues feel comfortable with and have the skills to use. There is no point plumping for computer-based training if no-one in the team has ever learned from a computer, let alone taught with one. Even if the writers have done so, will your support staff have the experience and skills to help learners working on CBT?

Of course, if a particular medium is essential, you may be able to overcome skill-deficits by appropriate training. Or you may hire expertise from elsewhere. However, you may not be able to afford either the time or the money.

Who controls the medium?

You may also prefer a medium you can control. Most teachers and trainers can develop materials for print, and even for audio-cassette, without much in the way of technical help. But once you are into video or computers, you are more likely to need help from media experts. This may be costly.

Furthermore, such experts will bring in their own production values and their own ways of using the media. These may not exactly suit your purposes but you may lack the expertise to contest them. This opens up the possibility of conflict between what they consider "good television" or "good CBT" and what you consider "good teaching" (Gallagher, 1978).

The more complex the media, the more control you may have to surrender. However, this may be acceptable to you up to a point or in certain circumstances—e.g. if it gives you a chance to acquire some of the skills of the experts.

Are the costs acceptable?

Cost is an inevitable constraint on your choice of media. On one hand there are the costs to your organisation. And these may be either once-off or recurrent. If you setting up an open learning centre (or a production facility), you may be able to afford to buy a number of video and audio-cassette players (or an off-set litho machine for print) but not a number of computer terminals (or a fully-equipped television studio).

Of course, you (or your learners) may have the necessary viewing equipment already. And you may already have, or be able to borrow or rent, any necessary production facilities. But you will still need to weigh up the relative costs (in staff time as well as cash) of producing materials for different media. These may differ greatly from medium to medium.

Relative costs

John Sparkes (1984) has estimated the following amounts of teacher/trainer time are needed to produce one hour's worth of learning in various media. (By "audio-vision" he means an audio-cassette plus printed material to look at while listening.)

- lecturing   2-10 hours
- small group teaching   1-10
- teaching by telephone   2-10
- video-tape lectures (for TVI)   3-10
- audio-vision   10-20
- text   50-100
- broadcast television   100+
- computer aided learning   200+
- interactive video   300+

He also points out that all but the first three items on this list will need input from technical experts, some of them in considerable quantities. This might explain why a similar comparison made by trainers at Barclays Bank agreed with John Sparkes's maximum estimate for print but suggested maximum ratios of 450:1 for CBT and 1400:1 for interactive video. I think they were rather more realistic also in suggesting a ratio of 100:1 for audio (even though this does not allow for any printed material to go with the tape).

And that's just **your** costs. But you may also need to consider what it might cost your learners to use various media. How much of the costs can you reasonably pass on to learners? How much might they be able and willing to spend on buying equipment and materials, or on travelling to a learning centre or doing practical work? Might the use of more expensive media mean that the programme is less open than you'd want it to be?

Perhaps the most reasonable approach to costs is always to ask: "Can another medium do an **acceptably** good job, more cheaply?" Thus, you may decide it is not worth spending months writing a state-of-the-art workbook on your subject when you could bring about similar learning by spending just a few days writing a study guide for a book that exists already and is cheap enough for your learners to buy.

Similarly, if you feel the urge to make an interactive video (or even a plain one), ask yourself whether your learners need moving pictures at all. Is it possible they might achieve comparable learning if you provided them simply with a sequence of still pictures together with your commentary on audio-cassette?

Combining media

Another factor you might consider in choosing media is how best to combine them. Learners working with, for example, the Open College, National Extension College or the Open University, may be on programmes that combine workbooks, audio-cassettes, video-cassettes, and perhaps computer-based training, together with tutor support.

Different media have different strengths (which we explore under the next heading below). Rarely can one medium provide everything that a learner needs in a learning programme of any duration. For instance, any pre-packaged medium needs to be backed up by human support. And even an all-singing, all-dancing medium like computer-controlled interactive videodisc may need the simple back-up of a printed booklet. Otherwise, learners may leave their "work-station" with nothing to remind them of what they have studied. West Midlands Travel (a coach company) has developed a number of interactive videos—but each is backed up by, at minimum, a workbook, practical exercises and assessment; and learners are supported by mentors who themselves have been trained for their role.

Remember also that a medium that suits some of your learners may not suit others. Some may prefer to learn by reading, some by listening, some by doing, some by working together, and so on. If several media are combined then perhaps there is more chance that all will get at least some of their preferred medium. I knew one Open University economics teacher who made a point of saying what he wanted to say in his printed workbook, then saying it again in sound on the radio and then saying it again, with pictures, on television. He argued that no one student would need it all three ways, but using all three helps ensure that everyone gets it his or her own best way.

Up to a point, learners may also find that changing from one medium to another can be quite refreshing. But they need to feel that each medium has something worthwhile to teach them. If we get too media-happy, learners may complain about "too much chopping and changing". They soon detect (and ignore) a medium that is not pulling its weight.

 You may think this would be a good point to make a note of any new thoughts you've had about selecting media for your learners.

What do different media offer?

Most research over the last twenty years or so suggests that media do not differ greatly in their potential for helping people learn. What makes a difference is not the medium itself but how well it is used and how keen the learners are to hear what it has to say.

Nevertheless, even if most media can do most things reasonably well, each does some things better than it does others. And each does some things better than other media do. So what are the peculiar strengths and weaknesses of each medium? In what follows we look at:

- Print
- Practical work
- Audio
- Video
- Computers.

Teaching with print

Despite all the high-profile "new technology", more open learners spend more time learning from print than from any other medium. It can take many forms—e.g. specially written workbooks, study guides, ordinary textbooks, reference manuals, job aids, pamphlets and leaflets, maps and wall-charts. It can provide the learner not just with the written word but also with, e.g. photographs and diagrams, graphs and statistics, checklists and tables.

Print has been the basis of distance learning ever since Johann Gutenberg invented movable type in the 15th century. That made possible the mass-production of books and the opportunity for people to learn on their own from teachers long dead or in distant lands.

Print excels as a medium that can convey complex ideas (e.g. arguments about the nature of the universe) or complex instructions (e.g. how to programme your video-recorder). Unlike more transient media (including a human teacher) it remains open to inspection. You can still see and ponder the first sentence of a passage even while you are reading the final one. Print can also touch the emotions (or so poets have always maintained) and even (remembering that the first mass-produced book was the Bible) people's attitudes and behaviour.

Most people can learn from print, if they think it's worth their while. They can do so anywhere—at home, in the workplace, down the pub or on the bus to work—and they need no special equipment. It also cheap to buy (compared with other media) and learners can personalise it by writing stuff of their own on the pages. Some learners, however, may have a school-bred aversion to print and even those who don't may not be able to read well enough to use it successfully.

From the providers' point of view, print is relatively easy to teach with (demanding no great media expertise) and it is cheap to reproduce. Print can help towards the attainment of most kinds of learning objectives (even those involving social and interpersonal skills) though it will sometimes be insufficient on its own.

The teacher or trainer also has considerable control over what might appear in print. In fact, now that computers are widely available with sophisticated word-processing software (or even desktop publishing software), she or he may even decide what each page looks like. (As I have done in this book, using Microsoft Word 4 on my Macintosh SE.)

Practical work

Not everyone thinks of practical work as a medium. But it's important to remind ourselves that learners can gain useful knowledge and skills by doing things in the "real world" as well as by working on packaged materials.

Practical work is essential for many subjects, especially when our objectives relate to work-related competences as well as knowledge. Even knowledge, however, may sometimes be acquired more easily and with deeper understanding and interest if the learner can carry out suitable practical work.

Practical work may involve equipment, e.g. fault-finding on electronic equipment or collecting and analysing soil samples. Or it may not, e.g. observing the behaviour of visitors in a zoo or interviewing colleagues at work.

If the practical work involves equipment, and learners are studying on-site, then facilities can perhaps be scheduled at suitable times. If they are studying at a distance, however, it may not be easy to bring them to a centre to equipment at the most opportune time—if at all. But the possibility is worth exploring—e.g. as a "one-day school" or a "summer session" in a local college. Another possibility, with some distance courses, will be to arrange for someone connected with the learner's job (e.g. a line manager) to organise practical experience—perhaps as part of their role as mentor.

Otherwise, or maybe additionally, we need to consider the second alternative—sending the equipment to the learner. Some Open University courses send a treasure chest of equipment to students in the form of a "home experiment kit". They may be sent chemicals, glassware, microscopes, rock specimens, seeds, and so on—even extending to an electric reed organ or a helium neon-laser for producing holograms. At the other end of the scale (as in one National Extension College course on elementary physics), the learner need only be sent household items like a duster, a comb, and a reel of cotton thread.

 You may like to make a note of any practical work your own open learners might need and how it might be arranged.

Audio teaching

Here we are talking about recorded sound—usually that of the human voice. But other sounds (e.g. those of engines or musical instruments) may also be relevant to some learning.

Sound can be a very powerful medium in open learning. In the early years of the Open University, radio was the chief means of delivering it. It still is in the distance learning systems of many third world countries. Nowadays, however, open learning programmes in the UK make far more use of the audio-cassette.

The audio-cassette is much more user-friendly. Learners don't have to be sitting by their radio at fixed times—often at dawn in the case of Open University broadcasts. They can listen whenever they like and as often as they please. They can also stop the tape and replay sections of it as often as they need.

There are three main ways of using audio in an open learning package:

- **Just listening**. Talks, discussions, interviews, acted scenes, natural sounds—material from which people can learn even when their eyes and hands are busy with other things, e.g. while driving a car or washing dishes.

- **Listening and looking**. Here learners have to use their eyes as well as their ears. They get printed material to use along with the audio-tape. It may contain diagrams, photographs, maps, charts, tables of figures, etc. which the audio will talk them through.

- **Listening, looking and doing**. Sometimes the audio may ask learners to stop the tape and write something in their workbook, or carry out some practical work with materials and equipment, or even with other people. When they switch on again the audio teacher will comment on what they have done.

What's so special about audio teaching? According to Hilary Temple (1991), course developers at British Telecom:

> ". . . are moving increasingly to the view that silent open learning is defective. The main benefit of sound is to reduce the number of printed words required to be read by the learner, whether these are on a page or on a screen."

But what about your learners? What might they get from an audio-cassette that they couldn't get so easily from a printed workbook?

I've asked a number of course developers why they use audio. Here are some of the things they said. Which might be relevant for your learners?

Possible uses for audio

☐ To give learners a relief from reading.

☐ To present new ideas to learners who don't care for reading.

☐ To help learners make best use of their time by giving them a means of learning while doing other things.

☐ To talk them through tasks like studying a map or a table of figures—where they might find it distracting to have to keep turning aside to look at written guidance.

☐ To help learners practise skills.

☐ To make the teaching more human and personal.

☐ To say things that aren't so easily expressed in print.

☐ To encourage or motivate learners.

☐ To touch learners' feelings and attitudes.

☐ To bring to learners the voices of people who would be unable or unwilling to say anything in writing.

☐ To provide "source material" (e.g. excerpts from an interview) for learners to analyse or react to.

☐ *Any other uses you can think of? (What?)*

(If you want to hear examples of these and other uses, listen to the tape of sample extracts in Rowntree 1990b.)

Open learners generally speak well of audio teaching. Here is what some have told me:

- *"It's like having your tutor in the room with you."*
- *"I get more sense out of the books now because I can hear the author's voice in my mind as I read."*
- *"The tapes are alive—they've got warmth and personality—and they cheer me up when the bookwork is getting a bit much."*

Fortunately, audio teaching is cheap and easy to prepare—without too much help from technical experts. And audio-players are quite cheap for learners to buy and convenient to use. Audio is a medium with enormous potential.

 You may like to make a note of any ways you might want to use audio with your learners.

Video teaching

Here we are talking about **moving pictures**, usually with accompanying sound. The television screen is now the most usual means of presenting moving pictures in education and training. These can take three main forms:

1. **Television programmes.** The typical educational television programme is around half an hour in length and is meant to be viewed from beginning to end without a break. It is heavily influenced by professional broadcast standards and formats—e.g. documentary or drama.

   A more basic form of "straight-through" viewing is provided by TVI—tutored video instruction. This is a low-cost operation in which the camera records a classroom lecture which is replayed for the benefit of groups elsewhere (Fleetwood-Walker & Fletcher-Campbell, 1986).

2. **Video segments.** Here, the videotape contains a number of separate clips, sequences, segments. Each lasts only a few minutes—some perhaps only a few seconds—and each is designed to trigger some kind of activity from the learner. Viewers are meant to stop the tape after each

segment to answer questions about it (perhaps rewinding to view it again first)—or, if they are viewing in a group, to discuss it with colleagues.

The video viewing may well be interspersed with reading, practical work, or learning from audio-cassette and there is no need for the segments to make up a continuous "storyline" as in material of Type 1.

3. **Interactive video.** This form of presentation uses special equipment (including either a computer or a bar-code reader) to give learners random access to thousands of still and moving pictures (or graphics and text) recorded on a videodisc (or, more rarely now, tape). Each learner may see a different sequence of images according to the signal he or she gives to the machine. For instance, several police forces are using interactive video to teach interviewing skills. Different learners see different versions of the next stage of a filmed interview according to which of several questions they choose to put to the person being interviewed.

Video can add an extra dimension to learning. Learners may be offered pictures in workbooks and sound from an audio-tape. But a video can bring them **moving** pictures, in full colour. And the sound—which may be people talking, or music or voice-over commentary—can work together with those moving pictures to give a sense of involvement, of "being there", that is difficult for other media to match.

As always, however, a potentially exciting medium can be used to less than optimum effect. Cullen (1985) reports finding four RAF trainees (whom he describes elsewhere as "highly motivated") soundly sleeping in front of their video-players while the tapes ran on.

I've asked a number of open learning developers about the purposes for which they use video. They mentioned a number of uses which I've listed below. Which of these might suggest possible uses with your learners?

Possible uses for video

☐ To show learners how to use tools or equipment.

☐ To demonstrate the skills they are learning—e.g. interviewing or anatomical dissection.

☐ To take learners through the stages of a procedure—e.g. a clerical task or a manufacturing process.

☐ To present a dramatic or musical performance—if it is important for learners to see as well as hear the performers.

☐ To analyse change over time, using animation, stop-frame, slow-motion or speeded-up pictures—e.g. the progress of a disease or the growth of a plant.

☐ To convey the three-dimensional qualities of an object—e.g. a building or a piece of sculpture—by moving the camera around it.

☐ To show a discussion or interaction between two or more people in which "body language" is important.

☐ To take learners into situations—e.g. into an intensive care unit or the cockpit of a jet plane making its landing—which they might not otherwise be able to enter.

☐ To provide "source material" for learners to explore or analyse, using principles or techniques taught in the course —e.g. a recording of scenes of violence at a football match.

☐ To help learners empathise with the people in a certain situation—e.g. with hospital patients or victims of crime.

☐ *Any other uses you can think of? (What?)*

If video is a medium you have not thought much about, you may find it interesting to watch one or two broadcast programmes and see whether they have any of the effects mentioned in the list above. Look in the listings magazines for Open University programmes or for any "educational" broadcasts that have "fact sheets" you can send off for.

Practical issues

Unlike audio, the production of video material is no do-it-yourself operation for the teacher or trainer with a couple of weekends to spare. It demands access to rather costly production equipment and considerable amounts of time for planning and editing. If you aim to produce video material of your own, you may need the help of professionals. Such experts may well have ideas that conflict with yours and you may need to surrender some control.

Enabling open learners to view the video material can also be more difficult and costly. On-site learners (e.g. those able to visit a learning centre) and distance learners pose different problems:

On-site learners may either be:

- brought together periodically for **group** viewing of material appropriate to the part of the programme they are **expected** to have reached, or

- given **individual** access to a video player whenever each learner is ready to view the material.

Group viewing has the advantage that learners (and tutors or mentors if they are present) can **discuss** the video material. It may also economise on equipment. The disadvantage, however, is that some learners may have got further through the programme than others. So the single showing of the video might come too late for some, too early for others—unless it is designed to be independent of the sequence in the rest of the course materials.

Individual viewing offers the learner more control. He or she can choose the most pertinent time at which to work on the video material. And, as with an audio-cassette, the learner can stop it and think about it, and replay bits of it as often as he or she likes—or as often as the video lesson itself suggests. However, the individual will be one of several; so a number of copies of the video material, and a number of playback machines, may need to be available. Furthermore, there will be the expense of providing accommodation, security, supervision, upkeep and, perhaps, an appointments system.

Distance learners may also be difficult to reach with appropriate moving pictures. If we can be sure they have access to playback machines, we can send them video-cassettes. If they don't have such access, we may face the expense of broadcasting material to them, perhaps via cable or satellite. Notice, though, that this may combine the disadvantages of fixed viewing times and lack of easy opportunity to discuss the material with others. It also inhibits the "video segments" approach.

 You may like to make a note of any thoughts you've had about using video with your learners.

Computer teaching

Computers can contribute to open learning in a variety of ways. For a start, they can control access to other media, like interactive video or CD-ROM and other databases. CD-ROM stands for "compact disc with read-only memory"—which means that learners can play back its contents but can't alter them. It is a storage medium that can hold vast quantities of information in text, pictures and sound—e.g. the whole of the *Encyclopedia Britannica* on a 12 cm plastic disc. (Many education and training databases—e.g. ECCTIS, ICDL and PICKUP—are now available on CD-ROM.)

Oddly enough, computers can also make it possible for people to talk to one another. They can help learners keep in touch with one another and with their tutors. This they do through computer-mediated communication, or computer conferencing, which we look at towards the end of this unit.

But computers are best known for providing direct teaching, using pre-programmed "courseware". Computer-based teaching operates under several names. The most common are computer-aided learning, computer-assisted learning and computer-based training (CBT).

CBT is very popular in industrial and commercial training on-site. (See Hawkridge *et al*, 1988 and Temple, 1991.) Rover, Jaguar, British Telecom, the Post Office, and B & Q are just a few of the many organisations whose "open learning centres" are well-stocked with microcomputers. The Open University also has several courses that call for students to use personal computers at home or in study centres (Jones *et al*, 1992). So what can computers do for the learner?

What computers can offer

If it is programmed appropriately, a computer can be the most powerful of open learning media—and certainly the one that can most easily adapt the pre-packaged teaching to the needs of an individual learner. After all, it can:

- store huge amounts of information
- select from it at great speed
- present the learner with a variety of stimuli, e.g.:
  ~ text and animated graphics
  ~ still or moving pictures
  ~ recorded sound
- respond to whatever messages it gets from the learner

- give immediate feedback to the individual learner
- respond differently according to the different requests or answers it gets from different learners.

Again in theory, computers can be programmed to use their teaching potential in three main ways:

1. **Tuition**. Here the programme requires the computer to act as a patient tutor or coach. It leads the learners through a sequence of material which they are expected to master. The computer can discover in what areas each learner has difficulties—then explain the ideas involved, using appropriate examples and exercises—and test the learners at each step to check how well they have understood.

   Different learners may be presented with different examples and test exercises, according to their earlier responses. And the program may "branch" different learners into different kinds of material according to the particular difficulties or interests they reveal.

2. **Simulation**. The second form of computer teaching uses the computer to simulate a particular situation or system with which the learner can interact. Thus the learner will be able to "experiment" in total safety with, let's say, a nuclear reactor, an ailing hospital patient, the processes of geological change, or the economic structure of the EEC.

   Learners can call up the information that will enable them to run the reactor, treat the patient, and so on, as they think fit, trying out their interpretation of the underlying principles. The computer will tell them what effects their decisions are having—especially if the reactor is about to go critical or the patient expire.

3. **Data-crunching**. Here the computer is used as a means of searching large amounts of data and/or of manipulating it at high speed. Thus the learner might ask the computer to search for certain figures or patterns in hundreds of census returns or to produce complex charts and graphs.

   In seconds or minutes, the computer may be able to provide learners with data that might otherwise have taken them hours or days to work out. Relieved of this drudgery and delay, learners can get on with the more important task of making sense of the data.

What are the costs?

What are the costs of using computer-based training and interactive video? To begin with, there is still a shortage of "generic" courseware—that is, teaching or training material of use to a wide range of users. So most organisations need to produce or commission their own. The British Telecoms and ICIs and B & Qs may take this in their financial stride; but small firms and cash-limited public sector organisations are likely to be more inhibited.

Experience in the Open University suggests that between two and four **months** of professional time are needed to produce a CBT exercise that will engage learners of varied ability for one **hour**. I've heard estimates of up to 450 hours per hour from commercial computer organisations.

With interactive video (involving the time of television experts as well as computer experts), the production costs are much higher—perhaps two or three times higher. Gange (1986) quotes development time ratios of between 700 and 1000 hours per hour of learning.

Such development costs can sometimes be justified—e.g. if large numbers of learners will use the material and/or their learning will be markedly superior. For instance, Temple (1991) tells of a British Steel interactive video on working practices in a steel mill that helped add £75,000 to the value of one team's production performance in a single year.

The delivery system for computer-based training and interactive video is also expensive. How many work-stations might you need to equip for on-site learners ? What would be the cost of staffing and accommodation? If your learners are studying at a distance and can't get to learning centres, can you (or they) provide equipment for use at home? Many of your learners will already have computers at home, of course. But the odds are they won't all be able to run the software you are developing. And very few indeed are likely to have the kit needed for interactive video, though a home market is predicted (sometime in the next ten years) for CD-I (compact disc-interactive).

 You may like to make a note of any ways (or new ways) your own learners might learn with the help of computers.

Teleconferencing

This is a medium for learning rather than for conveying pre-packaged teaching. That is, it allows the learner to interact directly with other people at a distance. As a result they may be able to seek help, discuss common problems and share ideas—and perhaps reduce their feelings of isolation.

Tele-conferencing can take any of three main forms:

- Audio-conferencing
- Video-conferencing
- Computer-conferencing.

Audio-conferencing

The telephone is often used in open learning as a means whereby the tutor can keep in touch with individual learners and clear up any problems they may be having with their programme. Audio-conferencing uses the telephone network to put **several** learners "on the line" at once (with or without a tutor) so that all can contribute and hear what others are saying. (See Robinson, 1990.)

Video-conferencing

The principle is the same as for audio-conferencing, but (at much greater cost) the participants are able to see one another (and any materials they are working with) on TV monitors. It is used, for example, by IBM as part of their system for training staff and customers (see Brian Robinson, 1990).

Computer conferencing

Here the participants communicate with each other through a network of personal computers (usually linked via public telephone lines). It works like a notice-board where people can leave statements or questions about a topic and read what other people have written whenever they choose to switch on their computer.

If you were a member of a conference right now, for example, you could "log on" and ask for comments from anyone who has had experience of a particular teaching medium you are thinking about trying. Unlike the other two forms, it is not usual to confer "live". So computer conferencing gives users more time to reflect on what others have said and how they might respond (if at all).

The medium can be attractive to professionals within a widespread organisation—e.g. a county police force or a firm with many branches—who want to keep one another informed, or pick one another's brains, without too much travelling. Such conferencing can even take place across firms—as it does in the UK confectionery industry, with firms like Cadburys, Mars and United Biscuits taking part.

Computer conferencing is already making an impact in distance learning—e.g. in a post-graduate occupational psychology course at Birkbeck College and on more than one course in the Open University.

Clearly, as Robin Mason (1990) points out: "this medium thrives on ease of access, and tends to wither and die when conditions for logging on are difficult." By this, she means learners are unlikely to make special visits to a learning centre. Nevertheless, the technology is getting cheaper and coming within the reach of household budgets.

Computer conferencing (or, more generally, "computer-mediated communication") has enormous potential for enabling "package-free" open learning. Learners would be able to question the experts (or other practitioners like themselves) rather than making do with what those people have seen fit to record in advance. This would have major repercussions on course design, staffing, costs, assessment, and a variety of other key aspects of open learning. And it could add a totally new dimension to "openness". (See Mason & Kaye, 1989.)

 Do you need to find any new ways in which your own learners might keep in touch with one another and with tutors—with or without computers?

Final remarks

Each medium has its unique qualities. But exploiting the unique qualities of the high-tech media can use up large amounts of time, money and expertise. Not all developers have been prepared to pay the price. So you may come across packages that use the media in degraded form. You may find interactive videos that allow little branching; CBT packages where the computer is simply an electronic page-turner;

videos whose message could have been conveyed more effectively in a booklet with text and still pictures; and even audio-cassettes doing nothing that could not have been done equally well in print. Watch out for media degradation.

When selecting media packages, you can never afford to take the developers' expertise for granted. They may not have chosen the most appropriate medium. And even if they have, they may not have used it to best advantage. (See the "Evaluating packages" section in Unit 5.) In particular, they may have given little thought to the "human media". To quote Fiona Munro (1989): "Enthusiasts are often keen on the production side rather than the support of the learner."

Whether vetting the media chosen by others or choosing media for packages you will develop yourself, it pays to keep your cool. Don't let the razzle-dazzle of new technologies blind you to your learners' real needs. Admit, by all means, that a certain medium may open up new teaching possibilities that you may want to exploit. But don't let the tail wag the dog. Keep in mind your teaching or training intentions and also your selection criteria. I list mine below. You may prefer others of your own.

- What kinds of learning do we want learners to do?
- Which medium (or combination of media) might best enable this?
- Can we make these media available to learners at a time and place that would suit them?
- How might learners feel about using these media?
- Do learners have the skills needed to use the media?
- Will support staff be able to work effectively with learners using these media?
- Shall we have sufficient control over the content and teaching approach of the media?
- What can we afford?

If you can't afford the medium you would really like, don't despair. Just remember the comforting words of Wilbur Schramm (1977):

> "If the medium that seems ideal for a specific purpose is not available, an alternative medium is likely to do almost as well."

What remaining concerns, fears or questions do you have about Media in Open Learning? Make a note of any that seem important enough to bear in mind when you do your desk work and field work on this topic.

Suggested follow-up work

Desk work

Thorpe & Grugeon (1987) contains articles about computer
based learning, learning from television and learning
from audio-tapes. It also has articles about tutors making
audio-tapes to support their distance learners and about
computer conferencing as a means for dialogue amongst
learners and between learners and tutors.

Robinson (1989) has one chapter (by Fiona Munro)
specifically about choosing and using media in nurse
training; though several of the chapters in the section
"The agony of production" also touch on media issues.

Paine (1988). The chapters with most to say about the choice
and use of media are those by Bates, Lougher and
Auchterlonie.

Temple (1991). Media issues pop up quite often and one
chapter, "Technology assisting learning", offers some
useful case studies of media use in industrial training. For
more industrial examples, see Hawkridge *et al* (1988).

The journal *Open Learning* has the occasional article relating
to media; but you are more likely to find the "newer" media
written about in journals like:

- ~ *British Journal of Educational Technology*

- ~ *Educational Computing*

- ~ *Journal of Educational Television*

- ~ *Interactive Learning International*

- ~ *Media in Education & Development*

- ~ *Educational Technology & Training International*

If you are particularly interested in CBT you may be
interested in a mixed media package developed for the
Employment Department; it is called *Using and Designing CBT*
and is available from System Applied Technology Ltd,
Howard Street, Sheffield S1 2LX.

If you want to know more about the very latest
developments—from CD-ROM and CD-I and DV-I through
multi-media to artificial intelligence and virtual reality—you
may find a useful source is *European Multimedia Yearbook*

published by Interactive Media International. The National and Scottish Councils for Educational Technology are also reliable sources of information in the form of free leaflets and priced publications.

Field work

- Interview one or two course developers or support staff who have used media with which you are not familiar. Get them to tell you what they believe that medium can do that other media can't—and ask them to show you some good examples of its use.

- Try to get hold of some learners who have recently used media that are new to you (or even media that aren't). What did they like about the media? What did they dislike? What do they tell you that might affect your decision about whether and how to use that medium with your own learners?

- Spend an hour or two trying to learn from a medium that you have never used before for learning. (This could be as complex as interactive video or as basic as an audio-cassette.) What does the experience teach you about using media with your own learners? For instance, what benefits might learners get from that medium that could not be provided acceptably well by cheaper and/or more accessible media?

 Remember to make a record of your desk work and field work in your portfolio.

Reflection checklist

 When you have completed your desk work and field work on this unit, please make notes in your portfolio using some of the following questions as a guide:

o What are the most important things you have learned during this unit? (You may want to look back at the objectives suggested at the beginning.)

o What has given you most satisfaction in this unit?

o What do you feel least satisfied about in this unit?

o Does this unit leave you with any unresolved questions or difficulties you feel you want help with?

o How might you try to get the help you need?

o What have you learned in your work with other people during this unit?

o In what ways were you able to draw on your previous experience during this unit?

o What have you learned about yourself—your own feelings and competences?

o What do you feel you need to do next?

Unit 5

The package in open learning

Most open learners depend on packages. What exactly are packages meant to do and how do they do it?

Can you buy them off the shelf or must you develop your own? Maybe you can adapt an existing package to suit your needs. Or perhaps you can write a study guide that will enable your learners to use materials that were never meant for open learning at all. These are the issues we consider in this unit.

Suggested objectives

As a result of working on this unit you could be better able to:

- Specify the kind of package your learners will need.
- Track down packages that may be suitable.
- Evaluate packages using appropriate criteria.
- Adapt packages that are not quite suitable as they stand.
- Write a study guide to help your learners use other materials.
- Weigh up the costs and benefits of developing a completely new package.
- o *Any objectives of your own to add?*

I suggest you now start a new section in your portfolio in which to keep a record of your ideas about Packages in Open Learning. From time to time, I'll print a box like this (with the symbol alongside) to prompt you to write something in your portfolio. I expect you will use some of these prompts and not others; and also that you will make occasional notes without my prompting.

The role of the package

Learning can be made more open **without** using packages—
e.g. by waiving entrance qualifications or by helping learners
develop projects based on their own interests. But I doubt
whether open learning could have become the force it has
without the use of packages. Packages usually foster one or
more of the key aspects of openness—e.g. being able to:

- learn without having to be in the presence of a teacher or
  other learners

- learn when and where one chooses

- learn at one's own pace

- choose one's own learning sequence

- assess one's own progress

- develop one's capacity for independence and self-reliance
  as a learner.

As a result, the package has, for many people, become the
feature that distinguishes open learning from ordinary
learning. They may even talk of "packaged learning". That's
all right in its way—so long as we don't forget the need for
human support. Packages can't respond to a learner's
individual concerns. For that, she or he needs to interact with
other people. Even where packages are essential, they are
rarely sufficient. That's a thought worth keeping in mind
throughout this unit.

What is a package?

Packages are materials designed so that learners can learn
from them without much help from a teacher. A package
may be a single workbook. It may be a videotape or audiotape
with a study guide. It may be a computer (CBT) disc or
practical kit together with back-up notes. Almost anything
that stores recorded information can be a package.

Packages don't have to use more than one medium, though
they often do. They don't even need to include more than
one item. What they do have to contain is some teacher's
teaching. Packages are pre-recorded, stored teaching.

So how does an open learning package differ from the
resources that teachers and trainers may use in ordinary
classroom teaching? How does it differ from textbooks,
reference manuals, videos, off-air recordings, and so on?

After all, it is possible to learn from these items also. Indeed, such items might even be **included** in a package.

The chief difference is that a package will have been designed with a more specific purpose in mind. It will be aimed at specific learners, specific objectives, specific competences. If it consists of more than one item, each will have a specific and separate role to play. Even if there is only one item (e.g. a workbook), support staff may be expected to help the learners in certain specified ways. If the package developers include existing resources, like textbooks or videos, they will "customise" those materials by adding a study guide that helps learners relate them to their specific needs.

What does a package need to do?

Packages are designed for learners who will have less access to a teacher than "ordinary" learners do. Unlike the author of a textbook, the package writer cannot usually assume there'll be a teacher hovering in the vicinity, guiding the learners about which sections to work on, giving help with the difficult bits and checking on how well they are learning.

Therefore, the package must do the teaching itself. That is to say, it must do whatever it can to help the learner learn.

The package contains a teacher in a state of suspended animation. Once the learner opens the package, that teacher is instantly at their service. What can learners expect from their teacher-in-a-package?

Here are some things that learners have told me they expect of a good face-to-face teacher. Which of them would you want your learners to get from the teaching in an open learning workbook or video or CBT package?

Expectations?

☐ Give me a clear idea of where we are going.

☐ Make sure I don't get lost along the way.

☐ Realise I can take in only so much between breaks.

☐ Be friendly and approachable.

☐ Use plain, everyday language.

☐ Use helpful examples (including pictures).

☐ Explain things clearly—and in more than one way.

☐ Give me a chance to draw on my own experience.

☐ Help me apply what I am learning to my own situation.

☐ Give me plenty of guided practice.

☐ Support me in trying out my own ideas.

☐ Help me to check my own progress.

☐ Summarise the main points from time to time.

☐ *Other expectations? (What are they?)*

You may feel that your learners will need virtually all of these services from their package. Well, that's all right. A well-designed package should be able to provide them. It should aim to give learners much the kind of help they might expect from their ideal teacher or trainer in a classroom. For if the package doesn't, who else will?

 You may want to make a note about what your learners are likely to need from a package.

How do packages teach?

Packages can be assembled from available materials by a tutor who knows the individual needs of his or her learners. But most packages are prepared to meet what are expected to be the common needs of a group of learners whom the package authors may never meet and who may not even know yet that they will want to learn with the help of that package.

Package teachers use a number of techniques to aid the learning of their prospective learners. These techniques can be seen most clearly in printed open learning workbooks and study guides. But they will also underpin the teaching in effective open learning videos and audio material and in computer (CBT) teaching.

If you've examined any open learning materials, you may know of these techniques already. (Look, for instance, through the sample pages from workbooks at the end of this unit.) These, I think, are the main "tricks of the trade" used by open learning writers to help the learners learn:

- Clearly stated objectives
- Advice about how to study the material
- Friendly, "You" & "I" style of writing
- Shortish chunks of learning
- Fewer words than usual per page (or screen)
- Plenty of examples
- Quoted remarks from other learners
- Illustrations used where they are better than words
- Headings to help learners find their way around
- Links to other media where appropriate
- Relating the material to the learners' needs
- Exercises that get the learners to do something
- Space for learners to write down their own ideas
- *Others? (What?)*

I'll now say a bit more about some of these features because you may want to look for them in selecting or developing an open learning package. Unless a package uses them properly it probably won't be much good to your learners.

Objectives

As you will know, objectives are meant to tell the learners what they might be able to DO as a result of their learning. All learning should enable learners to talk about the world in new ways and/or to act upon it in new ways. Objectives make clear just what these new ways are.

With most textbooks, and many classes, learners are never told what they're supposed to get out of them. With open learning they usually are. Authors of open learning materials may list the objectives for the whole course or programme at the beginning of the package. In addition they may list objectives for each separate section of the course, section by section. (I have done so myself in this book; compare the unit by unit objectives with the overall objectives on page 2.)

Once they know what they are learning to do, learners are in a better position to assess their own progress towards that goal. They don't have to depend entirely on someone else telling them how they are getting on. At the end of a package, or a section within it, they should be able to look back at each objective and say: "Can I now do that to my satisfaction?"

(Perhaps you are doing this with the Reflection Checklists as you work through this book.)

Objectives don't apply just to workbooks. Learners need them just as much if they are listening to an audio-tape or watching a video, or doing some practical work or computer-based training. They should still be able to get an answer to this same question: "What should I be able to DO as a result of this? What are the objectives?" They may also want to know how they relate to certain published "competences".

If you are selecting packages for your learners, you will be asking very similar questions. You'll probably want to reject materials whose objectives are quite different from those of your learners. You may also want to reject a package that gives the learners no freedom to challenge its objectives or choose from them—or indeed to pursue personal objectives.

(Note: We look at objectives also in Unit 2.)

Activities

"Activities" are often the most visible feature of open learning materials. They take the form of questions or suggestions inviting learners to do something.

They may be signalled in various ways. For instance:

- In some texts they are labelled, e.g. "Activity" or "Test Yourself" or "Self-assessment Question (SAQ)".

- In others there is no label but just a symbol alongside— perhaps a fancy letter A or a hand holding a pencil.

- *In yet other texts, you can easily spot the activities because they are printed in a different COLOUR or a different style of type.* Or maybe they have a blank space or a box for learners to write in.

- Sometimes there will be a rule of type across the page—to encourage learners to stop and do the activity before reading on. For example:

ɣɣɣ

Activities take many different forms, as you can see even among the sample pages at the end of this unit. They also ask learners to do different things and may take different amounts of time. Some will simply ask learners to read through a checklist and tick off the items they agree with. Some will ask them to write down their first thoughts on a topic. Such exercises may take only a few seconds. But others will take longer. In some subjects, learners may need to think through some problem or draw a diagram or work out some figures.

They may even be asked to get up and leave their package—to go and do something at work, around the home, or in the community. They may be asked to interview some colleagues, to observe what goes on in the local magistrates' court or to collect water samples for a pollution survey. (This is like the "field work" suggested in this book.) With activities of this sort, learners may spend longer on them than on reading the package.

What are activities for? The overall purpose of activities is to help the learners learn. But I've asked a number of authors why they use them and they've mentioned a variety of more specific purposes. I've summarised them below. Obviously, no one activity will have all these purposes at once. In fact, not all of these purposes will show up within every package.

Which of them might be important for your learners?

Activities may be meant to help the learner:

- [ ] remember the ideas in the package
- [ ] understand the ideas in the package
- [ ] make use of the ideas in the package
- [ ] think for themselves
- [ ] learn by doing
- [ ] bring in their own experience and examples
- [ ] reflect on their own thoughts and feelings
- [ ] obtain information that the package cannot provide
- [ ] apply their learning to their work or personal life
- [ ] practise towards important objectives
- [ ] monitor their own progress
- [ ] identify their strengths and weaknesses
- [ ] keep a record of what they have done.
- [ ] *Other purposes? (What?)*

Open learners generally seem to know what activities are there for. But that doesn't mean to say they do them. A colleague of mine recently did some research (Lockwood, 1990) into how students use activities in texts. Many students reported—with various expressions of regret and not a little guilt—that they either ignored activities or did something rather less taxing than the activity demanded. As one said: "I know they're there to help me think; but I haven't got time to think; I've got to get on."

It's worth paying critical attention to activities when selecting (as well as when developing) a package. Too often they seem to have been tacked on as a sort of design feature. Some provide only for what the Americans call "busy work". Even the best of activities cannot transform a set of uninspiring lecture notes into an effective open learning experience.

Four questions you may like to bear in mind while selecting or writing open learning materials are:

- Is each of these activities relevant to the objectives and worth doing (for at least some of my learners)?

- Is it essential for every learner to do every activity—or can they safely skip some? (Either way, they should be told.)

- How is the individual learner to recognise which activities he or she really must do and which can be ignored or just glanced at?

- What can I do to increase the likelihood that learners will make a serious attempt at key activities? (For instance, you might require learners to show certain results to their tutor or mentor.)

Feedback

Feedback is an important feature of an open learning package. We all need feedback in order to learn. It tells us about the results of our actions. It can therefore prompt our critical reflection, perhaps enabling us to do differently next time.

So, each activity in a workbook or CBT package is usually followed by some sort of information that helps the learner confirm or think again about the response they have made. With an interactive video package, say on infant teaching, the learner may get feedback to a choice they have made by being shown a film of what the child does next.

Feedback may take various forms. For instance, the author may give learners:

- the correct answer if there is one
- sample answers if more than one is possible
- responses that have been made by other learners
- the results of a choice they have made
- advice as to how they can assess their own answer
- questions about what they learned from the activity
- sympathy about difficulties they may have had
- reassurance about possible errors they may have fallen into.

In general, the author will try to help learners assess what they have done and perhaps compare their thoughts with those of the author or other people. Learners may be disinclined to spend much time on activities if the author doesn't feed them back some relevant comments. For instance, they may feel left in the dark as to whether they are working on the right lines. On the other hand, if the feedback is too extensive, learners may skip the activity and read the comments instead.

There will be times when the activity provides its own feedback. If learners are doing practical work, like wiring a 3-pin plug on a table lamp, the result they get will tell them whether they've carried it out correctly. The lamp either lights or it doesn't. (Though the thoughtful author may still give feedback in the form of a list of things to check again if the lamp fails to light up.) The authors of workbooks published by the Open College of the Arts seem to assume that their many drawing and painting exercises will provide a certain amount of feedback themselves—at least enough to sustain learners until they can get comments from a tutor.

Again, some activities (as with some of the field work in this book) may suggest that learners take what they have done— e.g. a plan they have outlined—and discuss it with other people. Their comments will act as feedback. That is, the comments should help them reflect on what they have learned and what they might do next.

Some packages include periodic self-tests to help learners measure their progress against all the objectives so far. Sometimes these will be a set of questions with the feedback available within the workbook or computer package.

Sometimes, especially with book-based distance learning courses, they may be "computer marked" (multiple-choice) questions and learners must send off their answers to get feedback. Thus the Open University has CMAs (computer-marked assignments) and National Extension College has MAIL (Micro-Aided Learning).

What ideas do you have about the part that activities and feedback might need to play in packages for YOUR learners?

Examples

Good open learning materials will include plenty of examples. The best teachers have always known that people may have difficulty with abstract ideas. Learners often can't really grasp new ways of looking at the world unless they are given plenty of telling examples. If I may give you an example, Jesus was well aware of our need for examples. He knew better than to lecture on ethical and theological principles. Instead he told stories about people like his listeners—and these examples brought the principles to life.

Open learning packages are usually full of new ideas, new theories and new methods—new to the learner, that is. They will all be capable of altering the ways learners see the world and the ways they operate in it. Whether they do so will depend to a large extent on whether the authors have provided examples that show how the ideas can work out in real life.

Examples may take several forms: e.g.:

- references to things learners already know (e.g. my parables of Jesus example above)
- anecdotes and stories
- case studies
- pictures (photographs, diagrams, maps, etc)
- audio and video material
- real objects (e.g. rock specimens or fabric swatches)
- graphs or charts and tables of figures
- calculations showing all the steps to a solution
- quotations from other people

- examples provided by other learners

- examples learners provide from their own experience
  (probably in response to an activity).

Obviously, different subjects call for different kinds of
examples. If your package contains the wrong sorts of
examples, or not enough, learners may find it lifeless and
dull. (Am I giving you enough of the right sort of examples
in this text?)

 You may like to make a portfolio note about the kinds of
example you would expect your learners to need.

Signals

The designers of open learning packages often pay a lot of
attention to layout and graphics. But they're not just trying to
pretty up the pages. They are using **signals** to help learners
find their way around the package and know what's going
on. For instance:

- **White space**. The pages of open learning workbooks are
  usually less crowded than other texts—so as to focus
  learners' attention (and avoid intimidating them).

- **Headings**. Big headings are used to break up the text into
  manageable chunks and also to give learners an idea of
  what each chunk is about. Smaller headings within each
  chunk do the same for its component sub-chunks.

- **Bulleted lists**. Lists (like this one) are often better than
  solid text for showing that a number of points are related.
  "Bullets" (•) or other devices (~) may be used to make
  them stand out more clearly.

- **Boxes**. Certain kinds of text—e.g. quotations or
  interesting side-issues—may be put in boxes to remind
  learners that they're meant to pay it a different kind of
  attention.

- **Icons**. Graphic symbols (or "icons", to use the jargon of
  computers) are often used in the margin to tell learners
  what sort of material they are about to deal with. The

icons alongside, for example, are the sort that might be used to indicate (in order):

~ an activity

~ using a video

~ using audio material

~ referring to other printed material.

Obviously, different packages use signals in different ways. Learners may need to be told how they work. This should be part of the study guidance given by the package.

Two different teaching styles

In selecting a package—or in planning one you will write yourself—you may want to consider its overall stance or philosophy or teaching style. You will find your own way of distinguishing between styles. However, I have noticed one distinction in my own package-making which I think you will find among other people's packages also. This distinction is between what I call the "tutorial-in-print" and the "reflective action guide". Both styles may appear in the same package, but usually one of them predominates.

Tutorial-in-print

The tutorial-in-print style is quite common among open learning workbooks and CBT packages. Learning from a tutorial-in-print is like having a good human coach or tutor, working with you one-to-one.

Like a good human tutor, the package tells the learner what they are supposed to get out of the session and then explains the subject clearly with examples that tie in to their experience. However, unlike a lecturer (but like a one-to-one tutor), the package does not present a monologue. Instead, like a tutor, it asks the learner frequent questions to check that they have understood the ideas being discussed and can comment on them or use them.

This approach arose out of programmed learning. It derived largely from the "branching" style of programmed learning rather than the "linear". Linear programmes usually presented learners with only a sentence or two at a time. By moving forward so cautiously, they intended that learners' responses—usually made by filling in a blank left in a sentence—would always be correct. (This approach is generally thought to have died out sometime in the 1970s. Recent evidence, however, suggests it is alive and well and keeping learners busy in some of the less imaginative CBT packages.)

Branching programmes, by contrast, tended to be relatively chatty and learners worked through them by answering a multiple choice question about the several paragraphs they would have read on each page—and getting additional explanation if their answer was not correct. The best branching programmes did simulate the kind of dialogue that may be seen nowadays in a tutorial-in-print (see Rowntree, 1966).

The tutorial-in-print style is perhaps most appropriate when there is a "body of knowledge" to be mastered. Here the aim is to help the learner take on board a new way of looking at things. The writer sets frequent activities to ensure learners are keeping up with the argument. These activities focus on ideas and usually involve writing something down or tapping computer keys. The writer is able to give quite specific feedback because he or she knows the kind of thing that learners will have written. The learning is assumed to happen while the learner is interacting with the package.

Reflective action guide

The reflective action guide, on the other hand, assumes that the important learning will take place away from the package. The material in the package is offered as a guide to action elsewhere—in real situations, perhaps with other people. The aim is not to have the learner master a body of knowledge but to attain personal insights or practice towards some kind of practical competence. Hence, we get the authors of the Open College of the Arts workbook on Art & Design saying: ". . . this is not an ordinary textbook. It is more like a set of instructions."

But the reflective action guide is not **just** a set of instructions—like painting by numbers or how to programme your video-recorder. It requires learners to think critically about the why and how of what they are doing—and evaluate the outcomes. I often mention the Lake District walking guides of Alfred Wainwright as a kind of reflective action guide. They have a particular interest for advocates of open learning in that they offer the reader a choice of several routes to the mountain tops.

More clearly open learning examples can be seen in project-based courses in the Open University and in Open College packages on management topics like Managing for Quality and Developing and Recruiting Staff. You may also be interested in a package called *Developing an Open Learning Package* (Rowntree, 1990b) which guides the user, step by step, through the stages of developing his or her materials.

The reflective action guide may have fewer activities than a tutorial-in-print but they will be more time-consuming. The reader may spend far more time on the activities than on reading the text.

Also, the activities are more likely to be related to the learner's own situation than to sample situations or case studies posed by the author. They are also less likely to involve writing or keying answers to questions about what the author has said in the package. On the contrary, they are likely to involve going out to do something away from the package—what I have called "field work" in this book. The learner may well be expected to interact with other people as part of an activity. The author cannot know enough about the learner's situation to provide specific feedback, so the learner must gather his or her own.

The reflective action guide may contain checklists and job aids. It may be intended for use "if and when" the user needs to carry out a particular task (e.g. climb Great Gable or carry out an appraisal interview)—a sort of "just in time" use—rather than the "front loading" use intended for much tutorial-in-print material—where the learner is expected to imbibe a body of knowledge which he or she may or may not need at some future time (e.g. in an examination).

The ultimate form of reflective action guide may be the "package" provided for learners doing an independent project in certain Open University courses. Here, a 20-page booklet may set up the learner for weeks of activity. It may contain guidance about how to choose a topic, sources of data, techniques of analysis, forms of reporting, the role of the tutor, and so on. But it may contain nothing of substance that has to be learned. The substance is all out in the real world.

As I suggested earlier, a lengthy programme may contain both tutorials-in-print and action guides. But confusion can arise if the authors have not been clear about what they were aiming for. I remember helping develop one package that was intended to help managers manage projects. Not unreasonably, its working title was Project Management. That title seemed to lead the writers into producing a tutorial-in-print that would have given learners practice in analysing the research on project management, applying the theory to case studies, and answering questions the authors knew the answers to. Unfortunately, it gave them no practice in managing projects.

So the course team changed the title to Managing a Project and asked the writers to produce a package that managers would not start on until they were about to take responsibilty for a project. The package would begin with a general orientation to project management (a sort of précis of the first version of the package) and then provide a developmental series of reflective action guides, each relating to managing a different phase of the project. The manager would thus return to the package at intervals over the ensuing months, whenever she or he needed guidance on a new phase of the project. Thus, the balance was shifted from "front-loading" towards "just in time".

In Unit 2, I discuss the dissemination v development models of learning described by Richard Boot & Vivien Hodgson (1987). You may want to consider how those models might relate to the two teaching approaches I have outlined above.

This may be a good point at which to look back over the points raised so far and make some portfolio notes about the kind of teaching you'll want in packages for your learners.

Obtaining a suitable package

In this second part of this Unit, I want to consider ways of obtaining a suitable open learning package for your learners. There are three main options which we'll look at in detail below:

- Use an existing open learning package.

- Build on existing NON-open learning material (e.g. textbooks or videos or government pamphlets).

- Plan and develop a custom-made package from scratch.

Make or buy?

The first of the above options is the cheap and easy way to get an open learning programme up and running—provided someone else has already developed a suitable package you can use. The second option—where you build your programme around materials that were not developed with open learning in mind—is rather less cheap and easy. But it is likely to be much more so than the ultimate option of developing all your open learning materials from scratch.

Shall we make or buy ? That is one of the first decisions to face an organisation setting up an open learning system. By now there are hundreds of thousands of open learning hours available in packaged form—many of them of excellent quality. Some colleges, at first through the FlexiStudy scheme and more lately also through Open College and other networks, have built their open learning business on materials published by National Extension College, Open College, and various other producers.

Yet many colleges and businesses still invest heavily in developing their own packages. Going round Britain as I do, consulting with various organisations on open learning, I am often aware of wheels being expensively reinvented. Let the government introduce a new Children Act, for instance, and you can be sure that most of the 40-odd police forces and even more social services offices will each have a team producing an update pack on the issue. Why is this?

I've asked a number of people I've worked with what they see as the pros and cons of developing their own packages. Clearly several had gone into producing their own because they hoped it might be easier than tracking down and evaluating packages produced by others. Some regretted making that choice. Here are the points they made:

The pros and cons of developing your own packages

Positive

- *"Better match with local needs"*
- *"Easier to update package"*
- *"Colleagues enjoy producing a package"*
- *"Staff seem better at supporting their own materials"*
- *"Our needs are too specific for generic packages"*
- *"Easier to find staff time than cash for materials"*

- *"Learners prefer a package produced in-house"*
- *"We all learn a lot of marketable new skills"*

Negative

o *"Costly in staff time"*

o *"Difficult keeping staff to deadlines and quality standards"*

o *"Pressures fray staff relationships"*

o *"Long delay before we can satisfy learners"*

o *"Pressure to sell to others to recoup our costs"*

o *"Learners rate our materials poorly against generic packages"*

o *"We don't have the production facilities for high-tech media"*

In general, the people I spoke with thought they had no choice but to produce their own materials if their needs were very specific—e.g. in training for jobs within a particular organisation. But all were very conscious of the cost and stresses of doing so—and of making what they'd see as a "professional job" of it. Collaboration with other organisations may or may not make the development process cheaper and easier.

However, unless you are in business to develop open learning packages, it is still wise to check what else is already available before you consider producing from scratch. One can pay a big price for scorning other people's material merely because it's "not invented here".

There is no shame in using other people's packages where they are appropriate. Some institutions—like FlexiStudy colleges and like the Open Learning Institute of Hong Kong which use chiefly materials from the UK Open University and other providers—have realised that their resources are better focussed on providing learners with a support system. Nor do major organisations (often with their own open learning development teams)—like British Gas, ICI and the NHS—have qualms about using management education packages from Open University, Henley Distance Learning, Open College, or whoever best meets their needs.

 What arguments might there be for and against making or buying packages in your own organisation?

Off-the-shelf packages

Ten years ago one could have been forgiven for not seeking out already published packages. Unless you wanted academic courses of the kind developed by National Extension College and the Open University, there was very little to find. Now, however, since the coming and going of Open Tech, the number of producers is enormous and still growing. Thousands of packages are already available, directed at a wide range of subject matter and competences. Yet more are published every week.

The trick, of course, is to find out just what is available, to decide what might be suitable for your learners, and then to get your hands on inspection copies. In what follows, I will suggest a number of ways of tracking down materials that may be suitable—starting off close to home and gradually widening your search. (I give addresses for all the organisations named in the Sources section at the back of this book.)

Your organisation

Have appropriate materials already been bought or made within your organisation? Trevor Sands (1984) tells how the Bradford College Mathematics Workshop got under way:

> ". . . my first priority was to attempt to collect together whatever individualised learning packages had already been produced commercially. The first place to look was in my own college, in locked cupboards. Some eight or nine years previously the college had . . . spent a fortune on programmed learning materials in many subjects areas in book, filmstrip and cassette form. Transferring the relevant mathematical materials to the Workshop gave a reasonable start to its development."

You may want to use your local networks to locate any such well-stocked cupboards that you may be able to pillage. The field work activities I've suggested in this book ought to put you in touch with people who know if anything is available in-house. If your organisation has a librarian or resources person, she or he might be a good one to start with.

Local sources

Next you might turn to other local sources for information about who is using what in your area, e.g.:

• Local colleges or other delivery centres.

- Local education authority (contact the organiser for adult education).

- Public libraries (reference section).

- Training Access Point (TAP) terminals or offices.

- Your nearest Training and Enterprise Council (TEC) or (in Scotland) your Local Enterprise Council (LEC).

- *Any others you are aware of? (What?)*

Other organisations like yours

Pay particular attention to other organisations (or sections within them) that are in the same line of work as yours. Some may not let you use their packages (or even see them) for reasons of commercial security. But others may be happy to let you use them (at a price)—especially perhaps if they will be able to use some that you are producing.

The Open Learning Directory

Consult a book called *The Open Learning Directory*. This is a catalogue of more than 2000 open learning packages updated every year. Many large public libraries will have a copy for reference. If they haven't, they should be able to obtain one or tell you where you'll find one—perhaps in a local FE college. You may want to ensure it is ordered for your own organisation's open learning library.

The *Directory* is divided into 18 subject areas—from Agriculture through Engineering to Social Welfare. For every package in each subject-area it tells you:

- what the package is about

- the intended learners

- what prior learning or qualifications (if any) are needed

- what level the package is at

- what qualification (if any) it leads to

- how long it takes to work through

- what learning materials you get

- what special equipment (if any) is needed

- what it costs

- what tutorial support is available (if any)

- who produces the package and/or how to obtain further information about it.

However, the *Directory* is firmly geared towards professional and vocational training. So you won't find packages that are more generally educational. No listing, for instance of the GCSE or A level subjects covered by National Extension College—or of the degree level packages in arts and social sciences produced by the Open University.

Producers' catalogues

You may want to gather catalogues from all the major producers of open learning packages—the Open University, National Extension College, Open College, and so on. Between them, they produce a vast range of academic, vocational, personal development and community material.

There are many other producers catering for learners in specific occupational groups—glass, knitting, electrical engineering, and so on. The *Open Learning Directory* has a section listing most of the producers and the main subject categories their packages cover.

International Centre for Distance Learning

If you want to spread your wings yet further and are interested in academic packages, contact ICDL. This is a documentation centre on distance education worldwide, based at the Open University but funded internationally. Its database carries details about courses and programmes (14,000 at present), about more than 300 institutions and about more than 3000 items from the literature of distance education. The database can be accessed either by online computer or by obtaining a compact disc from ICDL.

Other sources

Perhaps you know of numerous other sources. You may be able to pick up news of packages in your field by scanning the journals regularly and attending the occasional training exhibition or conference. As yet, no-one publishes a *What Package?* guide—but the Employment Department has made a start by producing databases (marketed by the Scottish Council for Educational Technology) that match available packages against the published NVQ/SVQ competences.

 You may like to make a note of how you could set about finding existing packages that might suit your learners.

Evaluating a package

Suppose you do come to hear of a package that seems to suit your general specification—relevant subject area, right level, appropriate media, acceptable price, and so on. The next step is to get hold of a copy and see whether it really is what you need. You may want to evaluate it from the viewpoint of both subject coverage and likely teaching effectiveness.

This step is not to be rushed, if you want to avoid making an expensive mistake. It may take some little while, especially if you have only one copy of the material and you want to involve others in the evaluation. And if your first impressions are favourable, you may well want to get comments from, e.g.:

• subject experts

• open learning experts

• learners' line managers

• tutors who know the intended learners

• the learners themselves.

Evaluation checklists

You may find it useful to work with a checklist when you evaluate. The one on page 145 shows some questions I might ask about a package. But you'll need to draft your own checklist, based on your own concerns.

In fact, you may want to give different checklists to different people. For example, you may want to ask:

• tutors to focus on whether the package seems likely to teach effectively

• subject experts to focus on whether it teaches what it ought to teach

• learners to tell you what they like or dislike about it and how they think it might be improved.

Perhaps you can meet with colleagues to pool your separate impressions of a package? This can also be a valuable staff development and team building exercise.

Adapting a package

Even the best package you come across is unlikely to be 100% right for your learners. You may decide you need to modify or adapt it in one of the following ways:

- **"Badging"**. The content and treatment is all right but you decide to present the material with your colours and logo (perhaps in a new box or ring binder) to reflect your organisation's image.

- **Study guidance**. You provide a Study Guide advising learners how best to use the package in your context—e.g. which sections are not relevant, where to go for help, tutorial arrangements, etc.

- **Local examples.** Again, the content and treatment is acceptable but you decide to add examples or case studies that are more closely related to your learners' interests.

- **New content**. Some parts of your syllabus have not been included, or parts of the content are unbalanced or outdated; so you add new material.

- **New media**. You decide your learners would benefit from an additional medium—so you produce, say, an audio or videotape to introduce or expand on a text-based package or a printed take-away "souvenir" of a CBT package.

In any such amendments, we must respect the original publisher's copyright. That is, you can give your learners new material **as well as** the package material. But you cannot freely print your own customised version of the package, interweaving your new material with the original. But if you do want a customised version of the package, you may be able to negotiate with the publisher—as Rover did in getting a computer-based version of the *30-hour BASIC* course that had been produced as a text by National Extension College.

 How might you organise the evaluation and adaptation of an existing package for use by YOUR learners?

Evaluating an open learning package

AUDIENCE
For whom is it intended? What prior knowledge, attitudes, skills (e.g. technical, educational, social) are required? Is its target audience sufficiently like ours?

OBJECTIVES
Are the learning objectives sufficiently similar to those of our learners?

COVERAGE
Is the subject-matter appropriate to our learners and the objectives? Is it accurate and up to date? Broad enough? Balanced? Any serious omissions?

TEACHING
Does it teach? Is it geared to learners working with less than usual help? Is it split into manageable chunks? Do learners apply and practice through self-testing activities? Is there adequate feedback? Are they given sufficient guidance on how to use the material? Are media used appropriately? What role for human supporters?

STYLE
Is the style of the material suitable for our learners—e.g. tone, vocabulary, sentence length, examples, use of pictorial material? Is it lively and interesting?

PHYSICAL FORMAT
Is it attractive in appearance? Legible? Durable? Portable? Suited to how it will be used?

REPUTATION
Does the material (and/or the producers) have a "track record"? Who has used it before? How well has it been received by other users?

COSTS
How much to hire or buy? What additional costs are there—e.g. video players, support system, staff development, adaptations to package? Is this within our budget and/or that of our learners?

AVAILABILITY
How easily/quickly can we obtain sufficient copies? Will it continue to be available?

LIKELY BENEFITS
Are learners likely to get what they would expect from using the package? Is the organisation?

ALTERNATIVES
How does this material compare with other existing material and with what we might produce ourselves?

Producing a "wrap around"

Despite your best searches, you may find that no suitable open learning package has yet been published. Must you then either embark on the long and costly task of developing your own package from scratch or else give up the idea of package-based teaching? Perhaps not. There may be a middle way:

Although you have not been able to find suitable open learning material, you may be able to find **other** usable material. That is, you may know of books, videos, audiotapes, etc that—while not produced with open learning in mind—do a pretty good job of getting your subject matter across.	**e.g. consider:** ~ textbooks ~ manuals ~ pamphlets ~ newspaper clippings ~ journal articles ~ commercial leaflets ~ videos/photographs ~ audiotapes/discs ~ practical kits ~ CBT packs ~ *Others? (What?)*

If so, you may be able to save a whole lot of time—and give your learners what they need—by writing a study guide that wraps around the chosen item or items and makes up for whatever they lack in open learning terms. And of course you may want to add new media.

So, depending on what you judge to be missing, your study guide might contain any of the following items:

- Study guidance
- Learning objectives
- Introductions/overviews
- Summaries
- Glossaries
- Clearer explanations
- Contrasting viewpoints
- Alternative examples
- Illustrations
- Local case studies
- Activities (especially locally relevant ones)
- Feedback on such activities

- Instructions for practical work
- Assignments for discussion with tutor, colleagues, etc.
- *Others? (What?)*

Again, you have to respect copyright law. You can't freely reprint newspaper cuttings and journal articles or make a scrapbook of whichever bits from texts and manuals you happen to like the look of. Either you or the learners must pay for copies of any items you use or you must negotiate with the owners of the copyright to let you reproduce their material in your own form.

Despite paying for copyright permissions, producing a wrap-around may still be cheaper than producing a complete package from scratch. Whether it is, of course, depends on how much work you need to do on your study guide. For guidance on producing study guides see Duchastel (1983), Kember (1991), Morris (1984) and Lewis & Paine (1986).

Made-to-measure packages

If you can't get a package off-the-shelf, and a wrap-around looks like more time and trouble than it's worth, you may decide to develop your own. There are three ways of getting a made-to-measure package:

- develop it in your own organisation
- collaborate with similar organisations
- commission an open learning producer.

Any of these options is likely to be trying and costly. Many excellent classroom teachers and trainers have found frustration in striving to pre-record their teaching for learners whom they will never meet. More than once I've heard remarks along the lines of: "I never really knew the subject myself until I tried to package it for someone else to understand." For guidance on developing your own package, see Lewis & Paine (1985b) and Rowntree (1990a, 1990b).

What about collaboration with other organisations? My own experience with such co-productions tells me they may result in a better package—but the greater scope for disagreements about content and approach may make the process quite slow and costly. The new Open Learning Foundation may have some useful insights to share with us when it comes to evaluate its experience of large-scale co-production.

Finally, there are many open learning producers (see the
Open Learning Directory) who may provide satisfactory value
for money. But you and your colleagues may still need to
invest a deal of your own time in choosing a suitable
producer, briefing them, contributing to the production, and
monitoring their work through its various stages. For
guidance on working with open learning producers—
especially in the area of CBT and interactive video—see
Rowntree (1990c).

 How do you feel now—is there a case for developing your
own packages? Or does one of the other two options
(existing package or wrap-around) seem preferable?

Unless you have special needs—and a good supply of money,
time and skills—the best advice may still be that offered by
Lewis & Paine (1985b):

> "The arguments for choosing one of the other options are
> thus compelling. Time, money and effort should be saved.
> The end product is more likely to be good. The energies of
> teachers and trainers can be deployed in areas where
> they are more likely to bear fruit, for example in devising
> flexible support and management systems."

Final remarks

I began this unit by pointing out that a package can foster one
or more aspects of openness. It seems only fair to end by
warning that packages can also be used to close down certain
other aspects. Packages can be used to empower people—but
they can also be used to blinker them, if not to indoctrinate
and manipulate. (See Harris, 1987; Boot & Hodgson, 1987).

An author could use a package to hammer home a single
point of view, giving learners no encouragement to
challenge it or develop their own personal angles on the
subject. (This reflects the "dissemination" approach discussed
in Unit 2.)

Such an approach—especially if backed by an assessment
system that rewarded only those who toe the party line—
would deny learners their autonomy. The learner could

become passive and unreflecting. No amount of choosing which package to study, and being able to tackle it where, when and at what pace one likes, would make up for closure in this respect. This would be open learning for closed minds. (At least, that's my view. Please feel free to think differently!)

If we have the will, the risk can be minimised, of course. Here are some possible ways of doing so. We can:

- use a variety of short packages by different authors (in preference to a monolithic production by one team)
- present conflicting viewpoints as in a debate
- require learners to compare and appraise
- ask learners to test views against their own experience
- set assignments that challenge ideas in the packages
- encourage and reward sound criticism
- get learners to exchange views and experience
- put more emphasis on independent project work and less on packaged teaching.
- *Others? (What?)*

I leave you to think of other ways in which you might ensure that pre-packaged teaching does not result in pre-packaged thinking.

What remaining concerns, fears or questions do you have about the use of Packages in Open Learning? Make a note of any that seem important enough to bear in mind when you do your desk work and field work on this topic.

Suggested follow-up work

Desk work

Thorpe & Grugeon (1987) contains two useful chapters—an article by Wendy Stainton Rogers on adapting existing materials and an account of a materials development project by Roy Webberley and Ian Haffenden.

Robinson (1989) has five chapters on package development.

Paine (1988) has only one chapter (by John Meed) that deals explicitly with materials and their development.

Temple (1991). The role and nature of packages is often touched on but no chapter discusses the topic at length.

In addition, you may find other sources you want to look at in the bibliography at the end of this book. For instance, if you are planning to develop open learning materials yourself I would recommend Rowntree (1990a)—you'll find a chapter outline at the end of this book; and Rowntree (1990b). If your role will be to manage the development of open learning materials, Lewis & Meed (1986) could be very useful to you, even though it was written before desktop publishing opened up so many new possibilities.

Field work

- Find out which staff in your organisation have experience of producing open learning materials. Get their views about the pros and cons of developing new materials compared with using packages that exist already. You might consider setting this up as a seminar to pool experience.

- Find and evaluate some existing packages, i.e.:
  - ~ Decide on a specification for the kind of package your learners need.
  - ~ Seek out some likely-sounding packages.
  - ~ Draft one or more checklists and evaluate the packages, if possible as a team exercise with other people.

- If you can find a more-or-less usable package, draw up a detailed list of what you would need to do by way of adaptation. (Try, if you can, to ask some learners.)

- If you can't find a suitable package, select some non-open learning materials and draw up a detailed contents list for a wrap-around study guide.

 Remember to make a record of your desk work and field work in your portfolio.

Reflection checklist

When you have completed your desk work and field work
on this unit, please make notes in your portfolio using some
of the following questions as a guide:

o   What are the most important things you have learned
    during this unit? (You may want to look back at the
    objectives suggested at the beginning.)

o   What has given you most satisfaction in this unit?

o   What do you feel least satisfied about in this unit?

o   Does this unit leave you with any unresolved questions
    or difficulties you feel you want help with?

o   How might you try to get the help you need?

o   What have you learned in your work with other people
    during this unit?

o   In what ways were you able to draw on your previous
    experience during this unit?

o   What have you learned about yourself—your own
    feelings and competences?

o   What do you feel you need to do next?

Sample pages from open learning materials

Materials play a vital role in open learning. Yet people in the business are usually so busy that they don't get time to look at any materials other than those being used in their own organisation. Sometimes, they don't even get to see materials used in other **sections** of their organisation.

This is a pity. I believe that we can learn a great deal about the design and use of materials by reflecting on how other people do it. It doesn't matter if their subjects and their learners are very different from ours. In fact, it may be helpful because it can concentrate our attention on **how** the materials are teaching rather than on **what**.

In my open learning workshops, I always have a session in which we analyse a range of materials from open learning packages. There's no space to do that here. But what I can do, in the samples that follow, is give you just a glimpse of the materials I keep on my shelf for reference. I would then urge you, as I urge my workshop colleagues, to go out and start building up your own collection of samples—from wherever you can beg, swop or even buy them. I suspect you'd find it a stimulating resource in your own open learning work.

You may well have no professional interest at all in any of the subjects dealt with in these sample pages. That shouldn't matter. Just ask yourself: "What is the author doing to help the reader learn?" and "What might be the pros and cons of using such an approach in my subject and with my learners?"

If you are examining the samples before you've looked at the section on "The role of the package" in Unit 5, I suggest you might usefully return to them after you have.

N.B. *All the samples are from workbooks, but some of these were for use with other media—audiotapes, videos, computers or practical work. The originals were all A4 in size, and some were printed in more than one colour.*

The contributors

The twenty sample pages that follow are from open learning materials produced by the organisations listed below and are reprinted here with their kind permission.

Activity 1 Your own house's face

The purpose of this activity is to begin a design analysis of your own house, starting from the outside (the 'face' your house presents to you and your neighbours) and, in later activities, working inwards to the plan and other details. (Estimated activity time: about ½–1 hour.)

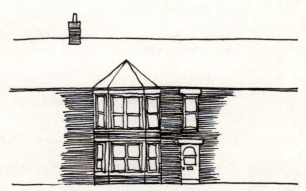

1   From memory (i.e. do it straight away, without first going outside to look) draw the front of your house. Don't worry about details that you cannot remember, but try to make your drawing as clear and as detailed as you can, although obviously you probably won't be skilled at drawing and your attempt may in fact be fairly 'childish'. Try asking other members of your household to make their own drawings, too, without looking at each other's until you have all finished. (As with all these activities, my own attempt is shown alongside.)

My drawing of the front of our house, from memory

2   Compare your drawings one with another. Are there any large differences between what you each remember and have drawn? Has someone in the family clearly got a better memory of all the details of the front of your house, or do you disagree among yourselves as to the details and their relative locations?

My daughter's drawing of the front of our house, from memory

3   Now go and look at the front of your house and compare the reality with the drawings. Are there any large differences between the reality and what is supposed to be represented on the drawings? Did you have a good visual memory of the front of your house, or have you not really looked carefully at it before? Try making another drawing from observation, to improve on your first attempt.

A photograph of my house (the one in the middle)

Retailing Basics

Hazard warning signs

Some products require special care when being handled or stored. Hazard warning signs appear on products to tell you what the hazards are.

If you have to use a product which is hazardous or if you may be exposed to one when cleaning up spillage, for example, remember to read the health and safety instructions which should appear on the packaging. This will enable you to deal with it safely.

It may be, for instance, that you should wear gloves or protective goggles.

 Go round the store looking for as many hazard signs as you can find.

Using the space below, draw four symbols which you have found and indicate what they mean.

1

2

3

4

8   TOLSTOY'S MORAL NEUTRALITY

8.1   'I have found', Tolstoy once said to a friend, 'that a story leaves a deeper impression when it is impossible to tell which side the author is on'. (See p. 45 for the full quotation.) As Tolstoy puts it, this might sound no more than a clever author's device; but I would suggest that it means something deeper.

8.2   Consider the question of 'taking sides' in a novel for a moment. It is surely very important in almost all the novels you have studied in this Course. (You will remember Graham Holderness's remarks about it in connection with *Wuthering Heights*; see Units 4–5). You can put it to yourself in this way: do the authors, at certain points in their novel, depend on your feeling *indignant*, or *gladdened*? Well, clearly, Jane Austen expects you to feel indignant at Mrs Norris's treatment of Fanny; Henry James expects you to feel indignant at Maisie's treatment at the hands of her parents; and George Eliot expects you to be gladdened that Dorothea, at a low point in her own fortunes, has the strength of mind to think of others.

8.3   Or you could put it another way: do the authors expect you to form *wishes*? Does Jane Austen expect you to *want* Fanny to be freed from oppression, and Turgenev expect you to *wish* that Insarov might not be doomed (as he so plainly is). I think you will agree that they do, and that this is the means by which they get you to make certain sorts of judgement for yourself.

Ask yourself, therefore: do you feel indignation, or gladness, or a wish that things could be different in reading *Anna Karenina*?

Discussion

8.4   Let us take indignation. Do you feel indignant, at Karenin's horrible letter to Anna? At Anna's neglect of her daughter? At Oblonsky's misdoings? For myself, I don't think that I do, or that I am meant to. Tolstoy *could* have made us indignant at these things with perfect ease, but it is not part of his plan to do so. Tolstoy places you, as a reader, at a point of vantage where you feel no wish that things should be different.

8.5   Does this mean that he is aloof and indifferent towards the fate of his characters —that he is treating them simply as a spectacle and intends us to do the same?

Discussion

8.6   I would say, not at all. He feels, and makes us feel, intensely for his characters, but this feeling is of a special kind: it is the feeling of kinship, of human solidarity, the sort of bond which unites the species and holds society together. He once wrote in his diary that 'The powerful means to true happiness in life, is to let flow from oneself on all sides, without any laws, like a spider, a cobweb of love, and to catch in it all that comes to hand: women old or young, children, or policemen'.[1] It is a good description of the way he writes; and this spider-like

---

[1] He made this diary-entry on 26 April 1856. (See Aylmer Maude's *Life of Tolstoy*, World's Classics ed., Dent, vol. 1, p. 151.)

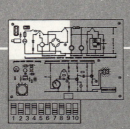

PRACTICAL
WORK   7

The picture shows the part of the
kit you'll be working on — the
bridge rectifier circuit. You'll also
need your multimeter and two
short wire links. Before you start,
make sure that you've removed
the wire from link LK1 after
Practical 6, and check that the
fault switches are all in their
correct positions.

1 Connect up links 3 and 6.

2 Switch on at the mains and at
your kit.

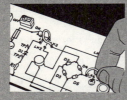

3 Set your multimeter to 20 volts
dc and switch it on.

4 Put the black meter probe on
test point TP4 and the red
probe on test point TP3, and
note the voltage reading you get.

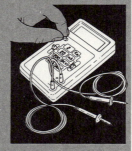

That's the end of the practical
work for this unit, so switch off
your kit and your meter and put
them away safely.

The voltage you just measured was
the output voltage of the full-wave
bridge rectifier on your kit. It
should have been over 8 volts dc,
much higher than the voltage you
got from the half-wave rectifier. In
fact, because the bridge rectifier
gives you twice as many pulses as
the half-wave rectifier does, its
output voltage is about 90 percent
of the ac voltage, compared with
the 45 percent you get from a half-
wave rectifier.

Home Experiment 2

To do the experiment you will need the following items from your Home Experiment Kit, Part 2:

Apparatus*

$100\,cm^3$ beaker

$100\,cm^3$ measuring cylinder

rack of test-tubes

$5\,cm^3$ syringe

2 dosing pipettes†

wash-bottle containing distilled water

spatula

Chemicals

sodium hydroxide

dilute hydrochloric acid (8.9%)

ferric nitrate (iron(III) nitrate)

potassium thiocyanate

Part 1

(a) Using your measuring cylinder, measure $50\,cm^3$ of distilled water into a beaker and add five pellets of sodium hydroxide, NaOH. Allow to dissolve.

(b) Add enough ferric nitrate, $Fe(NO_3)_3$, to a test-tube until the rounded bottom is full. Add enough distilled water to half-fill the test-tube, and shake until the solid dissolves.

(c) Add *one* crystal of potassium thiocyanate, KSCN, to a test-tube and add enough distilled water to half-fill it. Again shake to dissolve.

All three solutions are ionic. Note the colour of each solution and try to decide which ions are present: record these in Table 2.

TABLE 2   Observations for part 1 of Home Experiment 2

Solid	Colour of solution	Ions present
sodium hydroxide, NaOH		
ferric nitrate, $Fe(NO_3)_3$		
potassium thiocyanate, KSCN		

Now listen to the first part of the tape.

Extract from tape

"Now that you've prepared the three solutions, check your entries in Table 2. First, the columns: Both the sodium hydroxide and the potassium thiocyanate are colourless. But the ferric nitrate solution should be yellow. If you found any marked differences from these colours, you should make up that solution again, taking care that the test tube or flask is really clean—wash it well with distilled water before adding the chemical, and don't forget to wash and dry your spatula before using it.

Now what about the ions in these solutions? Well, you've already met sodium hydroxide, so I expect. . . "

The reception area

Start this section by carrying out the following activity which will help you assess what makes a good reception area.

ACTIVITY 7   Look at the following picture of a receptionist and reception area. This is not an ideal situation. What is wrong with it? Label the bad points shown in the picture.

Turn to page 36 for our assessment of this reception area. Look, too, at the picture on page 23 which offers a real contrast – a much more welcoming and attractive scene!

Part 5 Assessment Exercise

Part Five of the video, *Competence Assessment – Exercise*, shows the assessment of Andy, from Customer Service, while fitting Mr and Mrs Cartwright's fire.

Put yourself in the place of the assessor and observe Andy as he carries out the task you are assessing him on. This Element of Competence is 'Communicate with the Customer', a general task which many people in the Company perform.

This example should give you a flavour of the assessment process, rather than teach you specific assessment skills.

Before you watch the video, read the Performance Criteria on the facing page.

During Part Five you should tick any of these criteria which you observe Andy meeting. Put a cross against those criteria he does not meet, and leave blank where there is no evidence either way.

When you have completed watching Part Five you should compare your assessment form with the completed form on page 32.

Please note that some of the operational procedures in the video may differ from those in your region.

Now watch Part Five of the video,
Competence Assessment – Exercise.

SAA 3

Your answer must be **NO**. Marlene is a juvenile and therefore considered to be unable to give an informed consent.

1E

WPC Holmes starts the search but Marlene decides she would like her father present. The request is turned down by WPC Holmes who says there should not be a person of the opposite sex present at the time of the search as she wishes to remove Marlene's jacket and check inside her cardigan. Marlene accepts the decision and the search continues.

SAQ 4

Why was WPC Holmes incorrect in what she said?

Code A

Serving wine

The disadvantage of serving wines by the glass is that, once opened, they will not last. So establishments have to be sure, while extending their range, that the demand exists and wines will not go to waste. It is important therefore to make the customer aware of the range of wines that is available. Many establishments display notices to this effect, but staff can also help sales by telling customers what is on offer at the time the order is made

The need to display wines attractively in bars is probably more necessary than in restaurants where a wine list can be handed directly to the customer to show what is on offer. One solution is to place the whites and rosés in an ice bucket or special insulated holder on the bar counter or back fitting, and some red wines on racks clearly visible to the customer. Or white and rosé wine bottles can be placed in special cooling cabinets attached to measured dispensers. These cabinets are attached to the bar wall where they can be easily seen by customers

How wine is dispensed

Simply tilting the bottle into the glass is still the most common way of dispensing wine. Once the bottle is opened and exposed to the air, the wine soon becomes oxidised and undrinkable. With sales of wine by the glass, this would lead to a lot of wastage, but wine boxes, wine-cooling cabinets which dispense the wine through an optic or special wine measure, and wine-dispense systems which pump-up wine in pipes from a bulk container in the cellar, manage to solve the problem by preventing air from entering the wine as it is drawn off. Special bottle stoppers have also been developed to keep opened bottles of wine in good condition for longer than is possible with a plain cork.

Wine by the glass

Most licensees have adopted the code of practice on the sale of wine by the glass which stipulates the measures of still wines which can be served in a glass (see unit 2). It must be made clear, by a notice displayed where customers can see it, that the establishment has adopted the code. A variety of measures is allowed, both in imperial and metric, but the licensee must choose no more than two, both of which must be either metric or imperial measures differing from each other by at least 50 ml (2 fl oz). Many establishments choose to serve 125 ml because an exact number of glasses can be obtained from a 75 cl bottle.

 TO DO

Visit a licensed establishment of your choice and make notes on where (cellar/storeroom /cupboard/refrigerator/racks behind bar), at what temperatures and in what conditions (lying on their sides, upside down, upright on racks/shelves/in their original boxes) the different types of wine are stored (red/white/rosé/sparkling/boxed/screw top).

Then answer the following questions.
1. How many bottles of red wine are kept at room temperature and for how long before service? (The number of bottles may vary depending on the day of the week.)
2. How many bottles of white, rosé and sparkling wines are kept chilled, at what temperatures and for how long before service?
3. What is the average number of bottles of wine (red/white/rosé/sparkling) sold (a) on the busiest day, (b) on the quietest day?
4. From these figures, calculate the number each of red, white, rosé and sparkling wines brought to the correct serving temperature as reserves (in other words, will probably not be needed that day).

UNIT 4   THE INTERVIEW

Introduction

In this unit you will look at the art of effective interviewing. It sounds easy, but to be a good interviewer takes skill, self discipline and a knowledge of your own prejudices.

Purposes of this unit

When you have completed this unit you should be able to:

* create a suitable environment for an interview
* plan a structure for the discussion
* prepare individual questions based on the seven point plan
* take into consideration the importance of first impressions
* conduct the interview in such a way as to acquire the information needed to come to a fair decision
* close the interview effectively
* make a final decision and take appropriate follow-up action.

1 Why interview?

Interviews are the most common and, sometimes, the sole method by which organisations assess a candidate's suitability for the job.

Since so much depends on these encounters, it is worth asking how effective they are as a means of selection.

What can interviews tell you about a candidate's ability to do a job? – and what can't they tell you?
Write your ideas in the space below:

They can tell you	They cannot tell you ...

David, regional manager, clearing bank
'I'm very much in favour of interviews because you meet candidates face to face. I believe you can make an accurate judgement of their interpersonal skills and you have the chance to pose questions which can test this. The other factors are less tangible; you can get a sense of their enthusiasm – perhaps even their approach – and, most importantly, a sense of how much they want the job.'

Ronnie, distribution manager, sportswear manufacturer
'We use interviews almost exclusively – other methods are only used for top jobs. I think so much depends on the skills of the interviewer. The best interviewers can draw out much of the information they require, but most of us only interview sporadically. I've also found that interviews rarely help me to answer what for me is a big question: can they do the job in the way we want?'

Gwen, section head, petrochemical company
'My background is in personnel so I suppose I have a slightly different view of interviewing. I believe interviewing is the most effective way of selecting staff for most jobs but I feel it's very easy to have far too much faith in it as a single method. If there is no other method such as testing involved, always try to make sure that the application forms and preparatory work by selectors are as detailed as possible.'

Can you add anything else to the list as a result of what these managers described? After you have finished, compare your list with the one below.

They can tell you about:

- attributes such as appearance and manner

- motivation and how much the candidate wants the job

- interpersonal and communication skills

They can also ...

- enable the candidate to ask questions about the job

- give you the chance to find out more about specific points

They cannot tell you about:

- the candidate's practical skills

Other drawbacks ...

- inexperienced interviewers might not help the candidate to be seen in the best light

- interview nerves may inhibit an otherwise excellent candidate

Section 1:   Why trees and shrubs, and how to find out more about them

In this Section I'll look at why some gardeners prefer trees and shrubs to more formal garden designs. I'll also show you how to make a 'Looking good' list of plants for each month and how to collect information about each plant so that you can make sound recommendations to your customers.

Why choose trees and shrubs?

Many knowledgeable gardeners prefer to have borders that contain mixed shrubs rather than complex bedding designs and herbaceous borders. Why do you think this is? Try to think of 3 reasons and jot them down in the box below.

1.

2.

3.

You could have suggested any of the following reasons:

1.   Trees and shrubs offer an attractive, year-round display, with a variety of form, colour and height. The careful selection of plants will ensure:

   - something is in flower all year round (see the section in **Hillier's Manual of Trees & Shrubs**, page 567, and pages 33, 37 and 44 of **The Tree & Shrub Expert**)
   - a contrast of colour (variegated or evergreen leaves) and shape (bold-shaped foliage or fern-like leaves)
   - berries or stems for winter colour.

2.   A mixture of shrubs can cover the ground so as to suppress weed growth.

3.   Digging is unnecessary once trees and shrubs are established, and only light cultivation is needed. Read the articles on mulching and hoeing on page 107 of **The Tree & Shrub Expert**.

1: SOME IMPORTANT BUDDHIST TEACHINGS

The Four Noble Truths including The Eightfold Path

Do you remember *The Four Signs* (Religions page 195)? *Siddhartha Gautama* met four people and eventually came to *The Four Noble Truths.*

READ Religions pages 198 - 201

and then...

MAKE a dictionary list of the following:
dukkha samudaya nirodha magga

If possible look at the Buddhism in Focus 1 video.
LOOK at the picture of The Wheel of Life and read the accompanying explanation.

If possible read Looking for Happiness pages 22 - 26.

DESIGN a poster to show *The Eightfold Path.*
Try to make sure that it shows what each stage means.

The Five Precepts

A lay Buddhist lives by *5 basic rules* usually called *The Five Precepts.*

To find out about these:

READ Religions pages 204 - 207

WRITE out The Five Precepts.

IN YOUR TUTORIAL discuss how your life would have to change if you became a Buddhist. Are there any parts of *The Four Noble Truths, Eightfold Path* or *Five Precepts* which you would find particularly attractive, difficult, or with which you would disagree?

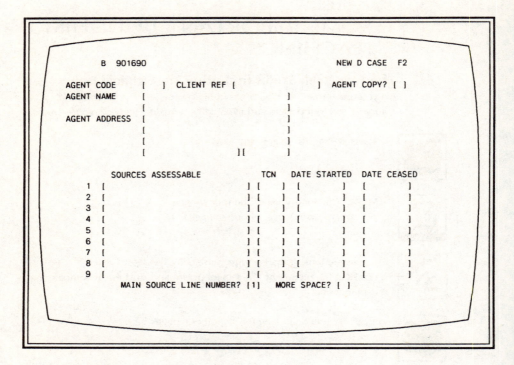

```
        B   901690                              NEW D CASE   F2

AGENT CODE      [   ]  CLIENT REF [              ]  AGENT COPY? [  ]
AGENT NAME      [                          ]
                [                          ]
AGENT ADDRESS   [                          ]
                [                          ]
                [                          ]
                [                   ] [         ]

        SOURCES ASSESSABLE           TCN   DATE STARTED   DATE CEASED
    1  [                       ] [   ] [            ] [           ]
    2  [                       ] [   ] [            ] [           ]
    3  [                       ] [   ] [            ] [           ]
    4  [                       ] [   ] [            ] [           ]
    5  [                       ] [   ] [            ] [           ]
    6  [                       ] [   ] [            ] [           ]
    7  [                       ] [   ] [            ] [           ]
    8  [                       ] [   ] [            ] [           ]
    9  [                       ] [   ] [            ] [           ]
        MAIN SOURCE LINE NUMBER? [1]   MORE SPACE? [ ]
```

Your screen now shows Format 2.

► Complete this screen

• Can you remember where to find the TCN? If not turn back to page 23

• Compare your completed screen with the next page
  before you press SEND

1 Introduction

Your project will be a very important part of your work on U206, indeed you may remember it vividly long after the other course materials have faded from your memory. The importance is not in terms of time spent – the project is only allocated 5 weeks and so must be small – but in the quality of the learning experience. In particular, your project will be a major part of achieving the third of the course aims – evaluating desirable courses of *action*. It would be improper for the course team to tell you how to act, or even that you should act, but we are asking you to develop skills by behaving as if you were going to act. We are asking you to investigate a local environmental issue, to write a short report and to draft a letter to an appropriate decision-making body advocating a particular outcome.

This task is intended to involve you in three ways which most of the course does not:

- the issue should be local, and preferably one where the outcome affects you directly
- we are asking you to draw on experience and skills which you already possess
- you will have to develop new skills of enquiry, interpretation and advocacy if you are to solve the problems you set yourself.

As a result of these factors, most students who do projects find that they generate much stronger feelings than the more passive learning elsewhere in the OU system. The job of this *Project Handbook* is to provide a framework to help you to take on this challenge successfully, so that you can emerge with strong *positive* feelings rather than the disappointment that can result when projects go wrong. We have written this booklet and scheduled feedback from your tutor to minimise the opportunities for error, but the nature of a project is that the ultimate responsibility is yours.

A word of warning is needed at this point: although the project will be yours and will be influenced by your values, there is no point in a piece of work which starts from your prejudices, selects information and views only if they accord with those prejudices and then attempts to hector decision-makers to accept them. What we hope you will achieve is an investigation which dispassionately seeks evidence and understanding and then uses that evidence, along with a justified set of values or goals, to argue for particular action.

To produce such a piece of work will be challenging, because it combines enquiry and self-analysis, but will be easier if you are sceptical about your own preferences as well as those of other people or groups who are involved. The issue of handling values as well as evidence is discussed at appropriate points in this booklet and links to Book One, Chapter 7.

1.1 Framework

The framework we are suggesting is one that divides your project work into four stages, each with assessment in a TMA and hence with tutor feedback. The stages are:

- choosing a topic
  TMA 01 (500 words max.) — 20% of mark
- planning your investigation
  TMA 03 (750 words max.) — 50% of mark
- collecting and interpreting information
  TMA 05 (1000 words max.) — 50% of mark
- reporting your findings
  TMA 07 (1600 words max.) — 80% and
  plus recommendations for action — 20% of
  (400 words max.) — mark

The suggested time allocations mean that about a third of your time should be devoted to each of planning, execution and report-writing. This is because careful planning is vital to success, and so is effective presentation.

1.2 Summary

To sum up the introduction, the project has the broad aim of carrying out an investigation of a local environmental issue and recommending action. To accomplish this you will have to achieve a number of linked objectives:

- develop skills in planning an investigation
- develop skills in finding out, i.e. gathering and interpreting information
- develop skills in report-writing.

Many of the particular ideas and skills needed for the project are used in course materials or taught through the other TMAs. It is the application of a wide range of ideas from the course to the particular project which justifies us in offering nearly a third of the continuous assessment marks for an activity which occupies less than a sixth of the course.

2 What kind of project?

By now you may be eager to get on with choosing a topic, but you may also be saying, 'I know what the objectives are and what the procedures look like but I don't know what you mean by a project.' So, before going on to discuss how *you* will choose (in Section 2.2), we are providing some examples which may give you a better 'feel' for what we

mean, as well as suggesting some possible 'ways in' to choosing.

There are several possible 'ways in' to choosing a topic. We have used three ways (and three authors) to demonstrate how you might go about making your choice: by your 'lifestyle'; by your 'surroundings'; by 'the media'. We know that choosing a theme may be the most difficult part of doing a project so these notes are intended to

Now try to mix a strip of colours which exactly match the colours in the strips you have stuck on the paper. Paint them on the paper so that they touch the printed colours. This will require much trial and error but will rapidly build up your experience of mixing colours. If you mix a colour that doesn't match the printed colour, ask yourself how you need to change it. For example, should it be more red or more blue? Should it be lighter or darker? Spend about an hour on this stage of the project, mixing and matching and remixing.

STAGE 2: PAINTING A SIMPLE OBJECT

[1½ hour]

Find a natural object (or more than one) which is colourful, small and relatively flat, for example, a flower, which you can put on your drawing board to match its colours just as you did with the magazine strips in the first part of this project. (See Figure 32) You may need four or five objects to provide a variety of colours. You can cut a slice through tomatoes, cucumbers, peppers, pomegranates, oranges or lemons to provide colourful cross sections.

Fix a sheet of A3 paper to your board and rest the board on a table. Lay the object on the paper. Draw the shape of the flower or fruit in pencil alongside the object. Concentrate entirely on mixing the colours accurately and paint them within the shape you have drawn. When you have finished, again ask yourself if the colours match. Do you need to change them, and, if so, how?

Figure 32
Arranging natural objects on your drawing board

ACTIVITY 30

start:

finish:

TE TOCA A TI - NOW ITS YOUR TURN

a. Listen to the tape and imagine that you are the first 5 people from ACTIVITY 28 in turn and when asked these 4 questions.

    1. *¿Cómo te llamas?*   2. *¿Cuántos anos tienes?*

    3. *¿Dónde vives?*   4. *¿Tienes hermanos?*

Answer aloud in the pause for each person. The correct answer will be given to you after the pause. Start with Alicia.

b. Now imagine that you are the interviewer and ask the 5 students from ACTIVITY 28 the same 4 questions. Ask the questions aloud in order in the pause after the bleep and the students will give their answers.

> *Now I can ask a Spanish person if they have any brothers and sisters*

ACTIVITY 31

TE TOCA A TI - NOW ITS YOUR TURN

a. Now write the answer to the 4 questions about yourself:

    ¿Cómo te llamas?   ....

    ¿Dónde vives?   ....

    ¿Cuántos anos tienes?   ....

    ¿Tienes hermanos?   ....

b. Practise asking and answering these aloud or pair up with a friend to practise.

c. Then fill in a form for yourself.

7.

Nombre :	
Edad :	
Pueblo :	
Familia :	

> *Now I can fill out a simple form asking my name, age and where I live*

Now try this out on yourself.

Activity 2: Practice in using a T framework

1. Consider your life at the moment and think of it in three areas
   a) WORK — how you spend your time, which may or may not be in a paid job
   b) RELATIONSHIPS — relationships you have with people in your life, outside and inside the family
   c) YOUR IDENTITY — you as an individual, who and what you are at this point in your life
2. Choose one area as a focus; they will overlap but it is helpful to concentrate on one — Ann's was work, though it involved her relationships and identity.
3. Record yourself under the headings of the T framework.
4. As you do it and read it over, does it clarify anything for you?
5. Try to share it with somebody who knows you well and see if it agrees with, or if it changes, their understanding of you.

Comment

Some students find this activity very useful for furthering their understanding of themselves; others find it difficult to do on themselves but easier to do on other people. Others, after trying it several times, don't find it useful at all, so, don't think you have to use it — the frameworks in this unit are suggestions for you to test and see if they increase your ability to help others, not straight-jackets! But do try them before you discard them.

The three areas I asked you to consider are useful ways of thinking about a client's concerns as they talk: where is the focus — on work, relationships or identity? As I said, they usually overlap, but these simple frameworks help you sort into manageable chunks the great mass of details clients sometimes bring. This sorting can help you to summarise and check out your understanding with the client. Here's another chance to try the T framework.

Activity 3: Using a T framework with a client

1. Select a client you are helping, or have helped, or somebody you know well and try writing out the T framework on that individual.
2. If you were going to do a session with them, what questions might the framework raise in your mind to 'explore' with them?

Comment

I hope you will try this out with clients when you get an opportunity. Some counsellors write up the framework and then use it to work with the client in a second session; others give it to clients as 'homework' to fill in themselves between sessions, others use it as a method of recording, to help them think about the clients and their needs — you may find other ways to use it.

Let's move on to another framework.

their needs they would like you to meet is an excellent way of providing a
more effective service.

*Sources of
information: the
patients themselves*

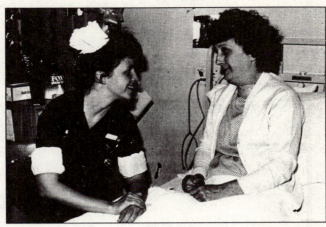

Activity 3.4

Select a maximum of four patients and ask them what they think their needs
are. You may like to stick to the group of patients you are most involved with
or go further afield and select a wider cross section. Whoever you decide to
ask, work out a few questions in advance such as:

- What needs do you have that are being met by the NHS?
- What needs do you have that are **not** being met by the NHS?
- Which of these needs do you think are the most important?

1st patient	2nd patient	3rd patient	4th patient
1			
2			
3			
4			
5			
6			

Compare your original list of needs in Activity 3.2 with the patients' lists.
Probably some needs appear in virtually all the lists while others appear only
occasionally. Of course, much will depend on what sort of patients you asked,
but you should be able to produce a new, expanded and, hopefully, fairly
comprehensive list of patients' needs. Do this now on a separate sheet of
paper.

The Problem Page

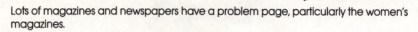

Skills you need <u>before</u> you begin:

- **Selecting the main points.**
- **Writing letters.**
- **Talking with other people.**

Lots of magazines and newspapers have a problem page, particularly the women's magazines.

The advice given is not perfect, of course, and it varies from one magazine to another.

1. Read the letter from the person who says:

    "My problem is that my whole life is a lie."

    Identify the three main points of the letter.

    Write them down in your own words.

> N.B. In the original workbook, this page was followed by one showing several facsimile letters from magazines and newspapers.

2. Do the same with the letter:

    "My grandson is spiteful to me."

3. Choose any one of the other letters on the page.

    Write an answer to the letter giving your advice to the writer.

4. With a partner do this *role play.*

    Ask your partner to be the person with one of these problems.

    Listen to them, comfort them and, if appropriate, give them advice.

    Ask your tutor to watch or tape record this role play.

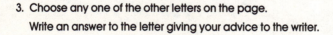

You can use this for Wordpower Stage 1 Unit 5 Element 4.

You can use this for Wordpower Stage 1 Unit 4 Element 2.

You can use this for Wordpower Stage 1 Unit 1 Element 1.

Unit 6

What does open learning cost?

Is open learning cheap learning? Not necessarily. But it may still give best value for money.

In this unit we explore the different costs involved. These look rather different according to whether you are producing open learning materials, delivering a support service or simply sponsoring learners. Whichever you do—and some organisations do all three—it's helpful to understand costs from all these viewpoints—and from that of the learners.

Suggested objectives

As a result of working on this unit you could be better able to:

- Decide what kind of costing you may need to carry out.
- Identify the costs involved in producing, delivering and sponsoring open learning.
- Show how the balance between fixed costs and variable costs and between cash costs and non-cash (hidden) costs affect a particular open learning project.
- Cost an open learning project of your own.
- o *Any objectives of your own to add?*

 I suggest you now start a new section in your portfolio in which to keep a record of your ideas about Costs. From time to time, I'll print a box like this (with the symbol alongside) to prompt you to write something in your portfolio. I expect you will use some of these prompts and not others; and also that you will make occasional notes without my prompting.

Why bother about costing?

Working out the costs of a learning programme can use up a lot of (costly) time and still leave you wondering whether you've covered everything of importance. That perhaps is why it is often not done.

Possible benefits

But even an approximate costing can help you (and ultimately your learners) in a number of ways. For instance, which of the following might you need to do?

☐ Decide whether your budget is adequate for the programme you want to set up.

☐ Justify the amounts you need to ask for if you are seeking new resources.

☐ Compare the estimated cost of the proposed programme with that of alternatives.

☐ Deal persuasively with people who have mistaken beliefs about how much (or how little) things are likely to cost.

☐ Assess the proposed costs of different items within the programme and decide whether the balance needs to be adjusted.

☐ Control the development of the programme by regularly comparing actual costs against budgeted costs.

☐ Convince those from whom you have obtained funding that it has been spent appropriately.

☐ Learn from your experience by comparing actual costs against budgeted costs once the programme is completed.

☐ Decide how much you need to charge learners (or their sponsors) for using the programme.

☐ Ensure that you are getting value for money.

☐ *Other benefits? (What?)*

Dangers to avoid

Open learning is still new enough—and various enough—for people to be unsure how to estimate what it will cost them. But we must try to be realistic. Some providers in the past have under-estimated the cost of producing materials or delivering support services. To protect their profit margins, they've either had to increase prices or skimp on quality. Either way, they end up with fewer, or less satisfied, clients.

Similarly, organisations introducing open learning into their staff training have often overlooked certain costs—e.g. the need for learner support—and have landed themselves with a system they cannot sustain.

Others providers have over-quoted. And some organisations have over-estimated the cost of using open learning—often because they've under-estimated the cost of alternative methods of training, or even of not training at all. Such over-costing may scare off many potential converts to open learning. Both under-costing and over-costing are bad news for open learning—and thus for potential learners who might have benefited from it.

What's your role?

Your approach to costing—and that of your organisation—is likely to depend on the role or roles you are playing in open learning. In the guide to open learning quality that I edited for the Employment Department (Rowntree 1990c), we identify four key roles: producer, deliverer, sponsor and learner. (A more recent guide—SATURN, 1991—has picked out the further role of "information provider".)

- The **producer** develops programmes and produces learning materials.

- The **deliverer** takes those programmes and materials and provides support services and facilities to help learners make best use of them.

- The **sponsor** pays for some or all of that learning.

- The **learner** not only does the learning but may also meet some of the costs.

Some organisations play one role only. For example, a small firm may pay for certain staff to study accountancy with the Open College or do an Open University MBA, but have no part in developing materials or providing support. An FE college may concentrate on delivery. A publisher may produce materials but offer no support.

Other organisations play two or more roles. The Open University and National Extension College both produce courses and deliver support. Forte Hotels sponsors its staff and provides them with mentors or tutors, but obtains its materials from outside. ICI and British Telecom not only sponsor their learners and deliver the support service but also produce much of their materials themselves.

Within a sponsoring organisation, however, any production and delivery are likely to be done by different departments. They therefore come out of different people's budgets—and that, as we'll see, is one of the reasons why cost-comparisons are not always as realistic as they might be.

Differing viewpoints

Producers, deliverers, sponsors and learners all see costs rather differently. In this unit, we'll be looking at costs from all four viewpoints. Even if you wear only one of the hats yourself, it could be useful to know how costs might look to colleagues elsewhere in your organisation or to outside suppliers and clients—and, of course, to learners.

Are you chiefly involved in producing, delivering or sponsoring? Or some combination? You may like to reflect on how your costing decisions may affect or be affected by those of people in any of the roles you are not active in.

 At this point you may have some thoughts you want to jot down in your portfolio.

Open v conventional costs

Many people think open learning means learning on the cheap. This may or may not turn out to be true. Whether it is cheaper than "conventional" learning depends largely on which media are used and how many learners are involved.

For example, an interactive video package for a small group of learners may be far more expensive than providing those learners with a number of classroom sessions. On the other hand, if the number of learners increases greatly and/or if the package consists of printed material only, then the open learning approach may be cheaper per learner than the conventional classes.

Options compared

The supremely cheap option would be large numbers of learners learning at home in their own time from books they have bought themselves (or which you have managed to buy at a huge discount because of the large numbers involved) and without any kind of help from tutors or other people who expect to be paid.

But most open learning is nothing like this. In some cases, it may involve a handful of learners learning in their firm's high-rent premises, on full pay (taking time out from production), using a computer-based multi-media package, supported by their line manager (who also needs to take time out from production) and a tutor from a local college.

Despite that, it can still be worthwhile. Such expensive learning may still be cheaper than the only available alternative. Indeed, perhaps because people are working shifts or are spread all over the country, there may be no alternative. Added to which, the results may be better than those of any other form of training. They may so add to quality or output, or save costs elsewhere, that their cost-effectiveness is unchallengeable.

Time is money

The chief cost factor in open learning is people's time—e.g.:

- the time of the staff who produce the materials
- the time of staff who support the learners
- the time of the learners themselves.

Staff time

In the production phase—while materials are being developed—open learning may need very much more staff time than is ever spent on preparation for conventional teaching. Just how much more depends on what media are being used.

In the delivery phase—when a programme is up and running and learners are learning—open learning usually needs less time from support staff than conventional teaching. This is because learners will mostly be teaching themselves, from packages.

But this is not always the case. For example, in a drop-in workshop with a teacher always available for consultation, there may be little saving of staff time—unless the teacher can cope with a larger group. And in a project-based programme, like several in the Open University, learners make relatively little use of packages and need much more time from their tutors.

Learners' time

In training within organisations—whether using open learning or not—the biggest cost is usually the time of the learners. The more time they have away from their jobs, the greater the cost of lost production or service to customers. This is often difficult to put a precise monetary value on. But one can get a minimum estimate simply by taking the amount of salary the person has earned during the hours of training.

This—like the time of line managers and other staff who might get involved in supporting learners—does not appear on the training department's budget. Such hidden costs may not get the attention they deserve.

Fixed v variable costs

The economics of open learning depends on the balance between fixed and variable costs:

Fixed costs (F): These costs are independent of how many learners you are dealing with. In fact, many of them are incurred before you even recruit any learners. They include such items as the salaries of managers and course developers; fees to outside suppliers; print, audio-visual and computing costs; equipment; use of facilities; warehousing; transport; rent, rates, heating, telephone, insurance, etc.

Variable cost (V): This is the additional cost of providing
for each extra learner. Every learner
will cost you so much for: a copy of the
programme materials; any individual
equipment needed; time from a
counsellor, tutor, mentor, assessor, etc.
(If, as a sponsor, you are also paying for
people's time while they learn, you
may also want to count the cost of lost
production—e.g. by taking salary as an
indicator.)

The effect of fixed costs

For producers, the fixed costs of open learning tend to be
higher than those for conventional (face-to-face) learning.
This is chiefly because of the high labour costs involved in
planning the programmes and developing packaged learning
materials. This stored-up labour then, in the words of
Greville Rumble (1988): "represents a form of capital
investment which replaces direct student-teacher contact
. . . In essence, capital replaces labour."

Deliverers too may face higher fixed costs for open learning
than for conventional learning. For instance, they may need
to set up a complex administrative system and/or equip and
run a technology-based open learning centre.

The effect of variable costs

The variable costs, on the other hand, tend to be lower in
open learning than in conventional learning. Each learner
perhaps needs a copy of the learning materials and some kind
of support from tutors or other staff. But he or she usually
needs less contact with support staff than conventional
learners do. And tutors in an open learning system are often
part-timers, and so cost less anyway.

When open learning is done on a large scale—as in a distance
education institution like the Open University—the cost
structure of teaching programmes can be strikingly different
from that in conventional education. Soon after the OU
started, one study suggested that its ratio of fixed to variable
costs was about 2,000:1—compared with 8:1 in other British
universities (Laidlaw & Layard, 1974).

Comparing cost structures

We can picture the difference between cost structures. The graphs on the opposite page compare the total fixed and variable costs involved in providing a conventional and an open learning programme for various numbers of learners.

Graph A shows fixed and variable costs in a conventional programme. Very low fixed costs, but total variable cost rises quite steeply as we increase the number of learners. (The graph is a simplification, of course. In real life, the variable cost line would probably rise in a series of steps—because every extra group of learners would mean that an additional teacher had to be employed.)

Graph B shows an open learning programme. The fixed costs are much higher than in Graph A. But the total variable cost rises much more slowly as the number of learners increases.

Graph C compares some open and conventional costs. It illustrates the cost comparison made by Abbey National building society when it introduced a computer-based training programme for clerical staff (reported in Coopers & Lybrand, 1989). The CBT programme had a huge fixed cost (more than £59,000) because computers were bought specially for the programme. This compared with a fixed cost of just over £2,500 for developing a conventional, one-day course.

However, because the CBT version took learners two hours rather than a whole day, the variable cost per learner was only about £6 rather than £67 on the conventional course.

Breaking even

Graph C shows us a "break-even" point. This is the number of learners beyond which an open learning programme becomes cheaper per head than the conventional programme. This is the point at which a large fixed cost is spread over such a large number of learners that thereafter the average cost of all the learners is less than in the alternative programme that had lower fixed costs.

In Abbey National's case, the break-even point was about 980 learners. If they'd had only one learner, that person's training would have cost more than £59,000. Even with 500 trainees, the average cost per learner would have been more than £120—still above the average cost using the classroom course.

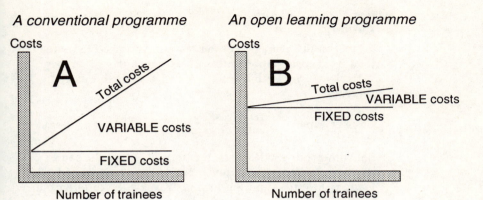

A conventional programme

A — Costs / Total costs / VARIABLE costs / FIXED costs / Number of trainees

An open learning programme

B — Costs / Total costs / VARIABLE costs / FIXED costs / Number of trainees

The Abbey National comparison

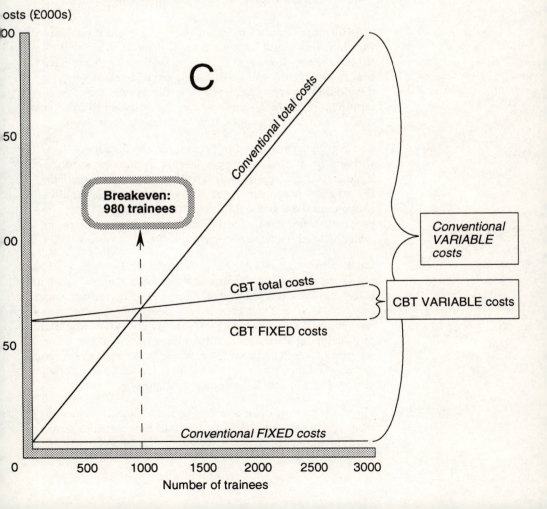

C

Costs (£000s)

Breakeven:
980 trainees

Conventional total costs

Conventional VARIABLE costs

CBT total costs

CBT VARIABLE costs

CBT FIXED costs

Conventional FIXED costs

Number of trainees

Average costs

To reckon the average cost per learner, you need to divide the total fixed cost by the number of learners and add on the variable cost for each learner. We can express this as a formula:

$$\text{Cost per learner} = \frac{\text{Total fixed cost}}{\text{Number of learners}} + \text{variable cost per learner}$$

So, with about 980 learners, this formula gives the same average cost for both methods. But Abbey National had 2,700 learners to train—and the formula reveals the difference in average costs for the two options:

Open learning (CBT)

$$\frac{£59000}{2700} + £6 = £28 \text{ per head}$$

Classroom course

$$\frac{£2518}{2700} + £66 = £67 \text{ per head}$$

This formula is also a simplification. For a more explicit formula, you might look up the one offered by Greville Rumble (1988). It recognises that, as well as a general fixed cost (which you'll still be incurring even if you stop developing new programmes—e.g. the system's administration costs—there is also the addition to fixed costs made by each new programme or course you develop.

The big distance education providers, like the Open University, minimise cost per learner by making sure they have large numbers of learners. This may mean restricting the number of courses. After all, each new course would add to the total fixed costs. But it might not lead to a proportionate increase in the total number of learners. In which case, the average cost would rise.

Smaller providers—whether producers or deliverers—will not be catering for such large numbers of learners. If they are to get a break-even point, it will have to be by reducing fixed or variable costs. Their only way of being as cost-effective as conventional systems is to look for low cost ways of obtaining or developing materials and providing support. For a useful account of how such a smaller provider can manage its costs, see what Chris Curran (1992) has to say about his experience at the National Distance Education Centre in Eire.

The costing of an open learning project is clearly a sensitive affair. We'll get our low costs per head by substituting up-front development costs for on-going face-to-face costs. If we skimp on the development costs, the materials will be poor. As a result, learners will either drop out (thus increasing the average cost per learner) or will need more tutor support (thus increasing the variable cost). The same may happen if we rely too much on packaged teaching and skimp on support. So, to get it right, we need to think about both fixed and variable costs at the planning stage.

The sponsor's advantage

Fortunately, the costs picture is a lot rosier from a sponsor's viewpoint. Clearly, Abbey National incurred production costs as well as delivery and sponsoring costs. If you are simply a sponsor—even if you are delivering as well—the balance between fixed and variable costs will be quite different.

You will be using off-the-shelf open learning materials rather than making or commissioning your own. Their development cost will not appear in your fixed costs. It will be reflected in the price you pay for each copy of the package —one of your variable costs. But since you are one of many users, that will be just a fraction of the producer's fixed cost.

This is why open learning can make economic sense to a small firm with few trainees. The break-even point (compared with conventional courses) can come quite quickly if they use off-the-shelf packages.

Coopers & Lybrand (1989) mention the case of a small paint manufacturer with 17 employees. The firm had only one person they wanted to train in the technical aspects of their work. To have sent him on an external course would have disrupted their production; to arrange a one-person in-house course would have been prohibitively expensive. Fortunately, a local polytechnic was able to meet his needs with an off-the shelf open learning package.

What are the prevailing attitudes to cost in your organisation? Is it essential to show that the cost per learner compares favourably with that in a conventional system? Or are the decision-makers willing to approve more expensive learning if it leads to bigger benefits? What are your views?

 This might be a good moment to write yourself a note in your portfolio.

Estimating your costs

The next few pages deal with how to estimate the costs for a particular open learning project—whether as producer, deliverer or sponsor. (And I shan't ignore the learner's viewpoint.)

Even if you play only one of these roles yourself, you may still find it useful to consider how costs affect people in the other roles. After all, their savings may be your costs, and vice versa. Ros Morpeth & Greville Rumble (1992) mention one side of this delicate balance in discussing the costs of a technician training programme that National Extension College developed for British Telecom. Bluntly, if the producer or deliverer's costs are reflected in too high a price, the sponsor will look elsewhere.

Production costs

You may be producing materials for sale, to a commission or for use in your own organisation. Whatever your purpose, here are the kinds of question you may need to ask:

Pre-production costs

1. What will be the cost of preliminary work before you even begin production? e.g.:

    - Carrying out market research
    - Talking with clients or advisers
    - Preparing proposals, specifications, etc
    - Training of new course writers

2. Will you need pump-priming money? If so, how much and from whom (and at what cost) will you get it?

Production costs

You may need to develop completely new materials from scratch. Or, more cheaply, you may be able to adapt existing materials (see Unit 5). Either way, questions like those below will surely arise. They may also help you in comparing tenders if you decide to sub-contract part of your production.

3. What might you have to pay people, either in-house or through using outside expertise, for the following?

    - Subject matter advice
    - Open learning advice
    - Learning design

- Graphic design (illustrations, typography, layout)
- Writing
- Word processing
- Proof reading
- Editing
- Copyright fees
- Photographs (specially taken or bought from a picture library)
- *Others? (What?)*

4. If you aim to produce audio or video tapes, what additional costs might you incur for the following ?

- Audio/video crew
- Audio/video producers' costs—e.g. editing
- Actors (fees depend on how well known they are)
- Music (can be very costly)
- "Stock shot" footage or sound effects from library
- Location work—e.g. fees, travel and subsistence
- Master tape
- *Others? (What?)*

5. If you plan to produce computer-based training or interactive video, what additional costs might you incur for?:

- Programming
- CBT design
- *Others? (What?)*

Post-production costs

6. What will be the costs of producing multiple copies of the material?

7. What will it cost to store them and get them to users?

8. What will it cost to pilot and evaluate (and improve) the material before use?

9. What will be the costs of packaging the material—e.g. box, dust cover, holder for audiotapes or videotapes.

10. Will you need to up-date and improve the materials in future years? If so, how will you budget for this?

Overhead costs

11. What will be the costs of managing the whole project?

12. What fraction of the general overhead will you need to charge to the project—e.g. administrative staff salaries, rent, rates, heating, insurance, transport, publicity, telephone, paper, postage, etc?

13. What will it cost to market or promote the package?

Selling on

Perhaps you need to sell your package—either to other units within your own organisation or to outsiders. If so, throughout this costing process you need to be asking yourself:

14. What price will "the market" be prepared to pay for the package?

15. Does the costing indicate that you will be able to produce at that price a package that will enable learners to reach the required standard?

16. If the market seems unwilling or unable to pay for a package that will enable learners to reach the required standard, can the project be worth going ahead with?

N.B. Even if you are producing materials for use by your own learners, you may want to consider re-packaging them for sale to outside users. Organisations like British Gas, ICI and several police forces are now recovering some of their production costs from external sales of materials that were designed originally for internal use.

Unless you consult colleagues, you may feel unable to answer many of the questions above. (How much will you need to pay a course writer, for example? And what do you know about printing costs and copyright fees?)

 You may want to write a portfolio note about how you might get hold of costing information for a production project you have in mind.

Delivery costs

You may be a sponsor thinking about delivering support for trainees within your own organisation. Or you may be delivering the programmes you also produce. Or you may simply be offering other people's packages along with support services to any individual learner or sponsor who is willing to pay for them. Here are some questions to ask yourself in costing the support of open learners:

Preliminary costs

1. What might you need to know about your learners before costing the delivery system, e.g.:

    *   Are they sponsored learners training at work?
    *   Are they self-financing learners studying at home?
    *   Will they need to attend your premises or a venue you have to pay for?
    *   Over what period of time will they be working on the programme?

2. What might it cost you to set up the delivery project? Clearly, much will depend on whether you are starting a new project within an existing delivery system or are setting up the delivery system from scratch. Either way, you may need to consider the costs of:

    *   Carrying out market research
    *   Analysing learners' needs
    *   Talking with sponsors or funding bodies
    *   Preparing proposals, specifications, etc
    *   Training support staff
    *   *Others? (What?)*

Variable costs

3. You may need to provide several different forms of support—either by using existing staff or by engaging part-time or temporary staff. Which of the following forms of support might you need to provide—and at what cost?

    *   Counselling—before, during or after the open learning
    *   Supply of package materials
    *   Alterations to packages to suit learners' needs
    *   Help because of special needs—e.g. disabilities
    *   Negotiating support from line managers
    *   Arranging for workplace practice
    *   Tutoring

- Assessment—possibly in the workplace
- *Others? (What?)*

4. You may also need to provide facilities and equipment. For example, what costs might you face in providing:

   - Premises to meet or work in
   - Computers and software
   - Audio or video players
   - Other equipment
   - Access to a fully equipped open learning centre
   - *Others? (What?)*

Overhead costs

5. What might be the salary costs of managing the delivery?

6. Might the project have some specific overhead costs—e.g. tutors' telephone bills or travel costs, the cost of obtaining feedback to evaluate your service?

7. Might you incur producer-type costs in adapting packages to suit learners' special needs? (If so, see the previous checklist.)

8. What fraction of the general overhead will you need to charge to the project—e.g. administrative staff salaries, rent, rates, heating, insurance, transport, publicity, telephone, paper, postage, etc?

9. What will it cost to market or promote your delivery service?

Pricing issues

Maybe you are also the learners' sponsor, or are commissioned by the learners' sponsor to provide a "made-to-measure" support service? If so, you may need to use your costings to convince yourself or your clients that the proposed service will offer value for money. (Could anyone else provide better value?)

On the other hand, you may be offering a standard "off-the-shelf" service (at an all-in set price) to support learners who are self-financing. They may be using a package you have also produced or one that has been produced elsewhere. Either way, you will need to cost your services, and arrive at an overall, standard price, in such a way as to balance what the package suggests by way of support against how much you believe the learners will be willing to pay.

Your preliminary research may be helpful in deciding a price. You may be able to offer the service at a lower price if you know that your fixed costs—e.g. marketing, evaluation, overheads—will be spread over a larger number of learners.

Without consulting colleagues, you may feel you can't answer many of the questions above. (For example, what might you need to pay per hour for a tutor's time or that of a line manager being used as mentor? What is your organisation's policy about recovery of overheads?)

How might you obtain all the costing information you need for a delivery project you have in mind?

 You may want to make a list in your portfolio of the people you would need to talk with.

Costs for a sponsor

If you are a sponsor, you need to know about costs in order to choose an appropriate form of training. But your focus is not quite the same as that of producers and deliverers. They are asking "What will our open learning cost?" You are asking "What are the costs of the most appropriate forms of training—and are the benefits worth paying for?"

This means making cost comparisons. Often it will mean costing open learning against a "conventional" means of providing the same training. Sometimes it may mean costing one open learning programme against another.

If you are to make fair comparisons, it is important to ensure you compare like with like. Many organisations have only a partial idea of what their conventional training costs. Costs like the lost output of trainees while training—which don't appear in the training department's budget—tend not to be taken into account.

Cash costs—where someone has to write out a cheque—are usually quite visible. Non-cash costs—like lost output or staff salaries and national insurance or share of the overheads—may get hidden. Some such costs—like lost output or sales—are income foregone rather than expenditure incurred. But they are still costs—often overlooked.

So open learning—where much of the cost is up-front and very visible—may sometimes seem to offer less of a cost-advantage than it actually does. It may, for example, appear comparatively expensive in cash costs yet still make for big savings in non-cash (hidden) costs.

The following questions are therefore meant to help you cost ANY form of training—not just open learning.

1. What options are available for meeting the training needs of the group of staff you are interested in? e.g.:

   • "Conventional" training :
     ~ in-house
     ~ external
     ~ a combination.

   • Open learning based on:
     ~ off-the-shelf materials
     ~ adapted off-the-shelf materials
     ~ made-to-measure materials
     ~ a mixture.

   • A combination of conventional training and some type of open learning.

Development costs

2. What does it cost your organisation to answer the questions above and the costing questions that follow? (Even costing has its costs—if only the salaries of the people who do it.)

3. How much does it cost to plan the training programme? (This might involve the time of your own staff or payments to a college or other outside provider.)

4. What are the costs of briefing or training any trainers, managers and mentors (and anyone else) who will be involved with learners in the proposed programme? (Count their salary costs as well as any other expenses.)

Facilities cost

5. You may need to rent or buy equipment—e.g. computers. If you buy equipment that may be used for more than one purpose, how much of the costs should be allocated to this particular programme?

6. You may need to provide on-site premises—e.g. use of a training room or an open learning centre. If so, what

share of the costs should be allocated to this particular programme?

7. What proportion of the costs of maintenance, insurance, security systems, etc might it be reasonable to allocate to the programme?

Running costs

8. Course fees or teaching costs. What might you need to pay to colleges or other external providers? Will your own staff contribute to the training? If so, count in an appropriate fraction of their employment costs (annual salary plus national insurance, etc) for the time they will spend doing so.

9. Will line managers or other specialists contribute to the programme—e.g. as mentors? If so, count in an appropriate fraction of their employment costs.

10. Might you need to pay examination fees or will your own staff carry out workplace assessment? If the latter, count in their employment costs.

11. How much time will trainees need away from the job? If you can quantify the loss of output, count it as the cost. If not, count in the appropriate fraction of their employment costs.

12. How much will you need to spend on learning or teaching materials—e.g. videos, books, open learning packages?

13. Might you need to rent premises elsewhere—e.g. in a hotel?

14. Learners may need to travel and stay away from home. What travel and subsistence expenses might the programme incur?

15. What will be the salary costs of administering the programme?

16. Must the programme make any contribution to general overheads—e.g. for rent, rates, telephone, etc—that is not included in the items above?

17. *Are there any other cost questions peculiar to your particular circumstances? If so, add them to the list.*

Can you see how you would obtain all the information you might need if you wanted to use this sort of approach to compare the costs of alternative forms of training?

 You may want to make a list in your portfolio of the people you would need to talk with.

Some cost comparisons

The kind of comparative costing suggested above should be of relevance whatever your role in open learning. Clearly, it is essential for sponsors. But you may also find it useful if you are a producer or deliverer providing materials or support to sponsoring organisations. In particular, you may want to make sure that they don't overlook the hidden costs that open learning might save them.

Coopers & Lybrand (1989) applied the comparative costing approach in a number of organisations that were using open learning during 1988. They studied ten organisations ranging from a large health authority to a small family bakery. These were all sponsoring open learners, delivering some or all of the support and, in two cases, producing their own materials. In all but one of the ten cases, open learning cost less per learner than the best alternative form of training would have cost.

In the Abbey National case, which we have already looked at, the cost of open learning was 42% of the cost estimated for the alternative method. In one case (Thistle Hotels) it was only 10%. Even in the case of Delco Electronics (who found open learning cost 7% **more** than the alternative), they still preferred open learning because it offered so many other advantages.

You may like to see one of the ten detailed comparative costings presented by Coopers & Lybrand in their report. The report, called *Relative Costs of Open Learning*, is now quite hard to get hold of. Fortunately, some of the key points it made and three of the case studies (Abbey National, Land Rover and Mathiesons Bakers) are repeated in OU/ED (1990). And another two of the detailed costings can be found in the costs section of Rowntree (1990c).

The example I show below concerns Citizen Newspapers (150 staff) who provided sales training for new recruits through a combination of open learning materials and face-to-face sessions. Unlike Abbey National, who produced their own materials, Citizen bought an off-the-shelf package consisting of six workbooks and six audiotapes. The costing below (1988 prices) compares their supported packaged learning option with the option of running an equivalent in-house course.

Alternative approaches to training for 68 sales staff:

	In-house course	Open learning
Cash costs	£	£
Open learning package	0	20,800
Television and videos	234	0
Travel expenses	4,273	1,068
TOTAL CASH COSTS:	4,507	21,868
Non-cash (hidden) costs	£	£
Lost sales (trainees' time off job)	75,992	18,998
Trainer time	3,978	1,224
Use of training room and facilities	584	193
Setting up costs	850	372
TOTAL NON-CASH COSTS:	81,404	20,793
TOTAL COSTS (for 68 trainees):	£85,911	£42,661
Average cost per trainee:	£1,263	£627

In this case, open learning costs are about half the expense of running a conventional in-house course. This is despite the high cash cost of the package (£306 per head). The savings come from the fact that the open learning needed less time than the six days a classroom course would have taken. And, in this case, learning time meant time away from selling. So, rather than just count the trainees' employment costs, Citizen were able to estimate and compare what the two approaches would have cost them in lost sales.

This is a very revealing example of why it is necessary to tease out and compare hidden costs. If training time had not been costed, open learning would have cost more than twice as much as the in-house course—£348 per trainee compared with £149.

Costs and benefits

So how paramount are costs in the minds of prospective users of open learning? According to Coopers & Lybrand:

> "The striking conclusion from the survey is that companies' decisions to use OL were usually not explicitly related to costs, despite the indication from the case studies that OL is often substantially cheaper. The most frequent reasons for choosing OL were the logistics of training—because trainees were scattered around the country, on shift work, or difficult to release from their jobs."

In most cases, the cost-advantage of open learning was so obvious that organisations made no detailed cost comparisons before choosing it. Will the cost-advantage be equally obvious in your context? If not, you too may need to highlight logistical benefits or improved productivity. For instance, when Forte Hotels introduced an open learning programme on wine service, they found that sales were 10% better than after a conventional course—and paid for the delivery/support costs within 15 weeks (Forte, 1991).

Surely, the ultimate criterion is not "How much does the programme cost?" It is "What benefits can we expect from the programme and are **they** worth the cost?" Even where open learning is more costly, we can often show that its cost-effectiveness is greater than that of other options.

Creative accountancy

Finally, to make the most of cost-effectiveness, you might do well to win the sympathy of a creative accountant. Between you, for example, you might:

- spread the capital costs of equipment or programme development over several years rather than just the first year of the programme.
- seek to get your budget some credit for gains the programme is likely to bring about elsewhere in the organisation—e.g. increased output or fewer complaints.
- where you are producing your own materials, predict the income from selling copies to other organisations and set it off against the cost of the programme.
- share the development costs with other organisations.
- *Others? (What?)*

A mini case study

Consider the following report from Roger Dobson (1988), formerly head of training at B & Q, the DIY retailing chain:

"Stocktake involves all our store employees, some 200 head office staff and a small number of casuals, in physically counting every item on every shelf of every B & Q store. Accurate, legible completion of stocktake sheets in accordance with disciplined procedures is essential. In July . . . a special team of training officers ran one-day seminars for some 600 key staff at hotel venues throughout the UK. We then relied on the key staff to train the rest of our store employees. We estimate that the cost of that exercise was £53,000 made up of travel, accommodation, trainers' time, production of material and delegate time. For the [following] January stocktake we adopted an open learning approach. We commissioned. . . two workbooks, one aimed at the Store Management Team and the other at nearly 10,000 store employees. There is a lot of evidence that the workbooks were well received and that many employees completed them at home. We estimate that the cost of the open learning approach was £11,500, made up of trainer time and production of materials. We have been able to compare a representative sample of stocktake sheets from the two stocktakes at 10 per cent of our stores and they have shown a 22.5 per cent reduction in error in January compared with July."

 Do you have any further thoughts about how you might get colleagues to see cost advantages for open learning in your organisation?

Costs to the learner

Whether as producers, deliverers or sponsors, we have a duty
to remember that learners too incur costs. There is no such
thing as a free course. Even learners who get their fees paid
will have to find their own resources of energy, commitment
and, especially, of time.

Open learners taking non-vocational courses—e.g. general
education, self-development, personal interest courses—will
usually be self-financing. They will be much less likely to get
subsidies or state funding than learners studying similar
subjects on conventional programmes. Many decisions we
might make—e.g. if we require learners to have home
computers—may seriously reduce the number of learners
who can afford what we have to offer.

With vocational learning (as Open College have discovered)
individuals are not so keen to invest hard cash in their own
training. This they usually see as the employer's
responsibility. What the individuals are investing—in rather
large quantities—is their own time. Some of the Coopers &
Lybrand cases, for example, would have been much less cost-
effective had it not been that trainees were studying at home.
In such cases, a hidden training cost (employment cost or lost
production time) is being shifted to the employee. As Hilary
Temple wryly asks, can this be what Open Tech had in mind
when they promoted the benefit of being able to learn "in
your own time"?

In fact, out of 50 sponsors of open learning interviewed by
Coopers & Lybrand (including the 10 case study
organisations), more than a third expected trainees to study
entirely in their own time. Another third expected at least
half the studying to be done in trainees' own time.

In many cases, the employer justified such expectations on
the grounds that learners were getting training they would
not otherwise have received. Thistle Hotels suggested this
approach for courses that primarily served the individual's
purposes—e.g. improving their promotability—rather than
the company's purposes. The personal development
programmes fostered by Ford, Rover and Lucas among others
might be similarly justified on the lines of "you put in your
time; and we'll put in our money".

The line between personal and company benefit may often be
difficult to draw, however. Doesn't the individual who is

"personally developed" become a more capable, flexible and productive employee?

We need to be sensitive to the ethics of expecting employees to train in their own time. What additional rewards should we negotiate with them in recognition of their help in cutting training costs? (Some organisations, for instance, use employees' success at learning in their own time as an indication that they might be motivated enough to justify funding them on more expensive block release courses.) And what alternative training must we provide for those whose domestic circumstances are not conducive to studying at home? How open can we be in suiting the approach to the individual?

 Will YOUR learners have costs you may want to help them with or compensate them for?

Final remarks

Open learning is not necessarily cheap learning. Sometimes —especially when high-tech media are used—it can be very expensive. Much depends on economies of scale. You won't want to invest huge amounts in developing a package if there are few learners who might benefit from it. But if someone else has already developed an appropriate package, you may be able to get it at a price you can afford.

Even relatively cheap open learning has often cost more than it appears to have done. I suspect there are many kinds of hidden subsidies. Colleges often don't charge full cost for use of telephones and word-processing equipment. Writers carry on writing a course in the evening and weekends, putting in far more time than they are paid for. Tutors too are often working for love rather than money.

The biggest hidden subsidy often takes the form of goodwill. We must be careful about taking people for granted— assuming that they'll carry on giving more than 100% out of pure commitment. Otherwise, we may one day find that we've been living with an illusion about the true cost of open learning.

One place it doesn't do to economise is on the support system (see Unit 3). As Open Tech and Coopers & Lybrand and many other projects have shown, poor support leads learners to delay completing their programmes or even to drop-out altogether. Every such learner bumps up the average costs.

Finally, you might like to stick on your wall a remark made by a colleague at one of the workshops introducing Open College. In talking about what Open Tech expected of their open learning providers, he said:

> "They want it quickly, they want it cheaply and they want it of high quality. Nobody can score more than two out of those three."

 What remaining concerns, fears or questions do you have about Costs? Make a note of any that seem important enough to bear in mind when you do your desk work and field work on this topic.

Suggested follow-up work

Desk work

Thorpe & Grugeon (1987) makes only a handful of references to costs, usually from the learner's viewpoint. However, the balance between a fixed cost (package development) and a variable (tutorial support) does underlie the important chapter by Sewart.

Robinson (1989) has nothing to say about costs.

Paine (1988) has a few chapters that mention costs (e.g. those by Fricker, Bates and Lougher) but there is no analysis.

Temple (1991) makes several references to costs in industrial open learning.

In addition, you may want to look at other sources I have mentioned in this unit—e.g. OU/ED (1990) or Rowntree (1990c). Some of the journals—e.g. *Open Learning* and *OLS News*—occasionally include case studies that make cost comparisons.

Field work

- Talk with people who have already run an open learning operation of the kind you are interested in. Even if they can't give you detailed figures, they will probably be willing to discuss how they set about estimating costs.

- Identify the likely areas of cost (cash and non-cash) in an open learning project you want to set up.

- Talk to colleagues in your organisation who can tell you how to reckon costs, or where to get appropriate data.

- Try doing a costing for an open learning project of your own. Get appropriate colleagues to comment on it and revise it accordingly.

 Remember to make a record of your desk work and field work in your portfolio.

Reflection checklist

 When you have completed your desk work and field work on this unit, please make notes in your portfolio using some of the following questions as a guide:

o What are the most important things you have learned during this unit? (You may want to look back at the objectives suggested at the beginning.)

o What has given you most satisfaction in this unit?

o What do you feel least satisfied about in this unit?

o Does this unit leave you with any unresolved questions or difficulties you feel you want help with?

o How might you try to get the help you need?

o What have you learned in your work with other people during this unit?

o In what ways were you able to draw on your previous experience during this unit?

o What have you learned about yourself—your own feelings and competences?

o What do you feel you need to do next?

Unit 7

Evaluating open learning

We may believe that open learning is, in general, a "good thing". But how can we be sure about any particular open learning programme? What is the programme like to work with? What do people feel about it? What kinds of results does it get? What unexpected snags arise? What needs to be changed? Is it all worth the time, money and effort?

These are the kinds of question to ask about open learning in action. If you omit to ask them, you could find that you and your learners waste a lot of time and money. Evaluation is the key to improving the quality of your learners' learning.

Suggested objectives

As a result of working on this unit you could be better able to:

* Argue the case for evaluating open learning programmes —both in general and in particular cases.

* Plan and carry out an evaluation of a single aspect of an on-going open learning programme.

* Plan an evaluation strategy for a new open learning programme that you are developing.

o *Any objectives of your own to add?*

 I suggest you now start a new section in your portfolio in which to keep a record of your ideas about Evaluating Open Learning. From time to time, I'll print a box like this (with the symbol alongside) to prompt you to write something in your portfolio. I expect you will use some of these prompts and not others; and also that you will make occasional notes without my prompting.

What is evaluation?

Evaluation has a lot in common with one of the themes of this book—reflection. It is an attempt to understand what is going on, to judge its worth and perhaps make decisions about it. We do it every day, in many contexts and at many levels. You can evaluate your diet, or the new staff-appraisal system at work or how the national economy is being run.

In education and training, evaluation has a special role to play. Here is the definition suggested by my colleague, Mary Thorpe (1988):

> "Evaluation is the collection, analysis and interpretation of information about any aspect of a programme of education and training, as part of a recognised process of judging its effectiveness, its efficiency and any other outcomes it may have."

Three comments

There are three things worth making clear before we go on:

1. Evaluation is NOT just another word for assessment. The quality of our learners' learning may well be one of the outcomes we need to evaluate. But many other factors may be equally worth looking at.

2. Mary Thorpe's phrase "any other outcomes" reminds us that evaluation is concerned with what happens rather than merely with what was meant to happen. It should be capable of picking up the unexpected—e.g. unwanted side-effects or interesting new possibilities.

3. By "a recognised process", she means that evaluation needs to be planned, systematic and openly discussed. Evaluation is not just keeping records or writing a final report. It is a public commitment to purposeful enquiry.

. . . and four questions

In this unit we look at four main questions about evaluation:

- **Why** bother to evaluate at all?
- **What** shall we be looking for?
- **How** shall we carry out the evaluation?
- **So what**—how shall we use the information we get?

Why bother with evaluation?

This is not such an odd question. Most "conventional" teachers and trainers don't get involved in evaluating their courses. Research commissioned by the Employment Department (Training Agency, 1989) suggests that only 15% of firms that train their employees bother with evaluation. And less than 3% try to judge whether the results of the training are worth the cost.

But we might be surprised to find there has been a similar lack of interest among open learning practitioners. In the words of Mary Thorpe (1988):

> "This is puzzling, when we consider that open learning is an *innovatory* approach to education and training, still in its early development stages. Surely we cannot be so confident about an innovation that there is no need to check whether aims have actually been achieved and our expectations justified?"

Whether innovating or not, we shall need to pay more attention to evaluation over the next few years—even in universities—as funding bodies seek evidence of quality before handing over more money. Evaluation is certainly essential if we are to maintain quality in open learning—let alone seek to improve it. This was one of our chief messages in the handbook *Ensuring Quality in Open Learning* which I edited for the Employment Department (Rowntree, 1990c).

So why might you want to evaluate an open learning programme? Various people I've worked with have made the following suggestions (among others). Would any of them apply in YOUR situation?

Possible reasons for evaluating

☐ Because it is expected of me.

☐ In order to justify expenditure.

☐ To obtain extra resources.

☐ To settle other people's doubts.

☐ To disarm any opposition.

☐ To get ammunition in case of criticism.

☐ To help in marketing the programme.

☐ To demonstrate acceptable outcomes.

☐ To detect any problems that arise.

☐ To monitor staff performance.

☐ To aid in staff development.

☐ To help in team-building.

☐ To improve the teaching and learning.

☐ *Your additional reasons (What are they?)*

Political reasons

Clearly, there are many reasons why you might want to evaluate your open learning programme. The first few in the list above are "political". Other people may need convincing that your approach is effective—especially if open learning is not yet well-established in your organisation.

You may need to prove to sceptical administrators, managers and other teachers or trainers that the results can be as good as, if not better than, those obtained by more traditional approaches. You may also have to justify your programme to whoever is providing funds to develop it.

The information you collect may also provide useful ammunition in marketing the programme—both within your organisation and outside it. That is, you may so impress people with the (true) tales you are able to tell them about your programme that they flock to sign up for it or to provide resources with which you can develop more.

Managerial

The second set of reasons mentioned above are broadly managerial. They are to do with checking to ensure that the programme is running smoothly, that people are working effectively and that acceptable results are being attained.

This kind of evaluation Roger Lewis (1985) prefers to call "monitoring". No programme can survive without it.

Educational

The final three reasons mentioned in the list are more educational. If staff are expected to take part in evaluation, it can help in their development as "reflective practitioners". It can also open up new ways of sharing experience among the programme team. Thus, team members are likely to run the programme, and develop new ones, more effectively in the future. But evaluation can also improve the learners' learning right now—by suggesting adjustments to your programme as it rolls along.

For whom are you evaluating?

People get involved with evaluation in various ways:

- You may find you are doing it alone, chiefly for your own purposes.
- You may be asked to contribute to an evaluation run by someone else.
- You may be one of a number of colleagues who make up an evaluation team.

Then again, the programme you are evaluating may be your own—or you may be asked to evaluate someone else's programme (one you have had no previous connection with). A few years ago, for example, I was asked by the World Health Organisation to join a medical colleague in evaluating aspects of the curriculum in an Egyptian medical school. I hesitated at first, knowing nothing of medical education or Egyptian academic practices; but it turned out that my innocence enabled me to ask questions that might otherwise have been regarded as rather too probing.

Whether you are alone or in a team, evaluating your own programme or someone else's, other people besides you are likely to be interested in your evaluation results. In the case I've just mentioned, the WHO officials and various factions among the medical school staff all had their different interests in the evaluation—as did the students.

Even if you are doing the evaluation chiefly for your own purposes, it is still wise to identify any other "interested parties" and negotiate your plans with them. If you show willingness to help them get the information they need, then they are more likely to support you and pay heed to your findings.

If you are doing the evaluation for someone else, then it is clearly vital that you make quite sure what your "client" needs. Though first you may need to decide who your client is—and this may not be as simple as looking at the signature on the cheque.

Consider the people listed below. Which of them might expect information from—or otherwise be influenced by—the evaluation of YOUR open learning programme or system?

Who might be influenced by your evaluation?

☐ Colleagues helping develop the programme

☐ Other subject experts

☐ Programme managers/administrators

☐ Tutors and mentors

☐ Trainers

☐ Influential persons or committees in your organisation

☐ Your existing learners

☐ Your learners' line managers

☐ The learners' sponsors

☐ Future potential learners

☐ Professional organisations

☐ Funding bodies

☐ Accrediting bodies

☐ *Others (Which?)*

Ethics in evaluation

Notice that many of the people who will be interested in the feedback from your evaluation are also people you may have collected your data **from**. For instance, you may well want to ask learners and line managers about their perceptions of the programme. And later they may want to hear how their perceptions fit into the overall results.

Ethical issues—like confidentiality and ownership—need to be negotiated before an evaluation gets under way. You may need to negotiate, for example:

• the focus and extent of the evaluation

• the people and situations to which you can have access

• the degree of anonymity to be preserved

• who should have access to the data

- the uses to which data may be put
- how people's contributions are to be acknowledged
- who can comment on the findings.

Many people besides yourself may have an interest in "your" evaluation. Granting them a share of its ownership is not simply ethical—it may also lead to a more open evaluation with results that mean something.

 You may want to make a portfolio note about the reasons you and your "interested parties" might have for evaluating.

What shall we evaluate?

Which aspects of your programme do you need to evaluate? Different interested parties will want information for different purposes:

- Colleagues involved in developing the programme will (like you) want to know if their course design is causing any problems.
- Subject experts may need to be convinced that the coverage is adequate and up to date.
- Managers will want data that enables them to keep the programme running effectively.
- Sponsors and funding bodies will want to know that they are getting value for money.
- Learners and tutors will want to know that their responses are being listened to. And so on.

In planning your evaluation strategy, you may think it worth asking your interested parties just what their concerns are. Otherwise you might find yourself halfway through the programme with no means of recapturing information that, if collected earlier, might have enabled someone to make an important decision—e.g. about how to lessen initial drop-out.

What the programme needs

Different programmes will also suggest different priorities. For instance, if this is your first open learning programme (or the first in your organisation) you may need to find out how its results compare with those of some previous course.

Alternatively, if this programme is simply the latest in a series, there may be some new feature—e.g. a new package or medium, or a new approach to briefing and training support staff—that you need to focus on. For example, when British Steel evaluated its computer-based training in health and safety (Temple, 1991), the evaluators were interested in such questions as:

> "~ Do learners using computer-assisted methods feel deprived of the social interaction and teamwork of conventional courses?
>
> ~ Is there constant interruption of the learning because it is too close and accessible to the workplace?
>
> ~ Is there resentment against computers and their association with formal control and monitoring systems?
>
> ~ Are there physical problems such as reading the screen, operating the keyboard?
>
> ~ How significant is the content and style of the training presentation?"

Performance indicators

"Performance indicators (PIs)" is one of the latest additions to educational jargon, promoted by the TVEI flexible learning initiative. You may find colleagues using it as a label for "things we want to collect data about".

Clearly, performance indicators need to arise out of the purposes and concerns of people in a particular programme context. But one users' guide to the evaluation of flexible learning (Morris & Twitchen, 1990) picks out ten "generic" PIs about which questions might need to be asked in any of a wide range of contexts:

1. Management commitment, support and planning
2. Monitoring and evaluation
3. Staff development
4. Teaching and assessment strategies
5. Time spent in contact between tutors and learners
6. The range of learning environments used

7. The extent and nature of learner autonomy

8. Selection and use of learning materials

9. The extent to which the curriculum is delivered by flexible learning approaches

10. The effectiveness of open learning in promoting the development of the learners.

Be selective

It is important to be aware of the wide range of things you could collect information about. But it's equally important to be selective. Information costs money. You can't gather data without spending time, effort and money. So don't plan to collect more than is likely to have a use. Otherwise, you won't be able to see the wood for the trees. You'll suffer from information overload—leading to what some observers call "analysis paralysis".

What performance indicators do you need to collect data about for your own purposes? What kinds of data do you need to collect to satisfy other people's purposes? The list below gives a number of aspects suggested by colleagues at a recent open learning workshop. The group tried to divide them roughly into aspects concerning the **process** of teaching/learning and aspects concerning its **product** (or outcomes or results).

Some of the aspects you might collect data about

Process aspects:

☐ Enrolments/Drop-out

☐ Numbers using facilities

☐ How packages are being used

☐ Workload of learners

☐ Staff development activities

☐ How programme staff respond to the unexpected

☐ Problems experienced by learners

☐ Problems faced by tutors/mentors/others

☐ How learners and support staff work together

☐ Ways people are modifying the programme

☐ Whether our practices are in line with our philosophy

☐ *Others (Which?)*

Product or outcome aspects:

☐ How learners and others feel about the programme

☐ What learners have learned (e.g. insights/competence)

☐ Effect on learners' job performance

☐ Whether the programme affects men and women in different ways

☐ Cost-effectiveness

☐ Acceptability to outsiders

☐ New needs revealed by the programme

☐ Long-term effects of the programme on the organisation

☐ Whether outcomes are in line with our philosophy

☐ *Others (Which?)*

Clearly, some of these aspects will be easier to evaluate than others. For instance, it will be relatively easy to discover the extent to which learners have attained certain pre-specified objectives. But one can overlook other, perhaps "unofficial", objectives they may have successfully pursued. I recall a course for nurses on how to **understand** research which several of them used as a course on how to **do** research.

Nor can we so easily be sure about how the programme will affect learners' subsequent job performance. And it will be even more difficult to decide what long-term effect it has had on the organisation.

However, if these more difficult issues are the ones your colleagues want information about, then your evaluation must somehow find something worthwhile to say about them. You may also need to watch out for, and be prepared to cater for, new concerns emerging (or perhaps lying half-hidden) as the programme rolls on. Linden Hilgendorf (1984) writing for managers of Open Tech projects, puts it like this:

"Most projects have multiple aims and objectives. A project has both general aims (e.g. to develop a greater responsiveness to training needs) and particular objectives (e.g. to produce six modules by Christmas). Some of the project's aims will relate to the task (e.g. to develop a more open access mode of delivering training) and some to the organisation (e.g. preserve the training department, develop the college's reputation). Not all of the project's aims will be explicit (e.g. assumptions about achieving a certain standard of output). All of these aims and concerns are important and need to be taken into account. Initially, only some of these aims may be clear to everyone involved and perhaps only a few objectives will have been specified. During its life the project will refine and redefine its aims and objectives in the light of experience."

It is also possible for some of the project's aims to be forgotten. Watch out, in particular, for the "drift from openness" (see Boot & Hodgson, 1988). In the early days of setting up a programme or system, we can be pressured into agreeing a number of short-cuts or compromises "just while we get things under way". Some time later we may realise that these have given rise to aspects of the system that are now deterring potential learners or denying them what they need and yet will be very difficult to change.

 How will you decide what to evaluate in YOUR system?

How to evaluate?

Until the publication of a paper by Malcolm Parlett & David Hamilton (1972), educational evaluation was dominated by a single strategy. This was the traditional strategy that sets out single-mindedly to measure the extent to which a project has achieved certain specific, pre-determined goals. Parlett and Hamilton called it the "agricultural-botany" approach— because it is similar to research in which, for example, plants might be exposed to different experimental treatments and their different responses compared statistically.

Parlett and Hamilton outlined an alternative strategy that has more in common with the "participant observation" approach of social anthropology. Here the evaluator enters into the project pragmatically, aware that objectives and priorities are constantly evolving and may differ from one person to another, but seeking to understand how things seem to the people involved and looking for a way to interpret the meaning of what takes place. See Hamilton *et al* (1977) for a wider discussion of this approach which has become known as "illuminative evaluation".

Towards a combined strategy

The two strategies differ in the kind of data they collect and the ways they collect it. The first is likely to be primarily interested in the formal assessment of learners and the statistical analysis of achievement tests and attitude questionnaires. Its approach is **quantitative**.

The second strategy, on the other hand takes a **qualitative** approach. It will emphasise sensitive observation, discussion and interviewing—and is likely to communicate its findings through revealing analogies and anecdotes.

The two strategies differ also in their focus. While the first asks, in essence, "Have the goals been achieved?" the second asks, more openly, "What has been going on?"

You may have a personal preference for one of these strategies rather than the other, as I do. That is by the way. Neither is right or wrong. Both quantitative and qualitative approaches may be needed for different aspects of a particular programme. Facts and figures may be relevant data; so may people's opinions and feelings. I recommend a strategy of "applied common sense" in which you pragmatically take what you need from both—and from any other approaches that emerge in the years to come.

So, pragmatically, let us consider two questions that urgently call for our attention:

• How shall we collect our data?

• When shall we collect it?

How shall we collect data?

How do we set about collecting evaluation data? To begin with, it's worth remembering that some data will thrust itself upon us, whether we seek it or not. Whether we notice it, and respond to it evaluatively, will depend on whether we realise its importance.

Casual data collection

Here are some examples of things we might happen to notice, or have brought to our attention. We might well regard them as calling for some sort of action.

- Learners are dropping out of the programme.
- One of our set books has gone out of print.
- Learners are being put on the course without consultation.
- The learning centre facilities can't cope with the demand.
- Some of the mentors feel their role has not been made sufficiently clear to them or others.
- Bad weather ruins an important field trip.
- Work done by previous learners is being plagiarised by the present group.
- Learners' line managers are not providing the support they promised.
- Learners are getting behind schedule on their projects.
- A new piece of legislation has made part of the programme out of date.
- Assessment results indicate ineffective teaching in certain sections of the programme.

Such items may arise from our own observations. Or they may be reported by learners, tutors, or anyone else (e.g. line managers) with whom we have contact. We may not always be able to do anything about the problems (or opportunities) indicated, but we need to keep a look out for them.

Systematic data collection

However, if we are to evaluate systematically we must do more than react to information that happens to come our way. We must seek out answers to specific questions about our programme—performance indicators or other aspects we have discussed with our colleagues. From whom shall we obtain relevant data and by what methods?

There are numerous methods of gathering data. Some of them—like conversation and observation—will be of most use if you regularly meet your learners and support staff in learning centres or at the workplace. Others—like reviewing routine records or assessment results and sending out questionnaires—can be used in any open learning situation but may well be the chief means of gathering data when learners are at a distance.

Some data collection methods

☐ Review of programme documentation

☐ Review of relevant literature/case studies

☐ Review of routine records and statistics

☐ Review of assessment results

☐ Observation

☐ Conversations

☐ Interviews

☐ Discussion groups/workshops

☐ Questionnaires

☐ Diaries or learning logs

☐ Learners' action plans

☐ *Other methods you have in mind (What?)*

Review of programme documentation

As an evaluator you will almost certainly be interested in the content and presentation of any learning packages or other materials. These may include not just workbooks and videos etc, but also such items as study guides and assessment instructions for both learners and tutors. (There is a section on evaluating learning packages in Unit 5.)

In addition, you may need to review what has been written about the programme's aims and objectives, its rationale, its support system, and so on. What kind of openness or flexibility is the programme aiming for? How does it intend to bring this about?

Clearly, if you played a leading part in developing the system, you'll have a good grasp of this already. If not, reviewing the documentation will help you understand what is supposed to be going on and explain it to other interested parties.

Review of relevant literature/case studies

You may be called upon to evaluate aspects of a system with which you are not already familiar—e.g. workplace assessment or computer conferencing. In such cases, and even if you are fairly familiar with the new aspect, you may want to find out what researchers have had to say about it.

Alternatively, or as well, you may want to look at case studies where other users report on their experience. Too often, unfortunately, these are self-promotional rather than truly informative. But some do reflect on the snags and unresolved problems as well as list the glowing successes. Such case studies may help you look afresh at your own data and thus make better decisions or give better advice.

Review of routine records and statistics

Most open learning systems collect reams of data as a matter of course—about learners, about staff, about use of facilities, about marketing, and so on. These may include items as various as biographies of learners and staff; statistics about numbers enrolling, numbers using learning centres and numbers dropping out; reports and letters from tutors, sponsors, clients and learners; minutes of meetings; etc.

The trick is to know where to find what you might need. For instance, if you are interested in the long-term effects of a programme you may also want to look at routinely collected data about, let's say, productivity, sales, absenteeism, wastage rates, complaints, enrolments for further training, and so on. Such measures are used by the Employment Department's independent assessors in making its annual National Training Awards (Employment Department, 1991). These go only to organisations that can demonstrate a connection between training and "business benefits".

Review of assessment results

How do your learners perform in pre-tests and post-tests; continuous assessment and end-of-programme examinations; written tests, multiple-choice tests and practical tests; oral examination and observations of their workplace performance? Such data may be vital not just in determining what has been learned but also in detecting weaknesses in the teaching. Statistics about how many learners tackle each assignment or test exercise during a programme may also warn about potential drop-outs.

Observation

If you can see your learners (and support staff) in a learning centre or at the workplace you may be able to do a lot of "evaluation by walking about"—and observing. You may be able to note how they tackle their learning and teaching tasks, singly or in groups. You may be able to observe how they apply what they have learned to their jobs.

Observation can be informal—you just make notes later about things you happened to notice. Or it can be formal— you may use checklists and coding sheets to direct your attention and record the perhaps complex activities you have seen. Either way, you need to take care lest your observation alters the events being observed.

Conversations

If you are in a position to observe your learners and support staff, you'll probably be able to chat with them as well. Informal conversations (perhaps in the bar or over a cup of coffee) can throw up all manner of feelings, concerns and danger signals that might take ages to emerge from more formal collection methods. These can then be investigated further. If you are collecting data in this way (or by simple observation) it's as well to let people know that you have a professional interest in what they are saying. Otherwise, they may accuse you of betraying their trust.

Interviews

An interview has been called "a conversation with a purpose". In a conversation you may be happy just to listen to what the other person thinks important. In an interview you probably set out to get their reaction to issues that concern you. An interview may be completely structured —perhaps by a questionnaire which you simply take the other person through, item by item. Or it may be semi-structured—based around some key questions, perhaps, but encouraging the other person to elaborate on anything that especially concerns them.

If you can't meet participants face-to-face, perhaps you can interview them over the telephone. "Cold" telephone calling was one of the approaches used by the National Extension College to coax responses out of pharmacists who seemed reluctant to reply to questionnaires about how they were getting on with a continuing education pack (Thorpe, 1988).

Discussion groups/seminars

Discussions or seminars with groups of learners or colleagues and other interested parties can be a cost-effective way of obtaining a lot of information in a short time. The sharing of views may also improve communication, develop team spirit and produce solutions to emerging problems. There is, however, the problem that a person's eccentric but interesting views may get side-lined in the pressure for consensus. Such groups also need some sort of agenda, or the discussion may go off at a tangent.

Questionnaires

Questionnaires are probably the most widely-used data collection method in all of education and training. Some cynics dismiss them as "happiness sheets", because they can give no hard information about what the person has learned, let alone about whether they can and will apply it at work or elsewhere in their lives. But questionnaires do have a role in collecting opinions, experiences and reflections—especially concerning "process" (what the programme is like to work with). For evaluating a distance learning programme they can be essential.

The design and handling of questionnaires is an art in itself. (Do you know the roles of open and closed questions? Do you know how to use the four types of closed question? Do you know how much enclosing a prepaid envelope can increase your response rate!) I can't begin to do justice to the subject in the space available here. If you need advice, I suggest you find out whether you can get help from someone within your own organisation who has experience in questionnaire design and survey techniques.

As for printed help, you may like to look at Gibbs & Haigh (1984)—a set of suggestions and sample questionnaires, many of which can be adapted to suit an open learning context. Also see Oppenheim (1986) a book whose aim is "to prevent some of the worst pitfalls and to give practical, do-it-yourself information that will point the way out of difficulties".

A colleague of mine has recently pioneered the approach of getting distant learners to interview themselves, talking their responses to a questionnaire into their own tape recorders (Lockwood, 1990). Their spoken responses generally seem to be more resonant than written replies to questionnaires.

Diaries or learning logs

These are a personal record of events and reflections that are kept up by learners (and sometimes by support staff) over the life of a programme. Evaluators won't normally expect to look at the log or diary itself (unless this is agreed from the start). Rather, the record-keeping is intended to encourage the learners in reflection, to involve them in the evaluation process and to remind them of issues they may want to raise with the evaluators. (The portfolio I've been urging you to keep could be put to this sort of use.)

If we are serious about helping learners take responsibility for their own development, I believe we need to involve them in evaluation. Evaluation can be presented as something they have a stake in rather than something that is done on them. In my book *Teach Yourself with Open Learning* (Rowntree, 1991) I encourage learners to evaluate their own open learning programmes—using checklists and a reflection log.

Learners' action plans

Learners can be encouraged to draft an end-of-programme action plan. (I've invited you to complete one at the end of Unit 9.) In this, they first need to consider what they have got from the programme. Then they can give examples of how they intend to apply it in their lives or work, identifying the factors that might help or hinder them, and suggesting performance indicators or criteria of successful application.

Primarily this is a learning exercise. But it may also help the evaluators tackle important issue like: "Has the training really done anything for the learner's quality of life or work-performance?" and "Are people able to put into practice what they've learned?" Clearly, the evaluators need to follow-up after a period of time to find out how the action plans worked out in the real world.

 Which of the methods outlined above do you think might be appropriate to YOUR situation?

When to evaluate?

Contrary to common belief, the answer to this question is NOT "When it's all over". It's true that some evaluation—of the programme's long-term effect on staff morale, for instance—cannot be done until after the programme. But even that had better be planned for well in advance.

You may have come across the distinction between **formative** and **summative** evaluation:

- Formative evaluation collects data that can be used to change a project while it is in progress. It helps form the project.

- Summative evaluation, on the other hand, uses evaluation data to sum up the project overall once it is completed.

But most of the data used even in a summative evaluation will probably have been collected in the course of the project. In fact, some of it may already have been used formatively.

Starting early

In fact, we may want to start evaluating even **before** the project is properly under way. We may run a "feasibility study"—to evaluate whether it is worth starting at all. And, if the project is to go ahead, we may want to interview those concerned about their hopes, fears and expectations. We may want to identify potential problem areas. We may want to record the way in which policies were decided. And so on.

Producers of open learning materials often attempt to evaluate those materials before they are used in programmes. This process—usually known as developmental testing or piloting (see Nathenson & Henderson, 1980; Rowntree, 1990a for details)—is aimed at improving the materials by getting the reactions of people like those who will later be using them in the programme.

Evaluation is usually meant to influence decisions. Many of these decisions will need to be taken while the programme is in operation. For instance, if our learners are dropping like flies, we need to know as soon as possible. Only then might we find some way of keeping them in the system—if that is in their best interests.

So we may need to collect data all the way through the project. If we don't ask people about their experiences, or record evidence of outcomes when they happen, there may be no way of obtaining the missing data several weeks later.

Sometimes there is a "window of opportunity" when people whose views you want to hear have reached a particular stage or are especially easy to get at. In the Open University undergraduate programme, for instance, summer schools provide the only opportunity to meet learners and tutors in large numbers. If the evaluators are not prepared for events like this, then they may miss a unique and non-repeatable chance to gather crucial information.

Planning even earlier

I've mentioned two evaluation tasks in the last few paragraphs—collecting data and using that data—e.g. to make decisions or to produce reports. But there is a third (and prior) task—**planning** for the collection and use of the data. This task clearly needs to be started at the very earliest opportunity. Like all plans, it needs to be flexible. It will develop along with the project. But you probably need to have some kind of strategy (e.g. Why? What? How? When? etc) right from the start. Otherwise, much vital data may escape for ever before you get it in your sights. You may simply fail to see the point of what your learners (or others) are telling you.

Nor is there much point providing data for decision-making if the time for that decision has already slipped past. Hence your evaluation plan may need to mesh with other people's plans, committee meetings, and the like. Barry Macdonald (1977) mentions how the National Development Programme in Computer Assisted Learning depended on step-funding. So the evaluation reports had to be timed to feed into key meetings of the Programme Committee.

 What is the time-scale against which you will need to plan and carry out YOUR evaluation?

So what?

The ultimate and overriding question in evaluation is "So what?" We may be collecting piles of data, by all manner of sophisticated methods, but what does it all mean? Data by itself is just a mass of facts and opinions. To turn data into relevant information—with implications for action—we need to analyse it. We need to look for trends and patterns. We need to **interpret** the data.

Using evaluation

This fits in with our initial aim in evaluation—to understand our open learning programme and what effects it has on learners and others who are touched by it. This might be enough if we were academic researchers. But, if we are professionals in education or training, our chief aim must be to use that understanding in doing things better and helping everyone (learners and staff) make the most of themselves.

I still go along with the vision of Robert Stake (1967):

> "A full evaluation results in a story, supported perhaps by statistics and profiles. It tells what happened. It reveals perceptions and judgements that different groups and individuals hold. . . It tells of merits and shortcomings. As a bonus, it may offer generalisations ('The moral of the story is. . .') for the guidance of subsequent educational programmes."

Except, of course, that evaluation should offer guidance on more than just "subsequent" programmes. It should be able to aid improvement and development at a number of levels. It should help improve:

- the current programme for current learners
- the current programme for future learners
- future programmes for future learners
- the open learning team
- the organisation as a place of learning.

In the long run, furthermore, if we talk or write about our evaluations outside our own organisations, they may influence practices and standards even more widely in the development of open learning in education and training.

Improving current or future programmes

An open learning programme cannot safely be launched and left to its own devices. However carefully you planned and however well you piloted, it probably won't work quite as you'd wish—especially on its first run. Evaluation should reveal where you need to develop and improve it.

For instance, on the opposite page you will see a set of recommendations drawn from the evaluation of a distance learning course by my colleague, David Hawkridge. For more extended examples of how evaluation has led to significant changes in programme materials and teaching approaches, see Nathenson & Henderson (1980).

Ideally, you will want the improvements you make to your programme to benefit learners who are **currently** working with it. If all you need do, for example, is give an individual extra help with their project, find them an extra sheet of examples, or keep the learning centre open for more hours, this may be quite feasible.

Some changes cannot be made fast enough, however. You might, for example, need to develop and print alternative workbooks, remake a video, or recruit and train a new type of supporter. Improvements like these would come too late for current learners and so would benefit only those taking the programme in later runs.

But the current programme, whether now or in the future, would not be the only one to benefit from evaluation. We may also be able to make **future** programmes better than they would otherwise have been. This is because, thanks to evaluation of each programme we work on, we can learn more about what works and what doesn't. Thus we acquire new insights that we can apply in later programmes.

Improving the open learning team

In fact, one can say that effective evaluation should help develop and improve not just the programme but also the people who devise and run it. That is, evaluation can feed into staff development. ("The motor-cycle you are working on is yourself."—Pirsig, 1972.)

Mary Thorpe (1988) gives a useful example—the Open University's scheme for monitoring the quality of tutors' written comments on learners' assignments. This evaluation

Some evaluation recommendations for a distance learning course

Evaluation findings | ## Recommended action

Evaluation findings	Recommended action
1. 40% of students consider workload on Units 3 and 4 to be at least double that of other units.	Remove the exercise on p.64. Eliminate items (c) and (f) from the reading list.
2. 30% of students report that local resources are not available for carrying out the mini-project in Block 4.	Provide a materials-based simulation as an alternative, but also ask tutors to help learners to get access to resources locally.
3. 52% of students do not find the tapes for Unit 3 to be useful.	Change the third assignment so that it is based on both the printed material and tapes, or eliminate tapes, or revise tapes so that they are more useful.
4. Students (12%) want extra help with the mathematical aspects of Unit 9.	Provide appropriate remedial material if available and ask tutors to check out their students' needs.
5. Reviewers of course (5) urge inclusion of alternative material to counter allegations of bias in Unit 9.	Do not alter materials. Include summary of reviewers' allegations. Add an alternative text to list of recommended books.
6. 70% of students complain of too many assignments.	Cut out essay C and replace essay E with a multiple-choice test for self-marking.
7. Less than 30% of students tackled either of the two integrative "course-as-a-whole" questions in the examination; and marks on those two questions averaged 20% below those gained on the questions of more limited scope.	Make the tackling of one integrative question compulsory in the examination; re-write final section of last unit so as to give students practice in reviewing the course to establish overarching principles and general insights.
8. Mentors (42%) concerned about how far to help with assignments that are to be assessed.	Arrange workshops at which to compare experience and refine the guidelines.

activity was originally intended as a means of managerial control. But eventually it became a spur to staff development. It was used to engage tutors in regular reflection about their own practice and discussions with colleagues about the quality of teaching. Hence, the emphasis shifted from identifying and correcting the tutors whose comments were inadequate to enabling **all** tutors to share and develop their understanding of best practice.

Improving the organisation

Whether knowingly or not, any college or company that goes very far with open learning is embarking on organisational change. In particular, it will almost certainly be transforming people's conceptions about learning and what it might have to do with them. Evaluation, if it is done openly and with wide consultation, can speed this process.

At the policy level, evaluation can reveal what the new approaches to learning and training might contribute to the organisation's "mission". For example, Temple (1991) reports how a British Gas evaluation of its open learning indicated that about one third of existing training (rather than the current 5%) would be more cost-effective if delivered by open learning. So evaluation enabled the company to decide new priorities and targets.

But, more pervasively, open and consultative evaluation—which is also central to the new approaches of "total quality management" (Oakland, 1989)—can help create a "learning organisation". In such an organisation, continuous training and self-development for all will be seen as both a means of economic survival and a path to personal satisfaction. "People here have seized on more new ideas in the last two years than they did in the last twenty" as one college lecturer told me. In addition, training becomes both a right and a responsibility for everyone—not just the gift of the training or personnel department. Managers become people-developers rather than simply resource-controllers.

Chris Feetham of Land Rover (OU/ED, 1990) gives us some idea of how this feels:

> "[The Open Learning Centre] has become an Employee Development Centre where an open learning style has replaced an open learning facility. . . What is incalculable is the awakening of talent which it brings. At Land Rover

we are in the process of exploring technical and
managerial expertise. We have found, much to our
surprise, that advertising such jobs internally we have
uncovered a wealth of expertise and ability which has
been dormant for years on the shop floor. The majority of
this new talent has been stimulated by open learning
opening a way to more demanding jobs. . . I would stress
that it is the open learning style which pays dividends
since it injects itself into the company's style and makes
the company more conducive to change and learning."

Communication

Without good communication, the results of even the most
thorough evaluation are likely to be disappointing. Usually, a
number of people will need to make decisions and take
action if the evaluation results are to have their full effect. So
we (the evaluation team) need to make sure that they all
understand it and can see realistic ways of doing something
about it.

The communication of evaluation is often skimped. Plenty
of time and money may be put into collecting data, leaving
too little for the vital tasks of discussing the implications of
the results and following up by helping people to do
something about those implications.

Written reports

Usually the evaluation team will need to write a report about
the results—maybe different reports for different users. Here
it's important to keep in mind our purpose. Our aim is not to
impress colleagues with our thoroughness but to get them to
take action (or sometimes to leave things alone). Experience
tells us that fat reports don't get acted on—A4 summaries do.
(We can always put the background material in an appendix,
and write it all up as an article for *OLS News* or *Open
Learning*.) You may like to track down Sagar and Strang (1985)
—an evaluation report that presents its analysis and
recommendations in snappy style with plenty of graphic
emphasis and dynamic layout, leaving decision-makers in no
doubt as to what the problems are and what might be done to
solve them.

Face-to-facing

But written reports, however well presented, are rarely enough. Receptionists whom learners find "forbidding" or tutors identified as erratic markers are not going to throw themselves into staff development just because some crusading evaluator hands them an analysis of the questionnaire returns. They need to own the problem before they can own the solution. So the evaluation team must expect to communicate also through sensitive, one-to-one discussions and through seminars, workshops and a variety of committee meetings.

In such gatherings, the focus is likely to be not on conveying the results but on identifying the most urgent problems or opportunities and agreeing what might be done about them. The evaluators may have a tricky role here. They will perhaps need to uphold a balance between truth, fairness and confidentiality while at the same time helping a group cope with conflicts of interest and avoid taking too simplistic a view of the results.

 What do you see as the most appropriate ways of using evaluation results in YOUR system?

Final remarks

Communication after the event is merely the icing on the cake. It won't make up for deficiencies in the way the evaluation has been set up and run.

Remember that evaluation is not always a popular activity. Gung ho innovators may be so sure of their new schemes that they don't see the need for it. Colleagues who are not so confident about what they are doing may feel threatened by what it might reveal. And others may suspect that they are just being softened up for yet another cost-cutting exercise.

The best way of ensuring maximum pay-off from evaluation is usually to involve all "interested parties" from the start. They need to know it is **their** evaluation which they help plan and to which they contribute throughout.

Let us end this unit, as we began, with the words of Mary Thorpe (1988)

> ". . . it should be a *collaborative* exercise, undertaken in the interests of *all* those engaged in the teaching/learning process, and open to their inspection, not "owned" by management. As to purpose, I take it as axiomatic that evaluation is for development—of learning and the quality of the learners' experience, of service and the quality of the curriculum the institution offers, and of competence and the careers of staff employed by the institution."

 What remaining concerns, fears or questions do you have about Evaluating Open Learning? Make a note of any that seem important enough to bear in mind when you do your desk work and field work on this topic.

Suggested follow-up work

Desk work

Thorpe & Grugeon (1987). Many of the chapters are evaluative in so far as they are summative reflections on experience. But only one article—that by Alan Woodley on "Understanding adult student drop-out"—addresses evaluation issues directly.

Robinson (1989). None of the chapters is devoted to evaluation though several mention evaluation findings in passing.

Paine (1988). Evaluation is mentioned here and there; but nowhere is it dealt with at length.

Temple (1991). Issues to do with evaluation arise in many chapters; and one chapter "Evaluating open learning's performance" provides a useful survey of the subject with a variety of examples from industrial open learning.

The journal *Open Learning* runs occasional articles relating to evaluation. And *OLS News* has often printed evaluation reports (especially from industry) over the years.

In addition, you may find other materials you want to look at in the bibliography at the end of this book—e.g.:

Thorpe (1988) is devoted to the evaluation of open and distance learning. It is still the best source of ideas if you want to further develop your professional expertise in this particular area.

Lewis (1984) is a collection of case studies, three of which give details about evaluation procedures.

Hamilton *et al* (1977) is a classic and very readable introduction to the theory and politics of evaluation.

Norris (1990) covers much the same ground and discusses the evaluation of such innovations as the Technical and Vocational Education Initiative and the National Development Programme in Computer Assisted Learning.

Field work

- Find someone in your organisation, or a similar one, who has more experience of evaluating open learning than you have. Get them to tell you how they set about it, what problems they faced, and what kinds of decision were made as a result of the evaluation.

- Negotiate with someone who runs an open learning system to carry out an evaluation of one aspect of it—e.g. how learners are using a new medium or how line managers support the learning. Design your questionnaires and/or interviews, collect your data and discuss your findings with your "client".

- Discuss the evaluation of the open learning scheme you are planning with colleagues who will be involved in it or affected by it. Aim to draw up an evaluation strategy covering questions like these:

  ~ What are the purposes of the evaluation?

  ~ Who owns the evaluation?

  ~ How might the evaluation contribute to managing and developing the programme or system?

  ~ What aspects of the programme will need to be evaluated?

  ~ What performance indicators may be relevant?

  ~ What kinds of data will need collecting?

  ~ Who will collect the data?

  ~ How and when will it be collected?

  ~ Who will interpret and report on the data?

  ~ What will the evaluation cost?

  ~ By when and to whom must reports be made?

 Remember to make a record of your desk work and field work in your portfolio.

Reflection checklist

 When you have completed your desk work and field work on this unit, please make notes in your portfolio using some of the following questions as a guide:

o   What are the most important things you have learned during this unit? (You may want to look back at the objectives suggested at the beginning.)

o   What has given you most satisfaction in this unit?

o   What do you feel least satisfied about in this unit?

o   Does this unit leave you with any unresolved questions or difficulties you feel you want help with?

o   How might you try to get the help you need?

o   What have you learned in your work with other people during this unit?

o   In what ways were you able to draw on your previous experience during this unit?

o   What have you learned about yourself—your own feelings and competences?

o   What do you feel you need to do next?

Unit 8

The pros & cons of open learning

Open learning was launched on a tide of enthusiasm and numerous pundits extolled its virtues. In this unit, we consider just who stands to benefit from open learning and in what sorts of ways.

But open learning is not beyond criticism. We also ask questions about whether open learning is doing all it might either for the development of individuals or for the development of an open society. What are the possible weaknesses of open learning?

Suggested objectives

As a result of working on this unit you could be better able to:

- Suggest ways in which more open learning might benefit your learners, your organisation, and you yourself.

- Anticipate dangers or unwanted side-effects in an open learning scheme.

- Suggest ways of averting or coping with dangers and side-effects.

o *Any objectives of your own to add?*

I suggest you now start a new section in your portfolio in which to record your ideas about the Pros and Cons of Open Learning. From time to time, I'll print a box like this (with the symbol alongside) to prompt you to write something in your portfolio. I expect you will use some of these prompts and not others; and also that you will make occasional notes without my prompting.

Where's the benefit?

Package-based training, distance education, open learning—whatever it calls itself, it has won a great many followers in recent years. Where is the attraction? Who gets what benefit from it? Perhaps the most obvious ones to benefit are:

- individual learners
- learners' employers
- providers.

Benefits to the learner

Here are some of the possible benefits that are often mentioned. Which of them might appeal to YOUR learners?

☐ **Access**. Some learners simply would otherwise not have been able to learn what they wanted to learn.

☐ **Flexibility**. Short, modular packages and "accreditation of prior learning" may mean that learners don't need spend time and money on topics they are already familiar with.

☐ Available **any time**—so learners can learn when they wish, rather than to suit someone else's timetable.

☐ Available **any place**—unless fixed equipment is involved, packages may be used in a learning centre, at home, or even while travelling.

☐ Own **pace**—individual learners are not held up or hurried on by other members of a group.

☐ **Private** learning—less danger of "loss of face" such as might be feared in certain kinds of group learning.

☐ More **choice** as to what they will learn in the programme and how they will assess their own progress through it.

☐ Better **quality** teaching—both in content and treatment than they might get from any local conventional course.

☐ A chance to use **media** that better suit their preferences or seem more motivating.

☐ **Individualised tutoring**. Support staff can respond to each individual's needs and interests, rather than aiming their discourse at what they hope is the "average" level of a group.

☐ *Other benefits? (What?)*

What are the chief benefits your organisation might offer learners?

Benefits to employers

Employers who sponsor open or distance learning for their staff may also may get a wide range of benefits. As Hilary Temple (1991) suggests, though, each may have different priorities:

> "One goes for the chance to train a large number of staff in a short time; another for parity of standards at different plants or branches throughout the country; a third for offering training to those who have never previously had access to it; a fourth because it is the only way of enabling trainees to accomplish an individual action plan; a fifth because they contrast the cost-benefit and visible qualities of open learning with that of conventional training; and a sixth to meet specialised needs which generic training programmes do not satisfy."

Whatever their main reason for getting into open/distance learning, employers may also benefit from knock-on effects. For instance, line managers may get more involved in training. And staff may begin to take more of an interest in learning and self-development throughout the organisation.

A major study of the use of open learning in 50 companies—ranging in size from 17 to 36,000 employees—was carried out in 1988 by the Open University and Coopers & Lybrand Associates. According to OU/ED (1990):

> "Although open learning was found to be substantially cheaper, the most frequently cited reasons for choosing it were:
> * because trainees were scattered around the country
> * because they were on shift work
> * because they were difficult to release from their jobs
> * because large numbers had to be trained in a short time
> * because the firm could not provide any other form of training.

Companies that used open learning identified:

- higher pass rates than before
- line manager's satisfaction
- better retention of information
- a better record of promotion
- an increase in the number of employees working towards vocational qualifications, from 43% to 75% of workforce.

Various firms in the survey also reported such business benefits as the following:

- financial performance improved in 70% of branches
- error rates in manufacture down by 3%
- reduced customer complaints
- 41% increase in the success rates of calls (sales engineering)
- 25% fewer "helpline" calls (microcomputer firm)
- sales increased by 50% (chemical industry)"

Many firms in the survey reported that open learning had made a measurable impact on business performance indices such as improved productivity and profitability. We may want to ask, however, whether the employees shared in these proceeds. After all, we are told that "Virtually all of the cost savings were achieved through the use of the trainees' own time . . . frequently at home".

Such productivity and profitability benefits are also reported by Forte (1991) as a result of an open learning programme on wine service for hotel and restaurant staff. In addition, they offer evidence of increased satisfaction among customers and of greater interest in further self-development among staff.

Benefits to providers

A specialist provider like the Open University or National Extension College owes its existence to open learning and distance education. For other providers, like further education colleges and training departments within a firm, the benefits sometimes centre around saving jobs and finding enough new learners to keep its existing courses running.

What the users say

The learners

"It's the versatility of open learning that appeals to me more than anything. I'm not tied down to a classroom. . . It fits in with my life." (Nursing sister)

"At school you had to learn. Here you learn and you enjoy learning. At school everyone learned the same thing. Here it's individual—it's good fun." (Supermarket trainee)

"With the open learning I've gained a lot of confidence. I can take on almost every job. . . it's given me the confidence to say, 'we don't need a contractor to come in to deal with this'." (Maintenance engineer)

"I was nervous about starting the course. My children take a keen interest and so does my wife. There's no classroom to put pressure on me." (Sales manager)

"When you're disabled you need time. Open learning let me take all the time I needed." (Computer student with multiple sclerosis)

The sponsors

"Open learning, available to anyone wishing to further their training and education, stands as an investment in Jaguar employees, both as individuals and as members of a quality workforce." (Sir John Egan, Chairman, Jaguar Cars plc)

"What we can do with open learning is to match the higher rate of change in our business units with training programmes which are adequately responsive and flexible. Open learning gives us a powerful formula for achieving change quickly." (Tony Gill, Chairman, Lucas Industries plc)

"If businesses are to expand, evolve and survive in today's climate of constant change, they need individuals who can take responsibility for their own development. It may therefore be that it is the system rather than the content of open learning which is of the greatest benefit to organisations."
(John Fricker, Head of Group Training, National Westminster Bank plc)

Here are some of the benefits that providers have mentioned to me. If you are concerned with providing open or distance learning, which of them might be relevant to YOUR organisation?

☐ Responding more easily to local needs

☐ Exploiting new sources of funding

☐ Catering for new types of learner

☐ Catering for greater numbers of learners without a proportionate increase in cost

☐ Cutting contact hours on existing courses

☐ Getting more use out of existing facilities

☐ Providing new development opportunities for staff

☐ *Other benefits? (What?)*

Whatever sort of organisation you are in, what are the main points you would make in arguing the case for more open or distance learning?

The price to be paid

Clearly, open learning offers many benefits. But, as always, there is no gain without some degree of pain. Open learning will not suit everyone. Some potential learners, sponsors and providers may feel they simply cannot meet its demands.

In Unit 9, I mention some of the costs involved for organisations in implementing open learning. Here I am referring not so much to the financial costs (which may themselves be considerable) but to the human costs. In particular, for most organisations, open learning means change. And the degree and kind of change is not always predictable at the outset. In the words of Ian McNay (1987), the introduction of open learning can be both "disruptive and revolutionary".

Learners too may baulk at the price to be paid. Again, I am not talking simply about fees, though these may indeed be a matter of concern to the learners. Equally or more challenging, however, is the matter of self-discipline. Not all potential learners will have the experience and motivation to control their own learning programme to the degree called for by many open learning schemes. Such self-discipline may be especially hard for learners whose near ones or dear ones (whether at work or at home) are unsupportive.

A mini case study

One of my colleagues, Sandy Sieminski (1992), has recently carried out some illuminating interviews in an FE college that is moving into open and flexible learning. One open learning programme it is running is for a Chartered Institute of Bankers qualification. Some quotations from a tutor and students will illustrate just a few of the kinds of pressures that open learners need to be able to survive.

First, a tutor:

> "There is no employer support. The students have to finance themselves. If they pass the exams they will get the money back for books and perhaps a bonus. But the days of day release have gone. If they can prove they can get the Certificate and go on to the Associateship. . . they've indicated that they're serious about their career, they're serious about the study side of things, and they're motivated. Then the bank takes a different attitude, but not until that stage."

And two of the students:

> "I find it hard sometimes because I have to have this commitment, this drive all the time and it's not always possible, especially if I've had a very hard day's work. When I first joined this course I didn't realise it was like a correspondence course, I thought it was just like evening classes. . . It demands that I give it 100%. . . I have to go home and say I'm going to study tonight and actually study and not do anything else, because I'm tempted when I'm at home to do something else. . . I'm so used to coming home and putting the television on. Once you switch it on it's hard to switch it off, so you mustn't switch it on at all. Sometimes I decide to go to the library straight from work and at least then I have two hours when there's no distraction whatsoever."

> "I was OK until I was told it is open learning and I can
> work at my own pace instead of having a deadline to hand
> work in. . . I found it very difficult to keep up to date with
> the work. Basically, the pressure's been taken off. . . One
> of the reasons that I'm here tonight is to have a word
> with Yvonne [his tutor] to sort out the problems I've
> been finding myself in. It's piled up. Recently I took a
> week off from work just to catch up. . . I need to motivate
> myself. At the end of the day, I think, it comes down to
> how much you want to further your career. . . I'm getting
> there, I've got until May to finish the course and I'll have
> to do it."

On the positive side, students seemed to be gaining
confidence in themselves as learners. As one said,
comparing open learning with school (where "you've got a
teacher standing in front of you waffling on and you're taking
it in"):

> "Whereas with this, you're literally expected to learn
> yourself, motivate yourself, sit down and gather
> information and take it in. So the things that I'm learning
> here are certainly staying in whereas at school they
> probably weren't."

And, as another said:

> "It makes me read books more often and it makes me
> want to understand. It makes me more attentive to my
> surroundings. It's not just the fact that you have the
> books to read, you also have to listen to the news and
> things about inflation and programmes about the
> economy. Before, it went past me. Now I'm more aware
> of what's happening and I want to find out."

For such benefits, learners may be willing to accept that
sometimes, as one student said: "You look at it and you think
'Oh no! I've got three weeks' work to do in one week, my God
how am I going to cope' and you just panic." Not too great a
price to pay, perhaps? After all, other kinds of learning would
also present problems—possibly worse ones.

Now let us look at some rather more fundamental concerns
about open learning and the dangers that may lurk behind its
beneficent front.

Where the dangers lie

Open and distance learning has already changed the lives of thousands of people, around the world. Every week, more and more are joining the procession behind MacKenzie's banner (see page 1). If we are to join them, we need to keep our critical wits about us and watch where we put our feet.

We cannot afford to regard open and distance learning simply as a technical fix. It is not a tool we are free to use in our own well-meaning way exactly as we please. As in any other area of human affairs, there may be hidden agendas, undeclared interests and unintended side-effects. Perhaps we shan't always be able to do anything about these factors. But we'd do well to keep aware of them for they can easily put us at cross-purposes with people whose aims turn out not to be the same as ours.

In the final pages of this unit I want to mention some concerns that are beginning to be talked about by open learning practitioners. Now that the first flush of enthusiasm has had time to dissipate, people are starting to ask if open learning is always quite the "good thing" it is usually portrayed as. (For example, see Boot & Hodgson, 1988; Edwards, 1991; Fox, 1989; Harris, 1987; Hirst, 1986.)

These concerns are to do with who pays for open learning, who can learn, who decides what is to be learned, and what effect open learning is having on the teachers and the taught.

Who pays for open learning?

To begin with, we have to recognise that open learning is largely a **government** enterprise. The Wilson government begat the Open University and the Heath government begat the Manpower Services Commission and the Thatcher government begat Open Tech Unit and Open College.

The current government still funds the promotion of vocational open learning through the Employment Department and subsidises the Open University through the same Funding Council as other universities. The open or distance learning activity in many other countries around the world is also underwritten by their governments.

Investment in open learning has many benefits for a government. Chiefly, it offers the prospect of updating or re-skilling the workforce at a speed that would be impossible by traditional methods. At the same time, the economies of scale and the shift to pre-recorded media promise vast cost savings. The combination of large numbers of learners and high visibility of projects—especially perhaps where new technology is upfront—can have high public relations value. In fighting for economic survival, a government can be seen to be big, bold and innovative.

To the extent that government is paying the piper, we can expect to find it calling the tunes. What sort of tunes does government want to hear? Usually the ones defined for it by industrial interests—that is, skills and competences capable of giving the economy "competitive edge". Here, the chief goal is not an educated population but a healthy economy.

Who can learn?

In the UK, open learning has been promoted by a government devoted to privatisation and the market economy. Students who choose open learning rather than conventional courses are likely to get very much less financial support (if any). For instance, three quarters of Open University students get no help with fees. (And the state subsidises the OU at only about 60% of the rate per student allowed to other universities.) This is in spite of the fact that most OU students are living at home (so no maintenance costs), working full-time (thus contributing to the economy) and paying taxes (part of which go to subsidise full-time students in conventional universities).

Thus, access gets biased towards the well-heeled middle-class and learners whose employers will pay the fees. The Open University has a "hardship fund" but this will never be big enough to invite an influx from the huge army of people who have more time than most on their hands and who may be more in need than most of a new stimulus in life—e.g. the unemployed, the house-bound, and the retired.

Instead, the OU, like other providers, is under pressure to seek out new (paying) "markets" and now runs one of the biggest business schools in Europe. Similarly, Open College has had to backpedal on providing vocational courses for unwaged or self-financing students and now operates chiefly through companies who will sponsor their employees.

So, who is meant to benefit from open learning? There has clearly been a shift of focus—from the needs of learners to the needs of their employers or sponsors. Open Tech Unit seemed to change its mind quite early about who the customer was. At the start (MSC, 1982), they said:

> "The main thing is that learner needs and circumstances are paramount and determine the system to be used in each instance."

But a year later we see the real customer emerging from the parentheses (Tolley, 1983):

> "Open learning provides the opportunity for the student to learn at a pace, time and place which satisfy the student's circumstances and requirements (or alternatively, the employer's circumstances and requirements)."

Perhaps you see no harm in such a shift of focus. Even in higher education, many people now seem to be committed to "the new vocationalism". On the other hand, you may agree with Alan Tuckett (1988) that:

> "The ability to attract students from the least powerful, least privileged classes and groups is a useful measure of the openness of a course, institution or system."

 If so, what can we (or our organisations) do to help make up for the built-in bias to access?

What can they learn?

Who decides the content of open learning? Who decides what is worthwhile knowledge in our supposedly democratic society? Increasingly, providers are having to bow to market forces. As Ros Morpeth (1988) points out:

> "It does not take much imagination to see that this will lead to an expansion in vocational courses which the government or employers are prepared to pay for and a reduction in courses which encourage students to think, question and learn for its own sake. Certain categories of students who do not have much economic power—for example, older people, women, ethnic minority groups and the unemployed—are bound to find that their needs are not given proper consideration."

Learning for life or for work?

More and more, the content of open learning programmes (like many others in education post-16) is being influenced by industrial interests. So what is the prospect for courses that encourage the pursuit of knowledge for its own sake? And what about courses that encourage critical reflection on moral, social and political issues or challenge the status quo?

Those who wield economic power in society are unlikely to encourage critical, non-conformist thinking. The public nature of open learning material even facilitates censorship. In 1984, for instance, the government's Education Secretary protested about alleged Marxist bias in some of the Open University's teaching materials (Richards, 1984)—and those materials were revised rather sooner than is usual.

Perhaps there will always be some employers with more liberal views about what knowledge is worthwhile—like the many police forces who pay the fees of officers to take whatever Open University courses they choose or the Ford "EDAP" programme which pays for employees doing general continuing education courses. But, especially in times of recession, training departments may have a hard time getting funds for schemes that have no obvious business payoff.

Such economic priorities may also be voiced by learners. So what? some may say. If we encourage open learners to choose what they want to learn about and they choose on the basis of what might improve their work prospects, who should worry? Those of us, perhaps, who believe that lifelong education—of a kind that we all need to live self-respecting lives in an open, democratic society—cannot be attained merely through education for work.

Neglected opportunities?

We may be especially concerned if the hype about open learning is blinding people to the underfunding of certain other educational opportunities that (for some learners at least) may be more appropriate. For example: The setting up of the Open University allowed other universities to offer fewer part-time degree courses.

Non-vocational and basic adult education is also short of resources. The 75 Open Learning Centres devoted to improving adult literacy and basic skills (ALBSU, 1991) are doing good work but are themselves too underfunded to make up for funding deficiencies elsewhere. Even the public libraries (once called "the universities of the people") are having to buy fewer books, reduce their opening hours and, in too many cases, close down altogether.

Richard Edwards (1991) implies that the economic promise of open learning may be something of a con, anyway. Open learning cannot make everyone a skilled worker because our post-industrial economy will never be able to provide skilled, secure jobs for more than about 25% of the potential workforce. Open learning will serve to promote the regular re-skilling of this core. But:

> "For the rest of the workforce, it will be there to support the movement of people in and out of employment, or to keep them busy with the revolving door. How real these opportunities are or whether they are taken up is not the point. Open learning is there to maintain the appearance of opportunity. . ."

Can it be true that the majority of the population cannot look to open learning to improve their long-term employability? If not, what can they look to it for? Is there a danger that market forces—directed at the work-worthy minority—may lead to only a restricted and unbalanced curriculum being available to potential open learners?

If open learning does get itself a lop-sided curriculum it will be so much less open. As Ian McNay (1988) points out: ". . . unless it is used to educate and not indoctrinate, to encourage people to be critical, not conformist, it will be closed before it has had the chance to become more than barely ajar."

 What are your own feelings about these issues? And do you know how your colleagues feel?

How will they learn?

We may be reasonably happy about who can get access to open learning. We may even feel they have adequate freedom to choose its content. And yet we may still have reservations about the actual processes of open learning. We may wonder about the possibility of unwanted side-effects.

Let's consider four typical aspects of open learning:

- Open learners work mostly on their own
- . . . and rarely in groups
- . . . using pre-recorded materials produced by teachers who do not know their life or work context and whom they may never meet
- . . . with support from people who did not produce the materials.

The individualism of the do-it-yourself learner

Open learning is usually a private affair. Course materials address themselves to the individual learner. The learner is given responsibility for his or her own learning. The individual needs to be self-motivating, self-directing and relatively self-sufficient.

It is interesting that this do-it-yourself approach came to maturity during the years of Thatcherism. That ideology deemed the individual responsible for his or her own fate. It denied the existence of social forces beyond the individual's control that might excuse any lack of success. Hence, for instance, it is the fault of individuals rather than that of society if they fail to become part of the skilled core workforce —especially since they've now been offered (user-friendly) open learning. As Richard Edwards (1991) puts it:

> "Being part of the core is the goal, as it is 'normal' to be a high skilled worker. Persons can strive for this goal, but if they do not achieve it, it is because they lack the skills. Education and training opportunities are available to them through open learning, as and when they need them, so the responsibility for not participating in the core of the economy lies with them."

Thatcherism also championed individual self-interest beyond the interests of any collective "society". Is there an underlying danger that open learning could promote a similar spirit of "I've got on all right, Jack—so the jobless can't have been trying"? If so, we may want to look for ways of making open learning more of a collaborative experience.

The perils of the package

Packaged learning can easily become passive learning— especially if the learners are to be assessed on what they have learned. The learner can become dependent, distanced from his or her own experience of the subject, concerned only to soak up the message or—slightly more actively but no more creatively—suss out which bits of it are likely to be assessed. Whatever the intentions of the authors, a package's well-structured exposition of carefully sifted ideas can encourage the learner in servile (if sometimes cynical) compliance.

The package—especially if it is glossily expensive—clearly embodies the wisdom of the expert (perhaps even a team of experts) whose view of things seems to be authoritative. Learners may feel too overwhelmed to challenge it or offer alternative views based on their own experience.

Packages lend themselves to what Richard Boot and Vivien Hodgson (1987) have called the "dissemination" model of learning. Here, they say, "knowledge can be seen as a (valuable) commodity which exists independently of people and as such can be stored and transmitted (sold)". This contrasts with what they call the "development" model whose purpose, they suggest, is "the development of the whole person, especially the continuing capacity to make sense of oneself and the world in which one lives".

It is easier to write packages that encourage people to learn what they are told than packages that help them make their own personal knowledge. Lewis Elton (1988) gives useful guidance on how to overcome this problem.

The absent group

People often find they are better able to challenge received ideas, and struggle towards new ideas of their own, when they can do so in company with other learners. One of the learners interviewed by Sandy Sieminski (1992)—not an open learner—reminds us of just what may be missing:

> "With the group it's easier, getting everyone's point of view, so you can come up with a better point of view. Because then you get to hear what everyone has to say. It helps us build close relationships with other students. Because we're a small group we tend to support each other, outside as well as inside the classroom."

Sadly, group interaction—allowing an opportunity to relate the package's ideas to a known context, to hear and perhaps grapple with other people's contradictory viewpoints or experiences, to articulate and get feedback on one's own, to engage in collaborative enquiry—is what the open learner gets relatively little of. In the absence of such live "process", many home-based learners may feel, as Winifred Hirst (1986) suggests, that packages are like fast food take-aways—seeming to lack that "real honest-to-goodness flavour".

Some sponsors of packaged learning may be quite pleased to ensure that learners are studying alone and learning what they are told to learn. Alan Tait (1989) reminds us why distance teaching was brought into higher education in Iran and Turkey. Reportedly, the rulers wanted to avoid the kind of political dissent that had been common where students spent time together on campus.

Most providers and sponsors of open learning have no such fear of the collective. But how much of it can we afford? The more often we expect learners to come together in groups, the more constrained (less open) some may feel. Contrarily, others may see it as the most attractive feature of the course. (And if we also expect those groups to have a paid leader, we risk eroding the cost advantages of open learning.) Yet if group meetings are infrequent, learners may not know or trust one another enough to disclose their thoughts and feelings or listen with empathy to others.

The human touch?

What about the human media—tutors, mentors, counsellors, and so on? Can they help overcome any tendency to dissemination in the package materials and undue deference in the learner? Can they provoke the learner to challenge the materials, relate them to their own experience and develop their own stance on the subject?

Quite possibly. Many Open University students have told me how their subjects came to life in arguing the toss with their tutors—either face-to-face, by correspondence or on the phone. Such tutoring in turn demands considerable attention to recruitment and staff development. Not all teachers take easily to the nurturing, developmental role. An unreconstructed pedagogue might simply add his or her weight to the dissemination model—increasing the learner's dependence on authorities.

The danger to teachers

Nurturing the teachers in an open learning system may be almost as important as nurturing the learners. Just as packaged learning can dehumanise the learners (in the sense that they may be reduced to dutiful data processors), so too it can de-skill and alienate, or even supplant, the teachers. Some people—perhaps those who suspect that the only open learning with a chance of catching on will be cheap learning —seem to hold out the ideal of a teacher-proof package, e.g. (Temple, 1988):

> ". . . without adequate support even quite satisfactory open learning material is badly received. The present solution is seen to be the proper training of teachers, trainers and tutors, whose services are, however, expensive for anything other than their technical expertise. A more economical far-reaching alternative is to develop better learning materials whose interactivity will provide the necessary support and to ensure that learners have access to—and are not embarrassed about using—peer groups and other 'non-experts' for most of their general needs."

The plight of the teachers in open learning can be seen as an aspect of what Otto Peters (1989) calls "industrialisation". He points out that large-scale distance education has been made possible only by introducing principles and practices developed in manufacturing industry—e.g. project planning, mass production of teaching materials, quality control, division of labour and mechanisation.

Those last two items may pose a special threat to teachers and, through them, to learners. Division of labour means specialisation within the workforce. The course-writers have to share the task of making a package with a number of other specialists—editors, graphic designers, educational technologists. And none of the course producers may have any teaching contact with learners. Indeed, the task of supporting learners may be passed to another set of specialists (e.g. tutors) who have had no say in deciding what is to be taught. Assessment may be controlled by yet another group of specialists (who neither plan nor teach the programme).

Otto Peters warns us that teachers may thus be alienated. Each one's involvement is limited and he or she is no longer responsible for the whole process. Thus teachers may be left feeling isolated and frustrated, coping with uncertainty and loss of control while, at the same time, learning new skills and keeping up the high level of motivation expected of them in what may be an innovative and risky undertaking.

As for mechanisation, open learning teachers and trainers may be only too aware that the ultimate form of mechanisation is automation. How long, they may wonder, before packaged learning puts us out of work altogether? Staff in colleges and universities, which the government is now demanding should process many more students without employing extra teachers, may increasingly find they are having to make the acquaintance of new packages rather than new colleagues.

Do you think that teachers or learners in your own learning system might suffer any of the side-effects mentioned above? If so, what might be done about it?

Final remarks

I do not want to end this unit on a down beat. In the last few pages we have warned ourselves about some dangers that **may** imperil open learning. It may lend itself to use as a tool of social control. Packages may promote dissemination rather than development. Isolated learning may limit exposure to conflicting ideas. Both learners and teachers may feel they've lost some vital spark of humanity and creativity.

But traditional education and training are not perfect either. That is at least partly why open learning has taken off. It still has enormous potential to transform people's lives. Can we overcome the dangers and harness that potential? Can we make learning more productive and satisfying—both for existing learners and for people who have never previously thought of themselves as learners and may even think of themselves as non-learners? Can we develop an open learning fit for the kind of society we'd like to live in? That is the challenge.

What remaining concerns, fears or questions do you have about the Pros & Cons of Open Learning? Make a note of any that seem important enough to bear in mind when you do your desk work and field work on this topic.

Suggested follow-up work

Desk work

Thorpe & Grugeon (1987). The first chapter considers the potential benefits of open learning but none examines the potential shortcomings.

Robinson (1989). The benefits and dangers are touched on in the chapters on delivering open learning and, in the final chapter, the author presents what she calls "the paradox of the success and failure of open learning".

Paine (1988) provides a number of chapters extolling the virtues of open learning and includes a few critical voices.

Temple (1991) is all about the potential benefits of open learning to industry.

In addition, you may want to follow up some of the sources I have referred to in this unit. One of the best ways of keeping up with current controversies is to devote a little time every few months to *Open Learning* and other journals.

Field work

• If your organisation has already embarked on open learning, what is it trying to achieve? Maybe there is a published statement of purpose or intent (e.g. a "mission statement")? Maybe you'll have to ask around. How do practices match up with stated intentions?

• Find some people (teachers or learners, inside or outside your organisation) who will tell you about their open learning experience. What do they see as its strengths and limitations—or dangers?

• Join with colleagues who are interested in talking about how open learning might be used to improve the world around us. Consider basing discussions on materials from this book or others you find useful; and maybe you can get more experienced colleagues to present some workshops.

 Remember to make a record of your desk work and field work in your portfolio.

Reflection checklist

 When you have completed your desk work and field work on this unit, please make notes in your portfolio using some of the following questions as a guide:

o What are the most important things you have learned during this unit? (You may want to look back at the objectives suggested at the beginning.)

o What has given you most satisfaction in this unit?

o What do you feel least satisfied about in this unit?

o Does this unit leave you with any unresolved questions or difficulties you feel you want help with?

o How might you try to get the help you need?

o What have you learned in your work with other people during this unit?

o In what ways were you able to draw on your previous experience during this unit?

o What have you learned about yourself—your own feelings and competences?

o What do you feel you need to do next?

Unit 9

Implementing open learning

Are you thinking of setting up an open learning project?
Perhaps you are already involved in one? This unit is about
making open learning work within an organisation you
know well. I hope it will stimulate you to write down your
thoughts and discuss with colleagues your ideas about:

- why open learning might be used
- what might be accomplished and how
- what might be your own part in it.

Suggested objectives

As a result of working on this unit you could be better able to:

- Identify a role for open learning within an organisation
  you know well.
- Decide what needs to be done.
- Do it effectively.
- *Any objectives of your own to add?*

N.B. If you are planning to read this Unit before some of the others,
that's all right—it should alert you to issues you may want to
follow up in the other units. But if you are reading it early on, I
suggest you come back to it again when you have completed
your work on the other units. It should then help you reflect on
what you have learned and how you might put it to best use.

 I suggest you now start a new section in your portfolio in
which to keep a record of your ideas about Implementing
Open Learning. From time to time, I'll print a box like this
(with the symbol alongside) to prompt you to write something
in your portfolio. I expect you will use some of these prompts
and not others; and also that you will make occasional notes
without my prompting.

Managing change

Your organisation may be a college or a company, a charity or a hospital, a civil service department or . . . well, only you know what. Similarly, open learning may be totally new to your organisation or, on the other hand, you may be working within an organisation in which open learning is already up and running. Furthermore, you may be making managerial decisions about open learning, or your work may be affected by other people's managerial decisions—or perhaps both.

The issues I raise in this unit are ones that should be relevant in all these cases. I assume merely that you are involved either in introducing a new scheme or in trying to improve an existing one. I leave you to decide what you might mean by a "scheme". This could be a single **programme** to fit within an existing system. Or it could be a complete **system** comprising, or capable of comprising, several programmes.

Open learning schemes don't just happen. Nor do they run themselves. They need managing. In the first part of this unit, I look at some aspects of managing the organisational change that open learning almost always involves. In the second part I offer some checklists you may find suggestive —either as a manager or as one of the managed (or as both). Either way, it could be in your interests to think about who should be doing what.

What kind of change?

The organisation that introduces open learning will almost inevitably find itself involved in organisational change. Not only is open learning a change in itself, it usually leads to other changes within the organisation. These changes can be far-reaching. In the words of Ian McNay (1987):

> "Open learning, at the extreme, can turn an institution upside-down. . . It can invert the control mechanisms in teaching and learning, putting decisions more in the hands of the student than the teacher. It can shift the whole budget of an institution from a staff-intensive service industry profile nearer to a production industry capital-intensive model. It can abolish timetables, exams and all the other familiar maps and milestones of institutional topography. It changes roles: it demands new skills and attitudes; it threatens vested interests; it

clashes with developed norms for measuring workload or allocating finance, and with established administrative practices. In two words, it can be disruptive and revolutionary."

How open is your organisation?

Clearly, a lot of stamina and energy may be needed if you are trying to introduce open learning into an organisation for the first time. Much will depend on how open the organisation has already become in other respects. For example:

	in a WELCOMING (open?) organisation	in a RESISTANT (closed?) organisation
• The nature of the work is	continually changing	very stable
• Organisation structures are	reshaped for each new project	fixed, hierarchical and bureaucratic
• Managers usually	consult staff and use their ideas	just tell staff what to do
• People's influence depends on their	ability and persuasiveness	position or rank
• Decision making is	decentralised	centralised
• Objectives or targets are	negotiated between staff and boss	imposed on staff by boss
• In planning and monitoring their own work, staff are given	considerable responsibility	little or no responsibility
• Staff are rewarded for	showing initiative	conforming
• Promotion is based on	achievement	length of service
• Staff development is	minimal or task-focussed	well-planned and career-focussed
• Communication is	frank, frequent and reliable	guarded, infrequent and unreliable

I leave you to decide whether your organisation lies chiefly in the WELCOMING or chiefly in the RESISTANT column above. Clearly, if you are working with a resistant organisation, your task will be that much harder. It will have bred (or attracted) staff who may not take easily to doing new things—especially if they involve fluidity, ambiguity and power-sharing (as open learning likely will).

Who might resist?

Individuals and groups of staff may resist open learning for a variety of reasons. For example:

- Tutors may say: "What am I supposed to do, if the package is doing the teaching" or "Is this going to make me redundant?"

- Learners may say: "Is it a second-best way of learning?" or "It looks like the teachers are making me do their work."

- Line managers may say: "I didn't get where I am today by being spoon-fed" or "You'll never persuade them to put the time in."

- Administrators may say: "It doesn't fit the system" or "It will be too difficult to control."

Such feelings are not to be dismissed lightly. You may share some of them yourself. They are usually held for very good reason and it can be fatal to ignore them. They will probably be simply the outward expression of more basic causes—the vested interests, the established practices, the ways in which members of staff are motivated, rewarded and managed.

Even within an organisation that has already adopted open learning, we can run into such barriers if we try to introduce a **new** form of open learning. If, for example, the computers and support systems are geared up to enrol hundreds of students once a year, we may be told they can't handle a programme that would enrol learners one-off whenever they want to start. Again, if our organisation insists that plans for programmes must be approved by committees that meet once every three months, what are our chances of tackling an innovative programme where the sponsor wants a programme in six weeks?

Analysing the forces

How does one cope with resistance? Many people start with the "force-field" analysis suggested by the psychologist Kurt Lewin. He saw the organisation as a "field" fought over by driving forces and restraining forces. The driving forces are those that enable or promote change. The restraining forces are those that hinder it. Unless the driving forces are stronger, in total, than the restraining forces, things won't change.

These forces can be internal or external. Here are just a few typical examples:

Driving forces	Restraining forces
~Support of top managers	~Lack of relevant expertise
~External funds available	~Unsuitable working practices
~Pressure to lower costs	~Tutors uneasy
~Spare physical premises	~Line managers sceptical
~Requirement to enrol more learners	~Uncertainty about external recognition

---

 You may like to make a list of the forces that would (a) help and (b) hinder the development of open learning in your organisation. Perhaps you can discuss this issue with colleagues?

Changing the balance

Recognising the forces is simply the first step. The second one is to decide which are the most and least powerful of the driving forces and which are the most and least powerful of the restraining forces. In total, the two sides must be equally balanced at present, or things would already be changing.

The third step is then to work out a strategy for changing this balance in favour of the driving forces. Only by so doing will you be able to implement the changes you want to make. In short, there are just two ways of getting your open learning scheme up and running, i.e.:

* strengthen the helping forces
* weaken the hindering forces.

Both may be necessary. It is not enough to strengthen the helping forces—e.g. by getting the big boss to wave a big stick. In fact, such approaches can cause conflict and this can strengthen the hindering forces.

On the whole, it is better to weaken the hindering forces— softening up the opposition and removing barriers. Then the helping forces can work more freely. Having the big boss (or bosses) fully committed to the proposed change can be useful, of course. In fact, it can be essential.

How might you weaken the opposing forces in your organisation? Again, this may be a question you would want to discuss with your colleagues. In my experience there are three main ways, very closely connected:

- Consultation
- Staff development/training
- Communication.

Consultation

Where open learning is concerned, the strongest restraining forces usually arise out of people's attitudes. Constraints like lack of funds and shortage of staff can ease miraculously if you can change people's perceptions of open learning.

People's attitudes to new schemes can be unhelpful for a variety of reasons, e.g.:

- They haven't been consulted about what is proposed.
- They don't see why the scheme is necessary.
- They believe such schemes have failed in the past.
- They don't trust the people who are proposing the scheme.
- Their cherished values seem threatened, e.g. "We'll lose the human dimension" or "The quality of learning will suffer".
- They fear loss of status, security, money, time, influence.
- They fear not being able to cope with something new or learn new ways.

Most of these reasons may stem from the first. Hence the need for wide consultation. How might you overcome the fears and concerns of all those individuals and groups whose goodwill is necessary to the success of your scheme? One way is by translating each of the features of your scheme into **benefits** (see Race, 1989). This is sometimes called "internal marketing".

Selling the benefits

Who are those people whose goodwill and cooperation you need? What might each one have to gain from your scheme?

- Potential learners may be persuaded that they will get more opportunities for personal development.

- Tutors that they will enjoy more stimulating relationships with learners.

- Line managers that they will get more productive staff.

- Administrators that they will get more opportunities to make their own decisions.

- Top managers that the scheme will contribute to the corporate "mission". And so on.

Needless to say, you cannot afford to peddle empty promises. The benefits you propose must be realistic. Furthermore, you need to be willing to negotiate. The people you are trying to influence may want to influence you back. That is, they may want to sell you a few benefits you hadn't thought of—like the opportunity to contribute to the shaping of policy for open learning in your organisation.

Sharing the ownership

Consultation is a two-way affair. The object is not just to sell. It may not be enough to persuade people of the virtues of your scheme. You will often want them to join in the "ownership" of it. In order to do this, they will need to have a share in making it. So let them see that their opinions are taken into account—e.g. get them to comment on plans, circulate their ideas, make sure your packages contain a printed acknowledgement of their contribution.

Whom would you need to consult in your organisation? What benefits would you bring to each one's attention? How might they be able to contribute to the planning or running of the scheme?

Staff development

Making sure people are well briefed and supportive is surely necessary to the success of your scheme. But it is probably not enough. In order to make it work, staff will need some open learning expertise or competence. Hence the likely need for training or staff development.

The specific skills your colleagues will need must depend on the nature of the scheme. Clearly the development of packages needs different competences from those involved in supporting learners. Supporting learners on package-driven courses may need a different set of competences from that involved in supporting learners on self-directed projects. And so on.

ADDFOL

Deciding what competences are required—and where to find people who already have them or can be helped to develop them—is a vital step in planning your scheme. One place you might look in order to check out your ideas is the "Scheme of Awards in the Development and Delivery of Flexible and Open Learning"—or ADDFOL, for short (see RSA, 1991).

This scheme is being offered by SCOTVEC in Scotland and by RSA and City & Guilds in the rest of the UK. It is meant to provide a range of vocational qualifications for teachers, trainers and managers working in flexible and open learning. The published "units and elements of competence" provide, in effect, a series of possible job descriptions. For example, the first six (out of 30) units of competence are:

"1. Select flexible and open learning materials

2. Adapt flexible and open learning materials

3. Provide entry and exit counselling to learners

4. Obtain and use feedback from learners

5. Implement record systems to aid learner progress

6. Provide learner support."

Each of the thirty units is then broken down into a number of "elements" of competence. Thus, for example, Unit 3 above breaks down as follows:

"3.1   Agree with a potential learner his/her needs, expectations and goals.

3.2   Agree an open/flexible learning programme to satisfy learner needs.

3.3   Provide guidance to learners on approaches to effective learning.

3.4   Provide guidance to learners upon completion of a programme."

Of course, you and your colleagues may wish to work towards a qualification in this scheme. Indeed, the chance to obtain a potentially marketable qualification may be one of those "benefits" you can entice people with. Be that as it may, the published competences may provide a useful list of possible tasks against which to check your staff development needs.

What further training needs?

But you may feel they don't go far enough for you. They give little indication, for example, of the social, political or interpersonal skills—"soft skills" (Spencer, 1979)—that may underlie some of the competences. For example, previous experience as a teacher or trainer may sometimes be counter-productive. Some colleagues may need help in making a major shift in attitudes if they are to work effectively in their new support roles—e.g. :

- from deciding what must be learned to helping the learner decide

- from conveying information to helping the learner learn

- from acting as the critical and impersonal expert to building relationships

- from using assessment to decide a grade to using assessment in order to help the learner learn (e.g. by written comments)

- from face-to-face teaching to teaching in writing or on the telephone

- from putting on a performance to nurturing a person.

It is worth thinking through the separate aspects of your open learning scheme and asking which of them have implications for your staff development programme. Here are just a few where "consciousness-raising" may be an essential prelude to acquiring new capabilities:

- **Learner-centredness.** How can you be sure that all staff—and not just those officially regarded as "supporters"—have developed an appropriately open and welcoming attitude to learners? The switch of emphasis from provider-driven to client-led systems may be difficult for some to adjust to—especially if your scheme is meant to reach out to new learners whose needs and abilities are very different from those your organisation is used to.

- **Interpersonal skills.** What new capabilities will you and your colleagues need—in negotiation, in handling internal committees and outside bodies, in preparing and presenting proposals, in running workshops and promotional events, in working with people in other organisations (e.g. companies or colleges) whose ways are different from yours—and so on?

- **Communication.** Your open learning scheme may require staff to communicate in new ways. People who teach excellently face to face cannot automatically be expected to teach equally well in print. Teachers who are used to live feedback from their classes do not always find it easy to write supportive comments on the work of a learner they have never met. Telephone tuition may also make new demands in some situations. Regarding the learner as a partner in communication rather than as the person being communicated to may be the biggest mind-shift of all for some teachers and trainers.

- **Teamwork.** Staff may also need to listen to one another in new ways. Open learning tends to involve people working in teams, with different members responsible for different bits of the planning, development and delivery. Staff who have been used to working independently may not take easily to having their ideas critiqued by colleagues or to providing criticism (supportively) in their turn.

- **Creative management.** Running such a team of professionals can make unusual demands on managers—recruiting the members, deciding who is to do what, briefing and training, fostering the shared norms and values that will sustain the team, encouraging creativity while ensuring standards are maintained—and all the while, perhaps, acting as a focus for the anxiety, anger and frustration that can arise among colleagues learning to cope with new ways of working. Successful open learning teams often run on the nicest of balances between individual autonomy and collective responsibility.

Approaches to staff development

There are several ways of helping open learning staff develop the insights, attitudes and skills they will need. For example:

- Learning on the job, with the help of a "mentor" observing and commenting on the individual's performance

- Regular group reflection sessions, perhaps facilitated by a consultant who knows the team but is not part of it

- Workshops with more experienced colleagues

- Workshops with outside specialists

- Going away on a course

- Information packs—containing details about the scheme, role descriptions, case studies of good practice, etc

- An open learning package (plus support)

- Enrolling as an open learner. Margaret Miers (1984, 1987) reports on what she learned from doing so as a tutor; but the kinds of insights she gained would be useful to anyone working in open learning. Being able to see open learning from the learner's point of view is possibly the most valuable "soft skill" one can have in our business.

- *Other approaches? (What?)*

In general, staff development is most effective if it is closely integrated with the work. Unfortunately, the work is often so hectic—with too much to do, deadlines looming, and pressure to get on to the next task—that staff don't feel able to take time out to reflect on what is to be learned from what they are doing.

Managers may need to build regular "learning from experience" sessions into the team's workplan. If so, they may want to make clear that all members of the team (e.g. secretaries, technicians and receptionists, etc as well as tutors, managers, etc) are expected to contribute. It can be useful to have some of these meetings run by an outside consultant to help the team get a fresh perspective on their work together.

If outside trainers are used, it is worth looking for ways of ensuring they have some continuing if intermittent tutorial contact with the team. For example, when I run workshops for writers of open learning materials I like to follow up by offering comments and suggestions on the materials they produce over the months that follow—and on the new

problems they meet in trying to practise what they have
taken from the workshop.

 What staff development needs do you and your colleagues
have? How might they be met?

Communication

Because open learning usually involves "division of labour",
colleagues can lose touch with one another. They can get so
enmeshed with their own specialist tasks that they omit to
notice the way their activities can affect the work of
colleagues (and vice versa).

Also, although it's almost a cliché to talk of "the loneliness of
the long distance learner", staff may also be lonely. A course
writer may be on his or her own for days or weeks, struggling
with what are sometimes the conflicting aims of how best to
communicate with the learners and how best to produce a
script that will both meet the standards set by the team and
avoid the sneers of experts elsewhere. Tutors and mentors
may likewise be working alone—separated both from those
who wrote the course and from colleagues who are
supporting learners—with little chance to see how others
tackle common problems or even share ideas with them.

Otto Peters (1989) writes of the potential for alienation in this
aspect of what he calls the "industrialisation" of teaching.
Opportunities for conflicts, uncertainties and distress are
abundant, and staff may themselves need support as much as
open learners do.

How can the necessary support be provided? You may have
your own ideas about how to ensure good communication
within the group. Here are my suggestions:

• Brief staff thoroughly and update regularly.

• Give relevant documents—e.g. programme specification,
  publicity leaflets, course materials, etc—to all who might
  conceivably need them.

• Provide staff with written guidance on their role—both in
  general and in relation to a specific task (e.g. how to mark
  a particular assignment).

- Encourage staff to get experience in other roles where appropriate—e.g. can writers do some tutoring, can support staff sometimes help prepare material?

- Agree on "humane" ground rules for exchanging criticism of one another's teaching materials or support activities—e.g. do it through the team leader, or in face-to-face discussion with the authors before going public.

- Hold regular evaluation or feedback sessions in which staff can air and compare experiences.

- Expect all staff to contribute to team meetings—secretaries, receptionists, technicians, etc as well as subject experts, tutors, media specialists, etc.

- Send round a regular newsletter in which staff can report experience, pass on tips, ask one another's advice.

- Put up a noticeboard on which staff can exchange ideas (or use the electronic version if they are using networked computers).

- Put on social gatherings (e.g. parties, lunches, visits to theatres or sporting fixtures).

- Talk to people—giving everyone, at least once a week, a chance to comment on how things are going.

- *Others? (What?)*

If you are setting up a new scheme, what might you do to ensure good communication? If you are already working in a scheme, how might communication be improved?

Open management

What's special about managing open learning? Is it significantly different from managing health care, catering, car production, or whatever? Perhaps not—the open learning manager will be as busy as others are with planning, setting targets, delegating, motivating, monitoring, communicating, and so on. **How** she or he carries out these functions, of course, will differ—but so it will from any management context to another. (See Rowntree, 1989.)

Management in many organisations is task-focussed. The needs of the immediate job or project are paramount. The needs of the people doing it concern the manager only in so far as they contribute to getting the task performed. It would be difficult to justify this focus in managing an open learning system. If the task we have set ourselves is ministering to the developmental needs of our learners, it would not be moral, in doing so, to neglect the developmental needs of our staff.

The open climate

Whatever else it does, the management of an open learning scheme must surely, in itself, embody the principles of openness. Open management depends on trust and a climate of mutual support and collaboration. Team members need to know that they can safely put forward their ideas. They will be listened to and will not be ridiculed or penalised. The team has no secrets from its members and everyone is kept fully aware of any decisions or information that directly affects him or her. Being confident of one another's support, the team can make the most of its energy and creativity.

Developing and maintaining such an open climate is no easy task for the manager—especially if team members have come from backgrounds in which openness is rare. However, she or he can set the tone by encouraging colleagues to take part in making important decisions. That is to say, decision-making should be done **with** staff rather than **for** them.

I was once involved with an open learning operation where staff had learned to do nothing until they were told exactly what to do. What they did, while competent, was uninspired and the climate was diligent rather than creative. It struck me as ironic that a system supposedly dedicated to developing the autonomy of its learners allowed little or none to its staff.

Open decision-making

Tannenbaum & Schmidt (1973) put forward a way of looking at decision-making that neatly echoes the transfer of power from teacher to learner in open learning. The checklist below is based on their ideas:

Which of the following looks most like the usual decision-making procedure in YOUR organisation or unit?

☐ **Telling**. The manager decides what to do and tells the team to get on with it.

☐ **Selling**. The manager makes the decision and explains to the team why it needs to be done.

☐ **Fine-tuning**. The manager decides what to do but invites comments from the team in case he or she can see ways of improving the decision.

☐ **Consulting**. The manager presents one or more tentative solutions to a problem and invites discussion of them before he or she makes the final decision.

☐ **Problem-solving**. The manager presents a problem, gets the team to offer possible solutions and then makes the decision.

☐ **Partly delegating**. The manager presents staff with the problem and lets them decide (within defined limits).

☐ **Fully delegating**. The manager expects staff to both define the problem and decide what to do about it (again within limits).

As you will have noticed, the progression runs from being very directive ("bossy") to expecting staff to take responsibility for their own work. This mirrors the kind of closed-open continuum we have learned to look for in teaching/learning systems. How much autonomy do we allow staff/learners?

Of course, it won't be appropriate to delegate all decisions to staff, any more than it is to delegate all decisions to learners. Some decisions are not worth bothering the team with. Or they need to be made more quickly than participatory methods would allow. But unless the team members are properly involved in making major decisions they may feel no great loyalty to them. They may also feel that they are regarded as no-account serfs. And, of course, the manager fails to draw on the experience and expertise within the team, thus reducing the quality of the decision.

If your organisation is already trying out something like "total quality management" (Oakland, 1989), what I am calling open management may seem quite familiar. Both would aim to empower staff and expect them to "own" the activities they are engaged on. Both see this as essential in an organisation that wants its staff to care about satisfying the needs of its clients or customers.

 Is management sufficiently open in your unit or organisation? What might be done to improve it?

Checklists

One or more of the following four checklists may help you in implementing your open learning scheme. They cannot be very specific because I know nothing of your individual circumstances. So please regard them simply as suggestive. I hope they will suggest to you a whole lot of further, more relevant questions. The best checklist is usually the one we devise for ourselves.

The checklists touch on four aspects of implementing open learning:

• Setting up your open learning scheme

• Developing a learning programme

• Supporting learners

• Running your open learning scheme.

Naturally, you may not be interested in all of these; and you may need to develop checklists on other aspects of your own. You will find they pick up issues touched on earlier in this unit and I sometimes mention another unit where the topic in question has been dealt with.

If you want some further suggestions you may like to look up the checklists I compiled for the Employment Department's handbook *Ensuring Quality in Open Learning* (Rowntree, 1990c).

If you are not responsible for answering such questions yourself, who is? Do you want to influence them or give them the benefit of your suggestions?

Setting up an open learning scheme

☐ What is the purpose of your scheme? Why is it needed? What benefits will it offer (and to whom)? How does it relate to goals, purposes, "missions" within the organisation? (Unit 8)

☐ Who are the intended learners? What do you know of their needs? How does the proposed scheme relate to those needs? Has the scheme been discussed with any learners? (Unit 2)

☐ What form will the scheme take? Which aspects of learning will be made more open? (Unit 2)

☐ What will the scheme cost? From whom will the funds be obtained? (Unit 6)

☐ If someone other than the learners (e.g. their employers) is expected to contribute to the cost of the scheme, how might they expect to benefit? How will you convince them? (Unit 8)

☐ What other resources will the scheme need—e.g. staff, equipment, premises, etc?

☐ From whom, within the organisation, must you obtain commitment and support?

☐ What support and commitment might you need from people outside the organisation—e.g, funding bodies, validating bodies, producers of learning materials, etc?

☐ How will the scheme be "marketed"—both with potential learners and with people whose commitment or support is needed both outside and inside the organisation?

☐ Over what time-period will the scheme operate? What do you see as key events or targets along the way?

☐ By what means—e.g. performance indicators—would you wish the impact of the scheme to be judged? (Unit 7)

☐ What problems do you foresee—e.g. resistance from vested interests, slowness in producing observable results, costs rising unexpectedly?

☐ How might you plan to avoid or cope with those problems?

☐ *Any other concerns? (What?)*

✍ You may want to make notes in your portfolio.

Developing a learning programme

☐ Who will decide the objectives and content of the learning programmes—e.g. the organisation, learners themselves, negotiation between the two? (Unit 2)

☐ What kinds of learning media and materials might be suitable? On what criteria will this be decided? (Units 4 and 5)

☐ Who will develop a specification indicating what will be expected from any learning materials? (Unit 4)

☐ How will materials be obtained—e.g. buy off shelf, adapt, develop custom-made materials? (Unit 4)

☐ If you decide to adapt or develop custom-made materials, will this be done in-house, by commissioning outsiders, or both?

☐ If the adapting or developing is to be done in-house, how many people need to be involved and what skills must they have?

☐ Will you find new staff (full-time or part-time) who have the necessary skills or will you expect existing staff to acquire them? If the latter, how?

☐ How will you settle on a budget, a procedure and a schedule for adapting or developing materials?

☐ How, and with whose help, will draft materials be piloted and improved?

☐ What arrangements will you set up for monitoring the materials in use, making any adjustments or additions that are necessary, and generally ensuring that their quality is maintained and, if appropriate, improved? (Unit 7)

☐ What problems do you foresee—e.g. lack of key skills, uncertainty about how much time is needed?

☐ How might you plan to avoid or cope with those problems?

☐ *Any other concerns? (What?)*

You may want to make notes in your portfolio.

Supporting open learners

☐ What kinds of logistical support might the learners need?—e.g.:

- Financial (e.g. time off work, fees, expenses)
- A place to study—e.g. learning centre, laboratory, workshop, etc.
- A place for learners to meet one another
- Use of equipment—e.g. telephones, computers, audio-visual hardware
- Transport
- Library or database facilities
- *Others? (What?)*

☐ What kinds of human support (Unit 3) might the learners need?—e.g.:

- Negotiating programmes with individuals
- Advising learners on learning how to learn
- Advising on use of equipment
- Conducting tutorial sessions
- Marking/commenting on learners' work
- Helping learners pursue individual projects

- Liaising with learners' line managers/sponsors
- Providing informal "mentoring"
- Keeping records of learners' progress and problems
- *Others? (What?)*

☐ Who might provide the necessary support? What benefits might they get from doing so? (Unit 3)

☐ What briefing, training or staff development might supporters need? How can it be provided?

☐ What systems or procedures are needed to co-ordinate the work of the supporters—e.g. by monitoring their work, keeping them informed of developing best practices, enabling them to share experience?

☐ What problems do you foresee—e.g. learners making new kinds of demands, isolation of tutors, conflicts with sponsors or line managers? (Unit 8)

☐ How might you plan to avoid or cope with those problems?

☐ *Any other concerns? (What?)*

✍ You may want to make notes in your portfolio.

Running your scheme

The running of your scheme is likely to involve both management and administration. Management refers to the setting of goals and deciding on corrective action if things are not going to plan or the plans need changing. Administration refers to the day-to-day operation of the scheme in accordance with the current plans.

In a small scheme, one person might be both manager and administrator. A large scheme will separate the functions and possibly have a hierarchy of people in each role. In the checklist below, I have listed some of the tasks involved in running an open learning scheme. The first set are broadly managerial. The second set are broadly administrative. And the third set are ones in which both administrator and manager might have an input. Who will do what in your system?

☐ Who will take responsibility for:
- Making policy decisions
- Setting objectives
- Obtaining budgets for open learning
- Monitoring expenditure on the project
- Monitoring quality in materials and delivery systems
- Identifying training needs
- Recruiting and developing staff
- Liaising with other agencies on open learning
- Deciding what action to take when problems or new opportunities arise
- *Others? (What?)*

☐ Who will take responsibility for:
- Publicising the opportunities for open learning
- Enrolling learners
- Dealing with enquiries and complaints
- Administering formal assessment/accreditation of learners
- Maintaining overall records of learners' progress
- Storing and maintaining equipment
- Ordering, storing and distributing learning materials
- Putting packages together from separate components
- *Others? (What?)*

☐ Who will take responsibility for:
- Co-ordinating support staff's efforts
- Keeping support staff informed
- Fostering a positive public image of open learning
- Monitoring day-by-day operation of the scheme
- Evaluating and improving open learning activities
- *Others? (What?)*

☐ Might you need outside consultants from time to time—e.g. for help with marketing, staff development or evaluation?

☐ What training or staff development might colleagues need to help them run the scheme? How can it be provided?

☐ What budget is needed for running the scheme? e.g.:

- Staff costs—full-time or part-time
- Fees to outside consultants
- Office space
- Reception room
- Interview room
- Study space
- Library
- Storage space
- Equipment
- Consumables (stationery, postage, blank tapes, etc)
- Telephone costs
- Reprographics
- *Others? (What?)*

☐ What problems do you foresee—e.g. departure of key staff, conflicts with people elsewhere in the organisation, new demands arising from outside the organisation?

☐ How might you plan to avoid or cope with those problems?

☐ *Any other concerns? (What?)*

You may want to make notes in your portfolio.

Your personal action plan

By now you may have a firm idea of the potential role for open learning within your organisation. You may also have a firm idea about how it might be accomplished—either by setting up a new scheme or by modifying or adding to something that exists already. Now comes the crunch question—what is to be your role? What are your personal priorities and how might you set about achieving them?

The pro forma opposite should help you think about what you need to do. Don't set yourself too long a time span—12 months is probably quite enough to think about. And be as specific as you can in your answers, e.g. not "improve communications" but "compile a monthly newsletter, keeping people informed of one another's activities and plans".

Naturally, you may well update those answers in the course of the next few months. Circumstances and priorities are always evolving. But it usually pays to think through some sort of action plan from the start.

If you are responsible for the work of colleagues, you may want to encourage them to produce personal action plans also. If so, they should be expected to discuss their plans with you—just as you will no doubt want to discuss yours with your boss (and perhaps with other colleagues).

 You may find it helpful to make a first draft of your Action Plan in your portfolio before discussing it with colleagues.

ACTION PLAN—where do I go from here?

1. The chief thing I would like to achieve during the next **12 months** is:

2. In order to achieve this goal:

(a)   I need to do the following **new** things
          —or old things **differently** (how?):

(b)   my **colleagues** (which?) need to do the following **new** things
          —or old things **differently** (how?):

3. The individuals or groups who might **help** me towards my goal are:

4. Possible obstacles that might **hinder** me in reaching my goal are:

5. Things I might do to **increase** the strength of the **helping** factors and **reduce** the strength of the **hindering** factors are:

6. What personal **strengths** can I draw on in this work; and what **new** capabilities may I still need to acquire?

Final remarks

In my experience, the most crucial need in implementing open learning is to keep in mind your sense of PURPOSE. Exactly what is it you are trying to achieve? As Otto Peters (1989) forcefully points out, open learning has brought into education and training a new wave of technology—not just of equipment but also of human systems.

Sometimes the technology takes on a life of its own and we forget what it's there for. We can find ourselves nurturing the systems or equipment rather than our learners. If we don't sustain our vision—if we aren't clear about our purpose—we can find ourselves (as I certainly have myself from time to time) working towards some related but different purpose.

You may, for example, start off intending to bring new kinds of learning to new (less privileged) kinds of learners. But, unless you keep on driving, your local restraining forces can push you back to delivering much the same old learning to learners pretty much like those who've had the lion's share of education and training in the past.

The price of open learning (like that of freedom) is eternal vigilance. In this real world of ours we must sometimes take, or go along with, decisions that do not accord entirely with our philosophy. For example, I recently had to accept that a course I was writing should have the usual final exam, even though I argued it was inappropriate to the ethos of this particular course. I simply didn't have the time or energy to fight the committees with enough left over to get the course ready on time for the students who were waiting for it. I compromised on that aspect in order to win acceptance for other more crucial innovations in the course.

Such compromises are often necessary to our survival—even though they go against our ideals. But we must remember that we have made them reluctantly and ensure they don't become set in concrete. As Richard Boot & Vivien Hodgson (1988) remark:

> ". . . measures taken initially for practical and expedient reasons can easily, almost without notice, become both policy and implicitly philosophy."

A supposedly innovative organisation or unit can get stuck in its ways very quickly. I remember staff in one faculty in the

Open University saying: "We don't do it like that in our faculty". And that was within twelve months of the university being set up. Traditions already!

So don't take anything for granted, not even your own earlier decisions. Some of them may have been taken reluctantly then—and even if they were right for then, they may not be right for now. If you want to be responsive to new learners and new needs, some old "traditions" may occasionally need to be replaced with new ones in order to achieve your purposes. Without a commitment to continuous change, your learning system may end up being less open than it was when you started.

What remaining concerns, fears or questions do you have about Implementing Open Learning? Make a note of any that seem important enough to bear in mind when you do your desk work and field work on this topic.

Suggested follow-up work

Desk work

Thorpe & Grugeon (1987) has little to say about the management (as opposed to teaching) aspects of implementing open learning. However, McNay's chapter runs through a number of useful ideas and the Webberley/Haffenden chapter is also worth looking at.

Robinson (1989) has several chapters that touch on implementation issues and one chapter discusses in detail the setting up of a production unit.

Paine (1988) has a number of chapters concerned with implementation, both in colleges and in industry.

Temple (1991) is rich in examples of how open learning has been implemented in organisations of various types and sizes.

Several other books (and packages) are worth a mention:

Thorpe (1988) contains much food for reflection on the links between evaluation and management—especially the final chapter and Conclusion.

Lewis (1984) is a collection of case studies carrying many insights into implementation that have lost none of their relevance over the years since they were written. See also Lewis (1985) for guidance on how to develop and run an open learning scheme.

Much of Dixon (1987) may also be useful if you are in FE —though you'd need to re-interpret some of its specific advice in the light of recent changes in that sector. NEC (1989) may also be helpful if you are implementing open learning in a college; and OPTIS (1989) if you are doing so in a sponsoring organisation.

The journal *Open Learning* occasionally carries case studies that give insights into implementation. *OLS News* often prints evaluation reports (especially from industry) that touch on implementation issues.

Field work

- Write reports, statements, suggestions to colleagues based on ideas you have had while working on this book.

- Run workshops in which to discuss such ideas with colleagues and explore the implications for your organisation.

- Draft your personal Action Plan for what you want to do about open learning over the next 12 months. Discuss it with your boss and/or colleagues. What arises?

- Design an open learning scheme and implement it.

 Remember to make a record of your desk work and field work in your portfolio.

Reflection Checklist

 When you have completed your desk work and field work on this unit, please make notes in your portfolio using some of the following questions as a guide:

o   What are the most important things you have learned during this unit? (You may want to look back at the objectives suggested at the beginning.)

o   What has given you most satisfaction in this unit?

o   What do you feel least satisfied about in this unit?

o   Does this unit leave you with any unresolved questions or difficulties you feel you want help with?

o   How might you try to get the help you need?

o   What have you learned in your work with other people during this unit?

o   In what ways were you able to draw on your previous experience during this unit?

o   What have you learned about yourself—your own feelings and competences?

o   What do you feel you need to do next?

Sources of information

Here are just a few of the national sources of information that may be useful to you. You will no doubt want to find more of your own. I suggest you also investigate local sources and keep an eye on the chief journals and regular events.

National sources

- British Association for Open Learning
15 Hitchin Street
Baldock
Herts SG7 6AL
(Tel: 0462-892417)
A trade association for producers and deliverers of open learning.

- Learning Methods Branch
Employment Department
Moorfoot
Sheffield S1 4PQ
(Tel: 0742-753275/594680)
Information about current Employment Department initiatives in open and flexible learning. Ask for its list of free and priced publications.

- International Centre for Distance Learning
The Open University
Milton Keynes MK7 6AA
(Tel: 0908-653357)
A documentation centre on distance education worldwide. Its database (available on compact disc) carries details about courses and programmes (14,000 at present), institutions and the literature of distance education.

- National Council for Educational Technology
Sir William Lyons Road
Science Park
University of Warwick
Coventry CV4 7EZ
(Tel: 0203-416994)
Many free and priced publications and resources available.

- National Extension College
18 Brooklands Avenue,
Cambridge CB2 2HN
(Tel: 0223-316644)

- National Open Learning Library
Birmingham Open Learning Development Unit
Unit 1—Holt Court (South)
Aston Science Park
Birmingham B7 4EG
(Tel: 021-333-3401)
Has 6000 items for inspection by visitors—but no borrowing.

- Open College
FREEPOST
Warrington
WA2 7BR

- Open College of the Arts
Worsbrough
Barnsley
South Yorkshire S70 6TU
(Tel: 0226-730-495)

- *Open Learning Directory*
Published annually by Pergamon of Oxford
Details of 2000-plus packages in professional and vocational training, plus information about package developers, delivery (support) centres and other organisations in the field.

- Open Learning Foundation
Angel Gate
City Road
London EC1 2RS
(Tel: 071-833-3757)

- Open University
  Milton Keynes MK7 6AA
  (Tel: 0908-274066)

- Open School
  Park Road
  Dartington
  Devon TQ9 6EQ
  (Tel: 0803-866542)

- Scottish Council for
  Educational Technology
  74 Victoria Crescent Road
  Glasgow G12 9JN
  (Tel: 041-334-9314/041-357-0340)
  *Many free and priced publications
  and resources available.*

- TVEI Unit
  Employment Department
  Moorfoot
  Sheffield S1 4PQ
  (Tel: 0742-753275/593857)

Possible local sources

- The adult education office of
  your local education authority.
- Your nearest further
  education college or higher
  education institution.
- Your nearest TEC (Training
  and Enterprise Council) or (in
  Scotland) Local Enterprise
  Council (LEC).
- Your nearest "Training Shop"
  (funded by the Employment
  Department as part of the
  "TAP" scheme and located in
  a number of large towns).
- The reference section of your
  nearest large library.
- Large firms (e.g. car or steel
  makers) or branches of large
  national chains (e.g. hotel,
  supermarket and DIY; banks;
  building societies).

Regular publications

~ *American Journal of Distance
Education* (Pennsylvania)

~ *Educational Technology &
Training International* (published
by Kogan Page)

~ *Distance Education* (Australia)

~ *ICDE Bulletin* (from
International Council for
Distance Education, Norway)

~ *Journal of Distance Education*
(Canada)

~ *OLS News* (from National
Council for Educational
Technology—see above)

~ *Open Learning* (published by
Longman of Harlow)

~ *Open Learning Today* (newsletter
of British Association for Open
Learning—see above)

Other education and training
journals such as *Adults Learning,
British Journal of Educational
Technology, Transition* and *Training
Officer* also have regular features
and articles about open learning.

Regular events

Any national exhibition or
conference to do with education
and training—e.g. Human
Resource Development at
London (April) and Education &
Training at Birmingham (July)—
may have items of interest. But
look out especially for the Open
Learning conferences organised
by CRAC and National Extension
College at Cambridge in July and
those on Educational Technology
organised by the Association for
Educational and Training
Technology at Easter (various
venues).

Bibliography

ALBSU (1991) *Open Learning Centres in England and Wales*, Adult Literacy and Basic Skills Unit, London

BAILEY, D. (1988) "Guidance and counselling in work-based open learning" in N. PAINE (ed) (1988) (see below)

BATES, A.W. (ed) (1984) *The Role of Technology in Distance Education*, Croom Helm, London

BATES, A.W. (1988) "Technology for distance education: a 10-year prospective" in *Open Learning*, Vol 3, No 3

BATES, A.W. (ed) (1990) *Media and Technology in European Distance Education*, EADTU and the Open University, Milton Keynes

BEATY, E. & MORGAN, A. (1992) "Developing skill in learning" in *Open Learning*, Vol 7, No 2, pp 14-22

BOBBIT, F. (1924) *How to Make a Curriculum*, Houghton Mifflin, Boston, Massachusetts

BOOT, R. & HODGSON, V. (1987) "Open learning: meaning and experience", Chapter 1 in V. HODGSON, S. MANN, R. SNELL (eds) (1987) (see below)

BOOT, R. & HODGSON, V. (1988) "Open learning: philosophy or expediency?" in *Programmed Learning and Educational Technology*, Vol 25, No 3, pp 197-204

BOUD, D. (ed) (1988) *Developing Student Autonomy in Learning* (2nd edn), Kogan Page, London

CANTOR, N. (1972) *Dynamics of Learning*, Agathon, New York (first published 1946)

COFFEY, J. (1977) *Open Learning for Mature Students*, Council for Educational Technology, London

COOPERS & LYBRAND (1989) *A report into the Relative Costs of Open Learning*, Open University/Employment Department, Sheffield

COX, S. and HOBSON, B. (1988) "User appreciation of open learning at Jaguar cars" in *Open Learning*, Vol 3 No 1

CULLEN, A.M. (1985) "An evaluation of a computer-based training package" in *Royal Air Force Education Bulletin*, Autumn 1985, No 23

CURRAN, C. (1992) "Cost factors in deciding on distance education and flexible learning" in *Journal of Higher Education Studies*, Vol 5, No 1

DIXON, K. (1987) *Implementing Open Learning in Local Authority Institutions,* Further Education Unit, London

DOBSON, R. (1988) "Tomorrow's training today" in N. PAINE (ed) (1988) (see below)

DUCHASTEL, P. (1983) "Towards the ideal study guide", *British Journal of Educational Technology,* Vol 14, No 3

ED (1989) *A Review of the Cost Benefits of Computer-based Training (CBT),* Employment Department, Sheffield

EDWARDS, R. (1991) "The inevitable future? Post-Fordism and open learning" in *Open Learning,* Vol 6, No 2, pp 36-42

EISNER, E. W. (1967) "Educational objectives: help or hindrance" in *School Review,* 75, Autumn 1967, pp 250-260

ELTON, L. (1988) "Conditions for learner autonomy at a distance" in *Programmed Learning and Educational Technology,* Vol 25, No 3, pp 216-24

EMPLOYMENT DEPARTMENT (1991) *National Training Awards,* Employment Department, Sheffield

EMPLOYMENT DEPARTMENT (1992) *Open Learning Directory,* Pergamon, Oxford

ERAUT, M. *et al* (eds) (1991) *Flexible Learning in Schools,* Employment Department, Sheffield

EVERISS, S. (1984) "Zoo animal management open learning scheme" in R. LEWIS (ed) (1984) (see below)

FAGE, J. (1987) "Foundation studies counselling and teaching—a case study illuminating the practice of integrated teaching and counselling for new learners" in M. THORPE & D. GRUGEON (eds) (1987) (see below)

FANSHAW, M. (1990) *Self-help Learning Groups: a Guide for Organisers,* National Extension College, Cambridge

FEU (1992) *Flexible Colleges: Access to Learning and Qualifications in Further Education* (two volumes), Further Education Unit, London

FLEETWOOD-WALKER, P. & FLETCHER-CAMPBELL, F. (1986) *TVI—a Handbook for Producers and Users of Tutored Video Instruction,* FEU, London

FLEXITRAIN (1990) *Being an Open Learning Mentor,* Flexitrain Ltd, Abergavenny (an open learning pack comprising two workbooks and an audiotape, commissioned by the Employment Department)

FORTE (1991) *Professional Wine Service Training,* The Academy of Wine Service, London EC4R 1QS

FOX, S. (1989) "The production and distribution of knowledge through open and distance learning" in *Educational and Training Technology International*, Vol 26, No 3, pp 269-80

FREIRE, P. (1974) *Education: the Practice of Freedom*, Writers and Readers Cooperative, London

GALLAGHER, M. (1978) "Good television and good teaching" in *Educational Broadcasting International*, December 1978

GANGE, D. (1986) "TVI in context—an individual view of distance learning in industry" in P. FLEETWOOD-WALKER & F. FLETCHER-CAMPBELL (1986) (see above)

GIBBS, G. (1988) *Learning by Doing*, FEU, London

GIBBS, G. & HAIGH, M. (1984) *Developing Course Evaluation Questionnaires*, Educational Methods Unit, Oxford Polytechnic, Oxford

GIBBS, G., MORGAN, A. & TAYLOR, L. (1980) *An Example of the Quality of Students' Understanding: Initial Conceptions of Psychology*, IET, Open University, Milton Keynes

HAMILTON, D. *et al* (eds) (1977) *Beyond the Numbers Game: a Reader in Educational Evaluation*, Macmillan, London

HARRIS (1991) *Open Learning in Public Libraries: an Evaluation of the Impact of the Funding*, Harris Research Centre, 34-38 Hill Rise, Richmond, Surrey TW10 6UA

HARRIS, D. (1976) "Educational technology at the Open University: a short history of achievement and cancellation" in *British Journal of Educational Technology*, Vol 7, No 1

HARRIS, D. (1987) *Openness and Closure in Distance Education*, Falmer Press, Sussex

HAWKRIDGE, D., NEWTON, W. & HALL, C. (1988) *Computers in Company Training*, Croom Helm, London

HENRY, J. (1989) "Meaning and practice in experiential learning" in S. Warner Weil and I. Gibson (eds), *Making Sense of Experiential Learning*, Open University Press, Milton Keynes

HILGENDORF, L. (1984) *Self-evaluation by Open Learning Projects: a Guide for Managers of Projects in the Open Tech Programme*, Tavistock Institute of Human Relations/HMSO, London

HIRST, W. (1986) "Melbourne to Manchester: a look at openness in some open learning situations" in *International Journal of Lifelong Education*, Vol 5, No 4, pp 327-46

HODGSON, V., MANN, S. & SNELL, R. (eds) (1987) *Beyond Distance Teaching—Towards Open Learning*, SRHE & Open University Press, Buckingham

HOLT, D. & BONNICI, J. (1988) "Learning to manage through open learning: a case study in international collaboration" in *Programmed Learning and Educational Technology*, Vol 25, No 3, pp 245-57

HONEY, P. & MUMFORD, A. (1986) *The Manual of Learning Styles*, available direct from Dr Peter Honey, 10 Linden Avenue, Maidenhead, Berks SL6 6HB

JACK, M. (1987) "SOLE—the Strathclyde open learning experiment" in M. THORPE & D. GRUGEON (eds) (1987) (see below)

JACK, M. (1988) "The Strathclyde open learning experiment", in *Open Learning*, Vol 3, No 1

JONES, A., KIRKUP, G. & KIRKWOOD, A. (1992) *Personal computers for Distance Education*, Paul Chapman, London

KEEGAN, D. (1990) *Foundations of Distance Education* (2nd edition), Routledge, London

KEMBER, D. (1991) *Writing Study Guides*, Technical and Educational Services, Bristol

KLEMP, G. O. (1977) *Three Factors of Success in the World of Work: Implications for Higher Education*, McBer & Co, Boston, Massachusetts

KOLB, D.A. (1984) *Experiential Learning*, Prentice-Hall, Englewood Cliffs, New Jersey

LAIDLAW, B. & LAYARD, R. (1974) "Traditional versus Open University teaching methods" in *Higher Education*, Vol 3, pp 439-68

LEWIS, R. (ed) (1984) *Open Learning in Action*, Council for Educational Technology, London

LEWIS, R. (1985) *How to Develop and Manage an Open Learning Scheme*, Council for Educational Technology, London

LEWIS, R. (1990) "Open learning and the misuse of language: a response to Greville Rumble" in *Open Learning*, Vol 5, No 1, pp 3-8

LEWIS, R. & MEED, J. (1986) *How to Manage the Production Process*, Council for Educational Technology, London

LEWIS, R. & PAINE, N. (1985a) *How to Communicate with the Learner*, Council for Educational Technology, London

LEWIS, R. & PAINE, N. (1985b) *How to Find and Adapt Materials and Select Media*, Council for Educational Technology, London

LEWIS, R. & SPENCER, D. (1986) *What is Open Learning?* Council for Educational Technology, London

LOCKWOOD, F.G. (1990) "Activities in Distance Learning Texts", PhD thesis, Open University, Milton Keynes

MACDONALD, B. (1977) "An educational evaluation of NDPCAL" in *British Journal of Educational Technology*, Vol 8, No 3

MACDONALD-ROSS, M. (1973) "Behavioural objectives—a critical review" in *Instructional Science*, 2, pp 1-52

MACKENZIE, N., POSTGATE, R. & SCUPHAM, J. (1975) *Open Learning: Systems and Problems in Post-secondary Education*, UNESCO, Paris

McNAY, I. (1987) "Organisation and staff development" in M. THORPE & D. GRUGEON (eds) (1987) (see below)

McNAY, I. (1988) "Open learning: a jarring note" in N. PAINE (ed) (1988) (see below)

MARSHALL, K. (1991) "NVQs: an assessment of the 'outcomes' approach to education and training" in *Journal of Further and Higher Education*, Vol 15, No 3, pp 56-64

MARTON, F. & SÄLJÖ, R. (1976) "On qualitative differences in learning: outcome and process" in *British Journal of Psychology*, Vol 46, pp 4-11

MASLOW, A. H. (1968) *Towards a Psychology of Being*, Van Nostrand, Princeton, New Jersey

MASON, R. (1990) "Computer conferencing in distance education" in A.W. BATES (ed) (1990) (see above)

MASON, R. & KAYE, A. (eds) (1989) *Mindweave: Communication, Computers, and Distance Education*, Pergamon, Oxford

MIERS, M. (1984) "How it feels to be a student" in *Teaching at a Distance*, No 25, pp 101-5

MIERS, M. (1987) "Reflections on the role of correspondence teaching" in M. THORPE & D. GRUGEON (eds) (1987) (see below)

MORGAN, A. (1983) "Theoretical aspects of project-based learning in higher education" in *British Journal of Educational Technology*, Vol 14, pp 66-78

MORGAN, A. (1987) "Project work in open learning" in M. THORPE & D. GRUGEON (eds) (1987) (see below)

MORPETH, R. (1988) "The National Extension College: present and future" in *Open Learning*, Vol 3, No 2, pp 34-6

MORPETH, R. & RUMBLE, G. (1992) "The technician training scheme at the National Extension College, United Kingdom" in G. RUMBLE & J. OLIVEIRA (eds) (1992) (see below)

MORRIS, A. (1984) *Writing Study Guides*, Council for Educational Technology, London

MORRIS, M. & TWITCHEN, R. (1990) *Evaluating Flexible Learning: a Users' Guide*, National Foundation for Educational Research, Slough

MSC (1982) *Open Tech Task Group Report*, Manpower Services Commission, Sheffield

MSC (1984) *A New Training Initiative*, Manpower Services Commission, Sheffield

MUNRO, F. (1989) "Choosing and using media" in K. ROBINSON (ed) (1989) (see below)

NATHENSON, M, & HENDERSON, E. (1980) *Using Student Feedback to Improve Learning Materials*, Croom Helm, London

NEC (1989) *Implementing Open Learning in Colleges*, National Extension College, Cambridge (a multi-media pack sponsored by the Training Agency)

NORRIS, N. (1990) *Understanding Educational Evaluation*, Kogan Page, London

NORTHEDGE, A. (1987) "The tutor's role in group learning", in M. THORPE & D. GRUGEON (eds) (1987) (see below)

OAKLAND, J.S. (1989) *Total Quality Management*, Butterworth-Heinemann, Oxford

OC (1990) "The line manager's guide" from *Being a Manager*, Open College, London

OPPENHEIM, A.N. (1986) *Questionnaire Design and Attitude Measurement*, Gower, Aldershot

OPTIS (1989) *Implementing Open Learning in Organisations*, OPTIS, Oxford (A mixed-media pack sponsored by the Training Agency)

OU/ED (1990) *How to profit from open learning—company evidence*, Open University/Employment Department, Milton Keynes

PARLETT, M. & HAMILTON, D. (1972) "Evaluation as illumination: a new approach to the study of innovative programmes", Occasional Paper No 9, Centre for Research in the Educational Sciences, University of Edinburgh, reprinted in D. HAMILTON *et al* (eds) (1977) (see above)

PASK, G. (1976) "Styles and strategies of learning" in *British Journal of Psychology*, Vol 46, pp 128-48

PAINE, N. (ed) (1988) *Open Learning in Transition*, National Extension College, Cambridge

PERRATON, H. (1987) "Theories, generalisation and practice in distance education" in *Open Learning*, Vol 2, No 4, pp 3-12

PETERS, O. (1989) "The iceberg has not melted: further reflections on the concept of industrialisation and distance teaching" in *Open Learning*, Vol 4, No 3, pp 3-8

PIKE, C. (1990) "Delivery and support—the keys to successful open learning" in *Open Learning: Moving into the Mainstream*, National Extension College, Cambridge

PIRSIG, R. (1972) *Zen and the Art of Motor Cycle Maintenance*, Bodley Head, London

RACE, P. (1989) *The Open Learning Handbook*, Kogan Page, London

RICHARDS, M. (1984) "OU's head on the block" in *Times Higher Educational Supplement*, 13 July 1984

ROBINSON, B. (1990) *Telephone teaching and audio-conferencing at the British Open University*, in A.W. BATES (ed) (1990) (see above)

ROBINSON, Brian (1990) "Open learning in IBM education" in *Open Learning: Moving into the Mainstream*, National Extension College, Cambridge

ROBINSON, K. (ed) (1989) *Open and Distance Learning for Nurses*, Longman, Harlow

ROGERS, C. (1961) *On Becoming a Person*, Houghton Mifflin, New York

ROSSETTI, A. (1988) "Open learning and the youth training scheme" in N. PAINE (ed) (1988) (see above)

ROWNTREE, D. (1966) *Basically Branching: a Handbook for Programmers*, Macdonald, London

ROWNTREE, D. (1975) "Communication is not just telling people things" in J. Baggalay *et al* (eds) *Aspects of Educational Technology VIII*, Pitman, London, pp 281-293

ROWNTREE, D. (1982) *Educational Technology in Curriculum Development* (2nd edn), Paul Chapman, London

ROWNTREE, D. (1985) *Developing Courses for Students*, Paul Chapman, London

ROWNTREE, D. (1987) *Assessing Students: How Shall We Know Them?*, Kogan Page, London

ROWNTREE, D. (1988) *Learn How to Study*, (new edn), Sphere Books, London

ROWNTREE, D. (1989) *The Manager's Book of Checklists*, Gower Press, Aldershot (Also published as a Corgi paperback)

ROWNTREE, D. (1990a) *Teaching Through Self-instruction*, Kogan Page, London

ROWNTREE, D. (1990b) *Developing an Open Learning Package*, Employment Department/Open University, Milton Keynes (a mixed-media pack sponsored by the Training Agency)

ROWNTREE, D. (1990c) *Ensuring Quality in Open Learning: a Handbook for Action*, Employment Department, Sheffield

ROWNTREE, D. (1991) *Teach Yourself with Open Learning*, Sphere Books, London

RSA (1991) *Scheme of Awards in the Development and Delivery of Flexible and Open Learning*, RSA Examinations Board, Coventry CV4 8HS

RUMBLE, G. (1988) "The economics of mass distance education"in *Prospects*, Vol XVIII, No 1, pp 91-102

RUMBLE, G. (1989) "'Open learning', 'distance learning', and the misuse of language" in *Open Learning*, Vol 4, No 4, pp 28-44

RUMBLE, G. (1990) "Open learning and the misuse of language: a reply" in *Open Learning*, Vol 5, No 3, pp 50-51

RUMBLE, G. & OLIVEIRA, J. (eds) (1992) *Vocational Education at a Distance: International Perspectives*, Kogan Page, London

SAGAR, E. & STRANG, A. (1985) *The Student Experience: A Case Study of Technicians in Open Learning*, Roffey Park Management College, Horsham, Sussex

SÄLJÖ, R. (1979) *Learning in the Learner's Perspective: II: Differences in Awareness*, Institute of Education, University of Gothenburg, Sweden

SANDS, T. (1984) "The Bradford mathematics workshop" in R. LEWIS (ed) (1984) (see above)

SATURN (1991) *Quality Guide for Open and Distance Learning* (Pilot version), SATURN, Amsterdam

SCHON, D. (1983) *The Reflective Practitioner: How Professionals Think in Action*, Temple Smith, London

SCHRAMM, W. (1977) *Big Media, Little Media: Tools and Technologies for Instruction*, Sage, Beverly Hills, Calif.

SEWART, D. (1987) "Limitations of the learning package", in M. THORPE & D. GRUGEON (eds) (1987) (see below)

SIEMINSKI, S. (1992) "Case study: City and East London College of Further Education" in course EH266, *Learning Through Life*, Open University, Milton Keynes

SPARKES, J. (1984) "Pedagogic differences between media" in A.W. BATES (ed) (1984) (see above)

SPENCER, L.M. (1979) *Soft Skill Competencies*, McBer & Co, Boston, Massachusetts

STAINTON ROGERS, W. (1987) "Adapting materials to alternative use" in M. THORPE & D. GRUGEON (eds) (1987) (see below)

STAKE, R.E. (1967) "Introduction" in R.W. TYLER *et al* (1967) *Perspectives of Curriculum Evaluation*, Rand McNally, Chicago

STRANG, A. (1987) "The hidden barriers", in V. HODGSON *et al* (1987) (see above)

TAIT, A. (1989) "The politics of open learning" in *Adult Education*, Vol 64, No 4, pp 308-13

TANNENBAUM, R. & SCHMIDT, W. (1973) "How to choose a leadership pattern" in *Harvard Business Review*, May-June 1973, pp 162-80

TAVISTOCK (1987) *The Open Tech Programme Development Review: Final Report*, Tavistock Institute of Human Relations, London

TAYLOR, E., MORGAN, A. & GIBBS, G. (1981) "The 'orientation' of Open University foundation students to their studies", in *Teaching at a Distance*, No 20, Winter 1981

TEMPLE, H. (1988) "Open learning: helped or hindered by Open Tech?" in *Programmed Learning and Educational Technology*, Vol 25, No 3, pp 241-4

TEMPLE, H. (1991) *Open Learning in Industry*, Longman, Harlow

THORPE, M. (1988) *Evaluating Open & Distance Learning*, Longman, Harlow

THORPE, M. & GRUGEON, D. (eds) (1987) *Open Learning for Adults*, Longman, Harlow

TOLLEY, G. (1983) *The Open Tech: Why, What and How?*, Manpower Services Commission, Sheffield

TOMLINSON, P. & KILNER, S. (1991) *Flexible Learning, Flexible Teaching: The Flexible Learning Framework and Current Educational Theory*, Employment Department, Sheffield

TRAINING AGENCY (1989) *Training in Britain*, Employment Department, Sheffield

TUCKETT, A. (1988) "Open learning and the education of adults", in N. PAINE (ed) (1988) (see above)

TVEI (1991) *Flexible Learning: a Framework for Education and Training in the Skills Decade*, TVEI Unit, Employment Department, Sheffield

UDACE (1990) *Open College Networks and National Vocational Qualifications*, NIACE, Leicester

UEA (1987) *Police Probationer Training: the Final Report of the Stage II Review*, University of East Anglia for HMSO, London

WEBBERLEY, R. (1987) "Skills training and responsive management", in THORPE & GRUGEON (eds) (1987) (see above)

WEBBERLEY, R. (1988) "Working in an Open Tech project and the Open University: some reflections" in *Open Learning*, Vol 3, No 3, pp 38-42

WRIGHT, S. (1989) "Supporting learners in the workplace" in K. ROBINSON (ed) (1989) (see above)

YOUNG, M. (1988) "Education for the new work" in N. PAINE (ed) (1988) (see above)

Index

*Another book about open learning
by Derek Rowntree*

Teaching Through Self-instruction
—how to develop open learning materials

*There is no one right way to produce quality open learning materials
. . . but there are plenty of wrong ways.*

This book should help you avoid them.

Reviewers' comments:

*"If you were only to buy one book on open learning materials you could
hardly do better than this one."*
Hilary Temple in *TRANSITION*

"Essential reading for all distance educators."
Geoff Arger in *DISTANCE EDUCATION*

*"Again and again I found myself not only agreeing with the author but
also admiring the clarity of his presentation and the aptness of his
examples."*
Janet Jenkins in *OPEN LEARNING*

Publisher: Kogan Page Ltd, 120 Pentonville Rd, London N1 9JN